MY GOD, IT'S CANCER

My epic journey with a late-stage
terminal cancer, sustained by outrageous
faith for healing through grace

COURTNEY A. MULLINGS

ISBN 978-1-0980-3861-8 (paperback)
ISBN 978-1-0980-3862-5 (digital)

Christian Faith Publishing, Inc.
832 Park Avenue
Meadville, PA 16335
www.christianfaithpublishing.com

Printed in the United States of America

With all my love to my dear wife,
Dorothy Rosalee Mullings.

CONTENTS

Foreword...7

Acknowledgments 9

Background..15

Chapter 1: Is Something Wrong with Me?.......................23

Chapter 2: Doctor, Doctor, Doctor 27

Chapter 3: Documenting My Journey 48

Chapter 4: New Realities..52

Chapter 5: Where Is God in This?...................................58

Chapter 6: Back Home...65

Chapter 7: Angry With?...71

Chapter 8: Learning to Adjust...82

Chapter 9: With My Mouth..90

Chapter 10: I Called It Cancer..96

Chapter 11: Which Spirits Do I Hear?............................100

Chapter 12: Called to a Place of Privilege.......................105

Chapter 13: Rationalizing the Cancer 123

Chapter 14: Bless His Heart...131

Chapter 15: May I Help Me? 133

Chapter 16: My Healing Brings 141

Chapter 17: Chemotherapy...148

Chapter 18: My First Chemotherapy................................153

Chapter 19: My New Normal 161

Chapter 20: By What Authority?......................................165

Chapter 21: On Faith..176

Chapter 22: Bearing My Own Cross 182

Chapter 23: The Power of Knowledge....................................192

Chapter 24: My Last Pain—New Hope 206

Chapter 25: The Body of Christ...214

Chapter 26: My Next Stage 220

Chapter 27: Bah, Humbug...226

Chapter 28: Setbacks or Opportunities 230

Chapter 29: Introspection in the Desert Place 234

Chapter 30: Giving Thanks..239

Chapter 31: Merry Christmas and Year-End Update 243

Chapter 32: Finished Work..247

Chapter 33: Through the Valley of Dry Bones 251

Chapter 34: Recovering from Transplant................................256

Chapter 35: After the Storm...262

Chapter 36: A Praise Offering 268

Chapter 37: Hold That Allogeneic Transplant for Now 273

Chapter 38: In Control 280

Chapter 39: The Substance of Faith 285

Chapter 40: Their Science, My Faith......................................288

Chapter 41: I Stubbed My Toe 293

Chapter 42: Those Were the Days..300

Chapter 43: My Caregiver 309

Reflections: The Voices...315

Lessons Learned 321

Next Chapter 327

Appendix I: About Cancer 333

Appendix II: My Journey to Date...351

References 355

FOREWORD

This book is exceptional! In writing about the physical trauma associated with his cancer, Courtney opens the door on the emotional and spiritual side of living with the disease. The book covers conversations with doctors and the medicines associated with his treatment, and the recounting of his experiences is priceless. If you know anyone living under the cloud of cancer, this is a must-read. Get ready to laugh, cry, and meditate as Courtney's journey opens your eyes to a true miracle.

Bishop H. Alan Mushegan

ACKNOWLEDGMENTS

C hallenged by the adversities that affected my life for the past three-plus years, I was only able to accomplish the monumental feat of completing this book by the leadership of the Holy Spirit. Granted, I received strong encouragement from many friends who read my Facebook posts and were convinced that I should compile them into a book so that others would benefit, as they did, from the experiences I related. But I lacked the motivation and was buffeted by doubt that I had the wherewithal to tell my story through this medium. In the end, it required the divine inspiration of the Holy Spirit to push past my hesitancy, and to guide and sustain me during this task.

With the help of the Holy Spirit, I was able to rehearse the convoluted episodes that marked my life as it teetered on the precipice of death. It has been a journey of absolute dependence on the benevolence of God and His grace that, through faith, I have emerged from near death to a wonderful new life, filled with great hope and great expectancy. I prayerfully submit my heartfelt gratitude to our Holy Father, God Almighty, for the guidance and leadership of the Holy Spirit, and offer myself as a living sacrifice for Him to use as He deems worthy. Thank You, most holy Lord God. I pray that all who read this account of mine will find strength and hope through Jesus Christ to overcome whatever challenges may confront them.

I am convinced that God assigns people strategically to accomplish His will, and my wife, Dorothy, is first among those whom I acknowledge as being divinely appointed to help me through my time of tribulations. Her dedication went beyond just physically nursing me back to health to ensuring that, through faith, I never lost hope. Through her, I experienced the most generous demonstration of the fruit of the Spirit as she was relentless in reinforcing my faith, making sure I never lost sight of the irrevocable promises of God. I will forever be in her debt, and I thank her profusely. Thanks too to my children, Marja and Orayne, whose love and care were always palpable, tossed as they were into the reversed role of caregivers.

My thanks to Bishop Alan Mushegan Sr., our spiritual leader for almost two decades, who prayed for us daily and never ceased to encourage me to fight in faith. He was our first point of call when things got rough, and it was he who would later prophetically declare that I would write this book. He made it his priority to read the manuscript over one weekend and gave me his full endorsement to publish it. Although vested with all the authority of leadership, he has been the very embodiment of a servant leader, and I acknowledge him before God and thank him.

My sincere gratitude to Pastors Harolene, Kenneth, and Mike, who were consistent in their care and advocacy to God for my healing. Their encouragement throughout my journey and willingness to read the manuscript were invaluable. Aside from the ministers of my home church, I learned a lot from the teachings of Pastor Creflo, particularly through his lessons of "Grace Life" series, witnessing him practice what he preached, and his personal testimony of eradicating cancer through faith. Pastor Bernard's "Faith in Practice" ministry and Bishop Jakes' "The Potter's Touch" teachings also influenced me and how I saw myself concerning the promises of God and my walk in faith. I acknowledge and thank them.

Ann and Glen Stevens are longtime friends and my Christian mentors. They were first on the scene even before my terminal diagnosis and were solid pillars of support. Ann's compassion was always evident. She rose to the challenge of transporting me to appointments and, along with Glen, defied every barrier to lay hands on me with prayers and encouragement at every opportunity. Glen's encouraging feedback after an early read of the manuscript was vital in my decision to move forward and complete the book. I thank them and their wonderful family.

My long-standing friend Hector was unflinching in his support. He found a thousand ways to cater to my finicky demands, tolerated my foolishness, and was always assuring me that God would pull me through. I thank him and pray that God will bless him tremendously.

Dr. Olu, my friend and brother in Christ, was always present. From my initial hospitalization to defying restrictions of home visits, he generally came bearing physical and spiritual gifts to encourage me. His encouragement throughout and early feedback about the manuscript provided an inspiring source of support, for which I thank him and pray God's favors for him.

Barry DeLisser, the author of the rousing novel *Think It Through*, was so helpful both from an experiential and spiritual perspective. He was the inspiration for chapter 41, "I Stubbed My Toe," and the "brother" to whom I referred. I thank him for never ceasing to inspire me with his willingness to acknowledge the goodness of God in our lives, and for his testimonies from which I benefited.

To my family and relatives who had to deal with the shock of my sudden illness and rallied to my support, I thank you. I thank my mother and sisters who, while struggling with their own personal and health challenges, were unrelenting in advocating for my healing, especially my sister, Evangelist Marian, who prophesied I would grow new bones. My Aunt Rose and uncles Bryan, Keith and Bevan, and Bevan's wife Claire, were perennial stalwarts. My aunt, in particular, was a source of strength for my faith. She always managed to find a scriptural reference to support my faith fight. Thanks to my favorite nieces, particularly Debbie, who insisted I write this book but keep it real. Katharine, Davia, Gabrielle and Ayana's consistent, inspirational words or prayers made my days more bearable. Jason, Stephan, and Israel were sources of inspiration, though they struggled to understand why their uncle had been dealt such misfortune. I pray that through the miraculous works of God in me their young lives will be impacted by the power of faith. I have the most caring and dedicated in-laws and my feeble attempt at expressing thanks to them falls short of what they deserve. I appreciate their love so much. Thanks to my wonderful, caring cousins and their families who, although dispersed across the UK, USA and Jamaica, found ways to embrace me with love. I especially thank Cousin Delores for not only praying but also enrolling me in her prayer group. Much respect to her grandson Nathan who, even while going through his bout with cancer, had the fortitude to establish the non-profit organization "Connected Through Cancer."

Big thanks to the hosts of friends who found unique ways to help me. Wonderful souls like BFF Linda, who provided me with ample supplies of wafer and juice so I could celebrate Communion while at home. I am grateful to Mark and Brenda, Dave and Diana, Woody, Yasmin, Judy, and the other Brendas, who, in various ways, rallied around me and consistently provided support from very early on. To Betty, Peggy, Floy, Joan and the countless number of people who sent me cards, even when I could hardly read and comprehend, let alone write a response, I thank you all for the demonstration of God's love through your kindness. My persistent encouragers—Andrea, Angela, Carol, Delores, Dave G, Doug, Edgar, Jennifer, Joan, William, Marjorie and Ron, Holmwoodites, especially my "batchies," and former Jamaica Telephone Company colleagues (xJTCers)—are among those who went beyond cheerleading me back to health and insisted I tell my story beyond Facebook. By writing this book, I hope I did you all proud.

Sincere thanks to the fantastic nursing team at Emory University Hospital who attended to my every need and to my brilliant and compassionate doctors, particularly oncologist Stephen Szabo (Emory University Hospital) and Carlos Franco (WellStar Hospital), whose expertise and care made a significant difference.

It was my friend Carlton's openness in a Facebook post that initially inspired me to follow his lead and start my own thread. I will be forever thankful that I could draw inspiration from him even as he too was experiencing his own health struggles.

Thanks to my faithful Facebook friends and church brethren who collectively represented my most significant source of inspiration. The support I received from my church and the individual ministries within it, such as The Men of Valor ministry, was a tower of strength that fed me constantly with messages of hope that sustained me spiritually. My Facebook following is rightly deserving of the credit for inspiring this book. To all of you who commented, liked, or used emojis to express your feelings for me at any point, I am in your debt. Through your words, I found the strength I needed to stay grounded in my faith, sustain the battle with cancer, and maintain my trust in God. I write this book as a tribute to you too.

Stephanie Hare was the consummate professional who artfully guided me through the maze of literary correctness in the initial stages of this book. I am extremely grateful to her for the enthusiasm and sensitivity with which she handled the early editing process.

We all have stories, but we are not all writers. This became painfully evident after consultation with my brilliant collaborator, dearest friend and confidant, chief editor Mel Stephens, to whom I am unspeakably grateful. She was brilliant at editing, formatting and structuring the material to meet the highest standards of clarity and readability. Mel meticulously guided me through the rudiments of style, grammatical propriety and the technicalities required to produce this book. Her diligence and comprehensive oversight gave life to this book. Merely thanking Mel, her husband Steve, and their daughter Anna-Kaye for their unwavering support is inadequate. Hopefully, Mel's impact on this book will bless her as much as the time and energy she devoted to this project.

I am convinced God uses whatever medium He chooses to reach those He wants to use in His service. I trust that by allowing me to use Facebook initially to provide my testimony and now this book, it will be an instrument to reach the suffering, hopeless and those in need of a timely word in finding peace and comfort, enabling them to give God all glory while enjoying His love through the gift of others.

BACKGROUND

What if, one day, you went to the doctor and came back with a diagnosis that turned out to be something that was on no one's radar? A disease spreading so fast that with each passing day the probability of your death increased exponentially? What if that critical disease gave no precursory notice or warning signs but snuck up on you without any drumbeat to herald its coming? How would you react when you realized that your life-sustaining bloodstream was the transport being used to diffuse the disease throughout your body and that the disease had already consumed sizable chunks of your skeletal mass and was on course to destroy your vital organs? How would you react?

Considering the advanced space-age science and technologies now available to the medical profession, with enough money, shouldn't it be a simple exercise of using your earthly resources to pay for your absolute cure? But what if the current science declares your condition incurable? Who would take your call for help and have the capabilities to guarantee your healing?

Would you have the confidence in a solution that could defy human facts and ensure your cure if you knew how to access it? Would God the Father be that Source with whom you have such a secure relationship that, in faith, He becomes your certain first point of call? When medical science declares a prognosis, which is based on evidence, quantifiable by statistics, and has been widely established as factual, does it make sense to confound such an obvious scientific reality with an abstract concept such as faith? To claim healing through the irrational and illogical idea of faith and be able to sustain such conviction, especially when every medical therapy continuously fails, require an indomitable fortitude in an authority that is beyond human reasoning.

The Bible teaches that with the smallest level of faith, it is possible to move a mountain. My mountain was a deadly disease. In June 2016, I was diagnosed with the most advanced stage of an incurable type of cancer. It was metastatic. Much damage had already been done to my body, and that form of cancer was fatal. One day I was healthy, the next I was hospitalized with a gloomy prognosis as a result of the late stage at which the diagnosis was made. The doomsday prognosis loomed ominously and presented me with the bleak outlook of never seeing my lifelong dreams becoming a reality and instead offered an easy pass to the great beyond.

Informed by my Christian belief, I chose the faith route, believing that the merciful God, through faith, would heal me. My journey in faith was not a simple wish-and-wait; as long as I remained in my human existence, I was plagued with the natural impulses of my human mind. I experienced the gamut of emotions from denial, to anger, to panic, to fear. Fear instinctively induced doubts in my mind and constantly painted pictures of worst-case scenarios. I had to condition my thinking to accept certain fundamental concepts. First, accepting the facts of my diagnosis, acknowledging that I live in the natural world where natural laws present natural phenomena of which sickness is one, then coming to an understanding of what should be my truth—that the ultimate resolution would be whatever the sovereign Lord determined and that, in faith, I would believe His promises, as written in the Bible, were meant for me. Finally, the faith process is nonprescriptive and unfathomable. The exact time of the healing I hope for in faith is not determined by me or anyone else.

The journey was an exercise in learning. I was taught the meaning of indomitable courage to stay committed to the faith objective, believing in the promises of our LORD. I had to disallow any circumstance that could cause discouragement, doubt, or wavering, trusting that there would be a definite time that God would reward my relentless and sustaining faith.

I dared to believe that God would help me to muster up the level of faith required, to access my healing through His grace, defying all predicaments portended by the facts. Little did I know that the "days of my faith" challenge would turn into weeks, months, and years and that the roller-coaster journey I was on would persistently confront me with challenges even to the very validity of my faith belief.

As my condition rapidly deteriorated, I was forced to come to terms rather quickly with the sobering realities of my progressive ineptitude. I became both physically and mentally incapacitated, unable to continue functioning competently on my own, let alone physically contribute to my care. I acknowledged the wonders of medical science and technologies but also recognized their limitations. Where science presented boundaries, grace through faith abounded limitless options and opportunities. According to current science, I would ultimately succumb to the eventualities of the disease in a short time. Through Jesus Christ, grace afforded me potentials, embedded in the mysteries yet to be revealed by God, including a cure for my affliction. In faith, I believed that God would unveil the remedy for my disorder to the domain of science. Although my situation was critical, I refused to accept that it was my death sentence; instead, I believed that God had allowed it. He is sovereign; He brought me into existence and determined when I would exit. When faced with death, I chose to believe that God could spare my life. I called on God in faith, knowing that through His grace I would be healed.

From the beginning of my illness, I had started to document my journey and continued to do so in real time through posts I shared on Facebook. It was like journaling publicly about my status. Unbeknownst to me at the time of my journaling, I was creating footprints of my faith walk. I did not know it then, but later, I realized I was bearing witness of God's love to me. From the hospital bed or the confines of my room, I was grateful to be able to share my real-time experiences with friends and family through social media.

My initial postings on Facebook were merely intended to keep my friends and family updated on my condition. They started out as vague lines from precepts I learned as a child, then moved to progressive status reports about my illness to include influences of my Christian faith. Because of the very gratifying feedback from friends of various dispositions and persuasions, I was motivated to be candid with every experience I had while going through the journey. In response, I learned that many of my friends had begun to come to terms with their individual mortality, fixing long-standing unresolved relational issues, and generally thinking of how they could be better people. Some readers were actually sharing my posts with others who were not Facebook subscribers.

The posts were my only outlet and connection with most people, but because of my impaired mental and cognitive state many of them were unclear and confusing. Regardless, there was an emerging chorus of encouragers, actively persuading me to document my journey in book form, as they believed it would be useful to a wider audience. But even if I wanted to write a book, I was physically and mentally incapable at the time. I also wanted to focus on sharing updates on my progress and not allow the thoughts being shared to be influenced by other motives.

It was never my desire to put myself through the daunting challenge of writing a book, particularly one that would put me front and center, albeit having God and His wonderful goodness as the focal point. The thought of me staying focused long enough to express myself, across multiple pages, was far too daunting a challenge. I was not prepared for the rigor it would take and the infinite public scrutiny to which I would be exposed. Even worse, I contemplated that my style of writing in book form might not satisfy the discriminating preferences of potential readers. If I ever wrote a book, I wanted to be so liberated that it would be an accurate reflection of my personality. You see, I was raised in a culture where, even though English was the primary language, "proper English" was reserved for the classroom or when it was explicitly mandated. Most of my countrymen and I spoke the de facto language, which is a unique form of patois.

Moreover, my last formal English class was in high school, and as a lifetime "techie," my English would be more appropriately written in numeric codes and schematics. Further, my natural childhood writing style was of a flowery and superfluous composition, layered with analogies and embellished with idioms and metaphors.

To skimp on the number of adjectives used in a sentence was, to me, literary suicide. However, in the work environment, I had to change my natural writing style. I had to adopt the bulleted PowerPoint, five-second elevator pitches, designed to capture the fleeting attention of busy C-suite executives. Initially, I felt as though I was sacrificing clarity for brevity. My penchant for reverting to my childhood writing style earned me a few demerits in the corporate world from my superiors. So, to write a book was never an option I would even consider. These paradigms, of mostly style over substance, made me question my competence to adequately yet comfortably express myself in the public domain.

Social media brought me poetic justice and provided me a means of communication; sick and challenged as I was. My grammatical mistakes were forgivable since abbreviations and emojis could mask my inadequacies, and I could escape the scrutiny of the writing police.

The postings I made on Facebook reflected my purest and most honest self and were maybe too transparent at times. In my vulnerable state, I feared I might have been too candid with my truths, which could potentially be embarrassing upon reading them later. As such, I was never motivated to review anything I had written when the chemo fog began clearing and I had regained some level of cognitive competency. I was, however, riding waves of encouragement from well-wishers to combine my postings into a book.

I eventually mustered up enough courage to commence reviewing what I had written. I wanted to get a sense of what my altered state of mind had produced. As expected, the posts were loaded with grammatical errors, awkward sentence construction, and quips, which even I had difficulty deciphering. Those unscripted posts were quite revealing of my pathetic, pitiful state. I later realized that most people might have struggled to decrypt what I was trying to convey. By reading them, I was able to relive some of the saddest moments of my life when I dealt with my most profound sense of despair, while piously reaching out to God in faith for complete healing. Each post was episodic, and each reminded me of roads that I never desire to travel again.

The freshness of these experiences made it difficult for me to resist the urge to editorialize each post and present a more contextualized framework. I wanted to provide clarity of the prevailing circumstances at the time, but it was more challenging than I initially thought as they evoked some raw emotions. Revisiting each post allowed me to relive all the emotions as though they were still quite fresh. All my senses would return to the places and times of the encounters: the sounds, smells, distasteful medicines, and pains resurfaced and clouded my mind. They were so palpable, I had to push myself through the emotional hurt the memories reintroduced.

Although ambivalent about the awesomeness of the undertaking, I began to venture beyond simply nurturing an urge and secretly started to make notes about each post. Not long after, one Sunday, our bishop made a prophetic revelation that I would write an impactful book. Emboldened by what I believed was a revelation from God, I feverishly expanded the work I was doing on the Facebook postings, convinced that I would write this book. Because I had previously documented my experiences while they were happening, I figured it would be an easy undertaking to formulate a big picture of each episode. It was easier said than done.

I wanted to maintain the integrity of the original posts without gross alterations. Because of how I had written some of the posts, I had to make slight modifications to individual sentences and phraseologies in a few of them. I also included materials that had been eliminated from the original Facebook posts because of their length.

This book contains either the exact postings or slight modifications of these posts, hopefully maintaining their authenticity and conveying with integrity the true message of my journey. The original Facebook postings in this book are indented to differentiate and set them off from other texts. The expanded comments to the posts are intended to provide a contextual framework or additional details of what influenced each episode that I posted. Having documented my experiences in near real time and sharing them in context, I hope to present a unique perspective—one that not just widens the aperture on the mind of the anguished and tormented but demonstrates how faith in God provides inspiration and purpose to sustain me through the adversities and trials. And how God interspersed my tribulations with joy and hope so that I would endure with great expectation for my deliverance and a prosperous future. I pray that God will receive all the glory for this effort.

At the time of writing, I was still struggling with the remnants of the disease and its impact on my cognitive capabilities, but I did not want to deprive the reader of me "keeping it real," even within those constraints. Sometimes it took me hours to compose a paragraph. The effects of the medications were exhausting, and coupled with the havoc of the disease, it did not take much for my brain to be saturated with information overload. The ideas I wanted to express were fleeting. As soon as I formulated a thought, I would lose it and had no way of recalling what I was previously thinking. That meant I would continuously have to disrupt my writing process and make random jottings so that I could reference them later. To merely express a thought, I had to consult dictionaries and other resources as my vocabulary had new diminished limits. But God wanted me to do this work, and He provided me the tools of the trade. Thank God for online resources. To whom much is given, much is required, and God has blessed me tremendously.

Nothing is impossible for God. A death sentence declared by science can only come to fruition if God says so. God is omniscient (all-knowing), and nothing happens without His knowledge and approval. He is merciful and provides grace for every need.

If my story brings comfort to anyone who is going through any form of terminal illness or helps caregivers and family members of the sick become more sensitized to the physical and mental challenges of the sufferer, then, I believe that writing this book would have accomplished God's will. By sharing my experiences, I intend to provide hope to the reader and glorify our Almighty Father. I sincerely pray that as you read this testimony, you will see the hand of God at work, as my faith keeps producing my healing. If there is any confusion, I pray that God will provide clarity through the Holy Spirit so that you too will be convinced that faith in God can produce in reality whatever you hope for prayerfully in faith. May the grace of our Lord Jesus Christ and the fellowship of the Holy Spirit guide you through the reading of my story.

CHAPTER 1

Is Something Wrong with Me?

*The secret things belong to the LORD our God, but
the things revealed belong to us and to our sons forever,
that we may observe all the words of this law.*

—Deuteronomy 29:29 (NASB)

I s something wrong with me? Something is wrong; I think some-thing is definitely wrong. At some point, I will have to let her know; she must see the magnetic resonance imaging (MRI) report. I cannot withhold it from her any longer. Nothing is striking about the main body of the report that we can't handle. I am not too bothered about what I regard as just a suggestion, an indication of something that is worth further exploration; nothing more. I comfort myself with the belief that it is purely a parenthetical comment; in fact, I hope that's all it is. Of course! There is a particular word in the report that is not filling me with optimism.

Whatever the radiologist meant, I know that my wife will help me put it in its proper context—it's a mere suggestion, nothing more. Like me, I know she will say that it is not anything particularly con-sequential, but it is undoubtedly worth the follow-up actions sug-gested. She will agree that this is generally what good doctors do out of an abundance of caution. It is not a diagnosis as such, just part of a holistic approach to patient care. I will be fine, and she will agree with me that it is not a big deal. My wife is a compassionate, nurturing soul, a consummate professional, and a nurse of distinction. Once she reviews this MRI report, I bet she will find that hidden nugget of hope and alleviate any fear that may have crossed my mind. "Everything is going to be all right dear, there is nothing to worry about, we see this every day," she'll say, right?

Amazingly, she went through the report rather quickly. Wow! That was completely unexpected—that reaction of hers. With her professionally trained eyes, I had to respect her ability to browse the content and pick out the salient points faster than I could. As a nurse, I appreciated her ability to quickly analyze and interpret the information, determine if there was anything needing attention, and outline the potential severity and consequences of the findings. But that ear-shattering shriek of hers, and her sudden collapse to the ground, left me torn to shreds. I went frozen stiff, my whole body shook, and my knees wobbled like jelly. I was too weak, too shocked and anguished to stand and pick her off the floor from where she had collapsed.

Over the swirl of confusion in my head, bone-chilling fear and anxiety, I deciphered some of the most crippling utterances from her, "I have never been alone in my life. We've always been together; how will I manage without you?" Those words struck at my very soul and pierced it deeply. My eyes started to well up. My focus then shifted from my selfish consciousness that something drastic could be impending for me, to an overwhelming wave of compassion. Here was the woman who had unconditionally devoted more than thirty of the best years of her life to me, now being challenged with the possibility of a drastic life change. Our family picture could be substantially altered.

That MRI report must be terrible then—in fact, far worse than I thought. Hopefully, it was just a spontaneous shock and a knee-jerk reaction on her part. The truth is, I was unprepared for such a response. The reality was, although a nurse, she was also human and my wife. She was emotionally connected to me, who was the subject of the report. I was not just another patient in her line of business. There was a dichotomous dynamic in play then. The compassionate, emotional wife confronted with the professional code and ethics that govern how to communicate with a patient. Not that I was her patient. That aside, it was my turn to react. I was shaking with dread, in fear of a worst-case scenario for us. That report was not a recipe for cupcakes but a statement of facts that could lead to a diagnosis with dire consequences.

The primary emphasis of the MRI report highlighted relevant and important findings showing severe damage to my cervical spine and lesions in the areas reviewed. There were, however, even more weighty implications in those few lines of comments that were unsettling. In my apparent state of denial, I concluded that they were merely implicit postscripts, even though they had caused much upheaval. I was contented and happy for them to remain mere suggestions rather than a professional diagnosis. I forced my brain to pick apart the report and fish for ambiguities, inferences, and vague insinuations that could counter the validity of the comments, but without success. I then tried to criticize the work of the learned professional who produced the report. He is a radiologist, not an oncologist and is not professionally qualified to make a diagnosis of the sort; as such, it was a simple suggestion. "Does this doctor remember that my original complaint was a pain in the neck and ribs?" "That isn't even a diagnosis anyway, it is just something he suggests that one should seek to follow up on based on his professional expertise." Admittedly, his reasoning was logical and made perfect sense to me. It was just not what I wanted to believe.

Somehow what was being implied did not add up for me. Just a few weeks ago, I was a regular at the gym and worked out aggressively. I have always eaten as well as I should and maintained a relatively clean lifestyle. I never did drugs, never smoked, or worked in any high-risk areas. Of course, the observations by the radiologist of bone spurs, lesions, and a fractured spine are logical reasons to be referred to an orthopedic specialist. My primary care physician summarily contacted me and advised me that he had arranged for me to see an orthopedic specialist immediately. Perfect! It was not an oncologist—what a relief! That sounded like a logical next step to me. With all the damage to my skeletal structure now diagnosed, it was no wonder my primary care physician prescribed the very serious opioid-based pain medications subsequently. These medications had to be some potent stuff since the prescriptions had to be hand-delivered to the pharmacist. The MRI report had validated the severity of the pains about which I had complained. To further compound the issue, the report included that dreaded word, which caused concern and heightened our state of anticipation and anxiety. That dreadful, blood-curdling word was from the angel of death's dictionary; it was "*metastasize.*"

CHAPTER 2

Doctor, Doctor, Doctor

*In my distress I called upon the LORD, and cried out
to my God; He heard my voice from His temple, and
my cry came before Him, even to His ears.*

—Psalm 18:6 (NKJV)

Shortly after receiving the MRI results, and before being hospitalized and ultimately diagnosed, my wife and I, being Christians,
deemed it imperative to seek God's intervention. We prayed and
asked God's healing and deliverance for whatever the final diagnosis
would be. We were confident that God already knew what the diagnosis was, the journey we would have to go through, and what the
outcome would be. We also knew that we needed to heed the advice
provided by health-care professionals and make individual choices
on our own. As a health-care professional, she understood that we
could be in error if we were too arrogant in our journey. The Bible
tells us in Proverbs 12:15 (NKJV), "The way of a fool is right in his
own eyes, but he who heeds counsel is wise."

James 5:14 (NIV) instructs us as follows, "Is anyone among you
sick? Let them call the elders of the church to pray over them and
anoint them with oil in the name of the Lord."

In obedience, therefore, we contacted the bishop and pastors
of our church. Our belief aligns with that of our local assembly that

God still performs healing, through His grace, if we exercise our faith. The following Sunday, our bishop was kind enough to agree with us in prayer. He modified the traditional order of service and invited me and two others, who were experiencing other illnesses, for prayers. That "altar encounter" was like none I had ever experienced.

There was no doubt that our bishop and pastors were "purpose driven" in faith, advocating God for our healing, and were determined to yield no ground to afflictions, whether or not our sufferings were of the devil or caused by anything that was not of God. We were anointed with oil, and our bishop prayed with every earnestness and faith he could. The entire congregation was in unison to seek God's mercy for us. The experience was transformative. The last conscious act I recalled for a while was my knees buckling, too weak to support the weight of my body and the power of the Holy Spirit taking control. I had a temporary mental departure from the natural world, barely conscious to appreciate what was happening in my surroundings, but I heard enough to perceive that the entire congregation was advocating God on our behalf.

Orthopedic 1

Yours, O LORD, is the greatness and the power and the glory and the victory and the majesty, for all that is in the heavens and in the earth is yours. Yours is the kingdom, O LORD, and you are exalted as head above all.

—1 Chronicles 29:11 (ESV)

For more than fifteen years, I have been cared for by the same primary care physician, so he has a good record of my medical history. He takes a very personal and holistic approach to the management of my health and well-being. I trust and depend on him for his professional guidance and sensitivity to my health-care needs, so I was in full agreement when he arranged for me to see an orthopedic specialist shortly after receiving the MRI report. It is incredible how anxiety and fear exaggerate things and times. The few days I had to wait seemed like an eternity. Where was Philippians 4:6 that I should have committed to memory for a time like that? It clearly instructed me, "Do not be anxious about anything, but in every situation, by prayer and petition, with thanksgiving, present your requests to God."

As I sat in the waiting area at the orthopedic office, my heart was pounding so loudly that I imagined everyone could hear it. Funny how, as a Christian, we can allow fear to strip us of our faith power. It didn't matter then how many times I had prayed or was praying; my faith belief was interspersed with fear. In faith, I was hoping that after the X-ray, the orthopedic specialist would find a way to patch me up and send me on my way. In fear, I pondered a thousand different options of worst-case scenarios. I could be crippled, unable to speak, or I could die. I was so relieved to get the X-ray process over with and the report of the orthopedic specialist, to set my mind at ease.

During the waiting period for the orthopedic appointment, my dear wife and I prayed even more than we did before. We had also previously enlisted prayers from other friends, families, and support groups, so there was abundant support for us even during the quiet period of pre-diagnosis. People continually assured us that they were praying and had asked others for prayers on my behalf, or sometimes physically visited and prayed with me. I vividly remember the day one of our precious friends in faith believing drove separately to the orthopedic appointment, stayed in her car, and prayed throughout the session.

The long-awaited moment had arrived. The X-ray images had been processed and analyzed by the doctor, and the revelations of his findings were imminent. After what appeared to be a rather quick review, he called me in to discuss the results. I can't remember how many times I prayed, or if I prayed at all, as I got up to receive the results in his office. I was too anxious to receive the report of man. The faith-man was subjugated, yielding prominence to the flesh man. When I write of "the flesh," I am not speaking of the physical covering of our bones. The flesh man is that sin nature that operates solely on human wisdom and sensual impulses and opposes the works of the Holy Spirit. The expression on the face of the orthopedic specialist foretold the diagnosis. The results were not good. I was way too discombobulated to comprehend or even hear the doctor's explanations.

I was tuned to different frequencies that had nothing to do with what he was saying at that moment. I had never seen a picture of what my healthy spine had looked like before, so there was no reference for me to compare the distorted, fractured mush that he displayed as representing my spine on the X-ray picture. It seemed as though there was a massive gouge in the upper section known as the cervical spine

"Oh well, that confirms it all," I concluded. From the little I gleaned, my cervical spine was severely damaged. I would need time to effectively unpack everything the orthopedic doctor was throwing at me at that time. I soon realized that he was referring me to another orthopedic surgeon at one of the most advanced teaching hospitals in the area. The fact that he was personally setting up the appointment on my behalf right there and then was disconcerting. My situation required an outrageous sense of urgency. My interpretation was that the fracture in my spine was too far gone for him to treat.

Dejected and still in a halo of disbelief, I somehow transported myself outside where our friend, who had accompanied us to the doctor but chose to stay in the car and pray earnestly, was anxiously waiting for us. She declared the revelation she had received from her prayers, that I would not die regardless of the results. That was so in line with what Psalm 118:17 declares, "I shall not die, but live, and declare the works of the Lord." With that assurance, I had some renewal of hope that the Lord would work some miracle to keep me alive. For that, I gave thanks and worship to God, our merciful Father.

Orthopedic 2

May the God of hope fill you with all joy and peace as you trust in him, so that you may overflow with hope by the power of the Holy Spirit.

—Romans 15:13 (NIV)

"What might be going through the mind of our young son who is now providing me physical support?" I pondered. He has a future to build that does not include being burdened by my circumstances. What must it feel like seeing me, the former backbone he has relied on since birth, so disheveled and weak? His father, so debilitated and in pain that he needs the physical support of his son. There I was, cautiously gripping my walking cane with one hand and desperately leaning on him for support as I tentatively limped from the car to the orthopedic office. "I should now qualify for accessible parking space, I think, this walk is far too long for me to endure with the excruciating pains I feel. It is such a chore to walk these days," I murmured. I talked relentlessly, mostly nonsense, in a vain attempt to distract my newly appointed tower of strength from focusing on me, and the burden he may perceive me being in the future.

I had never given any thought to how many people would be impacted and inconvenienced by my dilemma until now. I, Mr. Self-Made, Independent Man, was now so severely damaged by my debilitation that it almost brought me to my knees.

A sense of guilt enveloped me as I hobbled my feeble body at a snail's pace under the searing Georgia midday sun. I was desperately hoping my faithful pillar of support would be patient enough not to outpace me, as I would fall and even break my bones (if only I knew then how real the likelihood of me breaking bones was). This young man had just graduated from college a few days now, and he did not need to be saddled with my burdens. His life was just beginning, and I didn't want to impose on his progress.

I could not comprehend the traumatic shocks he had to endure because of the real-life episodes he had to live through in those days. He'd never seen me in such a debilitated state. I had always been Mr. Fix It; I think he or my daughter might have bought me the T-shirt for Father's Day some years ago that read: "Mr. Fix It." After all, I usually found a way to fix everything around the home, and they might have been under the illusion that I could overcome anything. The family had always relied on me to come through and deliver. I had worn the mask of the superhero in the home deceptively well, but there I was, limping like a wounded prey when I walked and leaning like the Tower of Pisa when I stood. I was becoming a piece of historical relic, I thought. I was weak, every joint hurt, my bones had a constant, dull, numbing pain that would not subside, and I could hear my bed calling me to rest.

While I awaited my turn to be called by the clinicians, I tried to make light of my circumstance with anyone who would engage with me. I joked around with anyone who dared to ask why I was wearing the bizarre, imposing neck brace, which was prescribed by the previous orthopedic doctor. I told them my flamboyant neck brace was a new male accessory that I was promoting. My comments and actions might have elicited a few brief laughs and additional dialogue, but my real motives were to create distractions so as not to concentrate on my dilemma and to save my son from boredom. As I stumbled into the examination room, I felt a sense of relief; I would be in good hands. That great Wiz Bang, glow-in-the-dark, prodigiously smart doctor would magically find the issue, fix me up, and I would be as good as new.

Another set of X-rays, but I didn't mind, I was in the presence of this super-brilliant orthopedic specialist. "Well, not again! He is not smiling; no eye contact with me." "Did they read the MRI report?" "I'm not hypersensitive, am I?" "Maybe this is how these super-brilliant, top-notch specialists must behave." "There you go, at least he is doing some physical or occupational-type tests on me to be convinced that I am well, and I shall do my best to extract the learnings out of him."

Those were some of the contemplations of my inquisitive, anxious mind on opioids. After hitting me on the leg a few times, he had me do some arm and finger strength tests, which, in my opinion, I performed with the utmost dexterity. Everything he asked of me, I did impressively—by my assessment. Aside from the little spinal injury thing, I would be declared fine—at least that is what I wanted to believe. I was betting that he had seen similar conditions a thousand times and fixed them all. I bet there was some nice little bright shiny gadget with some form of high-tech computer guided laser knife in his office, just waiting to make me whole again, at least I hoped. "I am entitled to my hope, am I not?" Such were my dreamland musings; I was shrouding myself in the classic cloak of denial.

So much for optimism. "Sir," the doctor explained, "the fracture of your cervical spine is very severe, it is very bad. Even attempting surgery could be a dangerous proposition. We would have to go through your throat and would be operating on small bone structures. It would be a very delicate operation, and there are so many things that could go wrong." For a moment, I wanted to believe that I could be hearing a conversation intended for someone else. Had I tuned in to the wrong frequency or was it just my luck to show up at the wrong time of day when the X-ray machines weren't taking accurate pictures? But then, even more dreaded news. "I think you should proceed with oncology treatment and see how that turns out, and we can take it from there."

"Where did that come from?" If someone had grabbed my head and viciously twisted it, even in its hypersensitive state, I would not have felt it. My spinal cord would have blocked all pain signals to my brain. I was numb, drained of all energy, and devoid of any emotions. Any hope for a false positive and that my diagnosis could be anything else but that which I feared most was rapidly diminishing. I had heard enough and didn't have the guts to seek any further clarification from the orthopedic doctor. The shock from the progressive revelations of successive doctors left me bereft of comprehensibility and devoid of any ability to reason. They were all now pointing in one direction.

I hung my head in anguish and took my leave of the orthopedic specialist's presence, hardly acknowledging him or anyone in my vicinity. This was in stark contrast to the lively, vivacious comic who had made such a joyful and highly expectant entrance earlier. It was challenging for me to come to terms with what I suspected based on the earlier radiologist's assertions. Now the waves of emotions were coming to the fore; I was panicking. Dispirited and anxious, I was faced with reality but still in denial about my next anticipated diagnosis. I knew enough to figure out what oncology meant. Twice, I was declared a lost cause and told there was nothing that could be done to impact my situation. Well, I had much; I could pray, and pray I did, because only God knows and could help me through my next encounter.

In the silence of my soul, I prayed with humility, appealing to God my Savior for mercy. As best as I can recall, it took the form of: "Oh Lord, my God, my Father, You have searched me, You know my heart, You have seen my deeds, only You have the authority to judge me, treat me as You please. You have the ultimate power to allow or disallow anything in or on me, even power over the evil of this terrible sickness that has befallen me. I was a sinner, but You saved me by Your grace. Judge me as is Your prerogative, but please be merciful to me when You pronounce my sentence. As for every wrong You find me guilty of, I beg Your mercies and forgiveness. Please do not cast me from Your presence or take Your Holy Spirit from me; otherwise, the damnation of hell will be my destiny. Lord, please help me through the next leg of my journey, and please provide me Your guidance. In faith, I walk, believing that Your grace is sufficient for me. I pray in the name of Jesus Christ." I believe that prayer may have been influenced by one that I read from I-Bible at some point during my illness.

Amid all my pain and disappointments, there were still my other external obligations. I still had a job, with several projects in progress. Would I lose my primary source of income? Did I have adequate insurance to ensure that I would be covered for the duration of my care? Would there be expenses incurred for procedures that I couldn't meet? Who would step up and take charge of my general obligations and duties at home? I had not done an excellent job at succession planning. I had not prepared a will. Things were moving too fast, too sudden for my impaired brain to compute so many permutations and assess the potential impacts. I was not prepared for a long-term illness. I couldn't afford to be a burden on my wife and my family unnecessarily. My wife has a full-time job and may have to become the sole breadwinner. It was unfair for me to impose on her whatever consequences my evolving state would bring. It was not the best time for me to try to address the complex issues that were confronting me. My health was foremost, and where I needed to focus.

It had become high time for me to deal with my current reality. I needed to move beyond the state of denial and schedule the dreaded but inevitable appointment with the oncologist. It was not that I had any prior familiarity with any oncologist to form an opinion; it's just that I hated to face the inevitable sound of the music that was playing for me that might validate the notes in the MRI report.

It was difficult for me to get a quick appointment within the hospital system, but I knew I needed one urgently. I was now experiencing excruciating pains in my upper spine and was compelled to accept any available slot anywhere I could get one. Desperation was setting in, and I was being consumed by pains and becoming increasingly distressed by the uncertainty of the unknown. My only comfort came from the knowledge that God loved me and that He would direct me to the place most suited for His perfect work in me. When I finally got an appointment, it was several miles away from my home, and I had to suffer two more weeks of increasing pains. Upon reflection, it was possibly the ideal choice among the options, and it had to be of God. The facilities at the hospital were relatively modern, and the hospital itself was among the best, complemented by the excellent care I received from some of the most attentive professional caregivers.

Two weeks away from my oncology appointment, and I could tell that things were not improving; I was rapidly getting worse. The pains were now all over my body and were beyond excruciating. I knew I was losing weight fast as I didn't have an appetite, and it pained even to open my mouth wide enough to eat. My memory was fading, and I was not able to think well or focus on anything but the pain in my spine. I was unable to fully recall too many details of what happened in the ensuing days. I could not even maintain a reasonably good conversation with anyone. I was getting weaker, more listless, and easily out of breath and exhausted. That would not be bearable for much longer. I had never coveted so much to see a doctor as I waited to be assessed by the oncologist.

One bright spark of light occurred when my daughter came to visit from the West Coast. Although I did not want her to see me in my current state, I was so glad to see her. She tried to bring some level of peace and comfort to me. I could sense her desperation to do what she could to help alleviate my condition. She sat on the floor next to my bed and, many times, watched me weep and wail profusely from the crippling pains—the first time in her life she was seeing me cry. Even if I tried, I had no pride left in me to exercise control. Literally, with my mouth wide open, I bawled uncontrollably like a terrified child. There she was, offering me every comforting suggestion she knew, fetching whatever she thought would ease my pain and darting off to the pharmacy late at night to get me whatever concoction or devices she and my wife thought would bring me some level of comfort. So, there I went, ruining the life of another person with my suffering. God knows how she endured watching me suffer, because she is a daddy's girl.

My constant prayers became more repentant as I sought forgiveness from unworthiness. The plight of Job became my primary biblical reference. As I thought of him, I could not fathom myself being anywhere close to his righteousness. I regarded Job as the epitome of virtue. So righteous was he that God allowed him to be afflicted and tested to extremes to demonstrate that a human being could be faithful to Him. Job was left to the torturous ways of the devil. Although he was righteous and highly favored, God allowed Job to endure human torment and significant personal losses. How much worse could it be for me then, being the relatively unrighteous person I was? Incidentally, I was more focused on Job's good work than on the power and potential of my faith. By comparing myself with Job, I became resentful of certain aspects of my sinful past and was angered by it.

Oncology

*Do not fret or have any anxiety about anything, but
in every circumstance and in everything, by prayer
and petition (definite requests), with thanksgiving,
continue to make your wants known to God.*

—Philippians 4:6 (AMPC)

On the day of the appointment with the oncologist, my son was again tasked with the burden of being my transporter. One of the few things I recall quite vividly was the immediacy of the decision to hospitalize me. That further affirmed my fears about my condition. Having never been in a hospital for more than a few minutes at any time, I was disturbed but somehow relieved.

I have never liked hospitals. I have a morbid fear of the place, no matter how clean and fancy it looks. Ever since I was a child, I have been horrified by the smells, the uniforms, the needles, the bandages, the wheelchairs; everything about hospitals spelled death to me. I am not sure if it was because my grandmother, to whom I was very close, died while hospitalized when I was a youngster. What irony that I should marry a nurse and hate hospitals. Weirdly, deep in my psyche, maybe it's because I hoped that she would keep me from being hospitalized. My outlook about the institution, however, began to change when the oncologist commented that my attitude was such that I would pull through my ailment. I was thinking, "Flesh and blood did not reveal that to her." For the first time, a clinician, a specialist in her field, had declared that I was not beyond repair.

Hospitalization 1

And we know that all things work together for good to those who love God, to those who are the called according to His purpose.

—Romans 8:28 (NKJV)

The first phase of a new and enlightening escapade was the speed with which the oncologist made her decision to hospitalize me. First came the wheelchair. I've never been toted around in a wheelchair before. It struck me then that I was sick, but in my confused and convoluted mind, I allowed myself to bask in the luxury of being wheeled around by someone else. It conveyed the sense of the good life. I had finally arrived, but really, I hadn't expected it would be in a hospital! Where was my anticipated mansion and all its opulence? After more than forty years of working almost non-stop in the pressure cooker of corporate life, with long nights of planning, meetings, strategy sessions, and rising to the aggressive demands of the technology environment that had become my life, I was finally going to have some rest, in the luxurious resort known as a hospital. There would be no work-related pressures from instant messaging and presence technology that typically tracked me down no matter where I was.

From the look of things, I would be in the hospital beyond the weekend. So on Monday, someone else would have to respond and take responsibility on my behalf. This time, I felt no guilt for being absent from work; my recovery was now the priority. The compulsion to feel accountable for unfinished work slid way down my pecking order, giving rise to the need to focus on healing and recovery. My place, then, was in one of those beautiful little motorized hospital beds. There, I would live out a childhood fantasy of impulsively raising and lowering the bed at will, just for the fun of it. It was time to be catered to by a host of caring and loving professionals, who would serve at my beck and call during my stay. In the solace offered by my quiet room, I would be undisturbed and have the pleasure of drifting away in blissful solitude.

What a mistake that was. Who fooled me? There would be no peace in my valley, no warm island breezes to caress my cheeks on the beach, and no extended sleep fest. The minute my head touched the pillow, I was swarmed by an ever-changing, keenly focused hive of professionals, whose glancing smiles and pleasantries were as brief as the fleeting wind. "They must know something that I don't." "Why do they avoid eye contact with me?" "Am I dying?" "Why else would so many different professionals be taking turns at me, in such short order, to perform all those different examinations?" They reminded me of worker bees, always in flight, then perching on me. They would come buzzing into my room with drill squad precision, executing their plan of care, only to be replaced by others as soon as they exited. "This is the big one! I'm dying! You hear that, Elizabeth? I'm coming to join you, honey!" (Sanford and Son). In my case, Elizabeth is my grandmother's middle name.

As I pondered the awesomeness of the responsibilities the team was entrusted with, I contemplated how much my life hinged on the accuracy and competence of those professional caregivers—with a single error, I could die. They had the burden of ensuring that regardless of the volume of work, absolute accuracy was paramount as my life depended on what they documented. Imagine the potentially dangerous consequences of substituting a B for an A blood type and having that wrong blood type transfused in me. At that moment, I became conscious of the plight of my diligent wife, whose twelve-hour shifts usually turn out to be fifteen hours. Weary and tired as she struggled home, I often wondered what could cause her to be so delayed every night. Through what I observed, I gained a new level of appreciation and sympathy for her and her professional peers. These were among the myriad of fleeting thoughts flooding my anxious and excited mind and, fortunately for me, they filled the gaps that would otherwise be occupied with the dreaded consequences of my impending diagnosis.

Although it was too early to be conclusive about my diagnosis, it was clear that something was seriously wrong with me. I was terrified by what I believed the medical professionals suspected. The suspense of not knowing was worse than the pain.

Meanwhile, it occurred to me that hardly anyone outside of close family and friends knew of my recent status change. I am not sure if I had told more than five people that I was ill. I had taken vacation leave from work, so my absence could have been interpreted as business as usual. After pondering how I would break the news to friends, I recalled reading the candid account of a friend about his illness. He had used Facebook to convey his story, and I was very impressed by the openness and honesty with which he gave his account. I realized that it could be a means for me to control the narrative about me en masse. My initial post on Facebook reflected the state of my soul. I was reaching out somewhat cryptically to convey a message of what could be my last days. Although philosophical, it shows that I was reflecting on my mortality; I was swinging from a spiderweb that could break at any time. I was aware that I could be meeting with my Creator soon. The post drew on what we call a "memory gem" or "precept" that I learned in school when I was probably five years old. It reads:

> *The clock of life is wound but once / And no man has the power / To tell what time the hands will stop / At late or early hour. (Robert H. Smith)*

How ironic it was that I had to go fishing in the kiddies' pool for rationale and comfort, now that I was weakened in health and dejected in spirit. "Once a man, twice a child." I didn't rationalize it then, but maybe in the depths of my psyche, I had to delve that deep into my childhood repository to find something simple that was relatable to even a child to convey the sense of regression I felt. That simple phrase communicated more than I imagined to several of my followers and friends. It was simple yet profound. It was my best characterization of my state of mind as I sought to answer the question: "Is it my time?"

Meanwhile, back at the hospital, the next intruder to disturb the quietude of my anticipated hospital vacation was a young technician, all businesslike and professional. He requested that I extend my arm. After scanning my armband and having me verify that it was, indeed, me, he proceeded to hook me up to his mobile diagnostic thingamajig. He then went on to puncture my arm with that dreaded weapon called the needle. I hate and fear needles beyond comprehension, but it was in my best interest to oblige him just this once. If only I could have imagined it then; that this was just the beginning.

The routine of poking, probing, and stabbing me with the horrific, dreaded weapon called the needle to extract from my depleting supply of blood was now set in place. At various times, night and day, they came dutifully wielding their little tech-enabled trolleys, sticking thermometers in a mouth that I could barely open, pinching my fingers between the small clamps, strapping Velcro bands around my arms then checking my blood pressure, and launching attacks at me with that detestable weapon of massive pain—the needle. "Why do they need these large quantities of blood from me? I mean, at 2am! Didn't they just take some from me at 10pm? I promise I won't allow

anymore at 5am tomorrow." I lost track of how many times throughout twenty-four hours I had the pleasurable company of these wonderful professionals whom I perceived as torturers. After a while, I
got into the habit of rudely greeting them as vampires under my
breath when they launched their attacks on me late at night. They
took it in their stride, and I do apologize to them now, even though I
knew they understood I meant it in jest. Between snoozing, I would
anticipate the ceremonial procession of blood-seeking professionals
as they made their timely march with such clocklike precision, as
though responding to some inaudible Pavlovian bell.

The practice became so repetitive that a willing arm of mine
would automatically be extended as soon as I heard the door open,
or the rattle and squeak of the nerve-racking trolleys. Even as I slept,
they wouldn't need to ask; my submissive arm would already be
there, as I muttered in my sleep, "Hello, vampire," in response to
their warm and cheerful greetings. Ignoring my discourteous, delusional ramblings, these wonderful caregivers would perform their
duties professionally and quietly. They simply desired a submissive
body with a willing arm extended and an open mouth to insert a
thermometer before extracting what I thought were massive amounts
of my blood. They would send the blood samples to the labs so that
real-time analysis could be performed and the critical decision made
for my care and well-being. I am so grateful for these professionals.

The strong medicines I was being administered were wreaking havoc on me. Amazingly, I was aware of my sudden cognitive
decline. My memory was so affected, I was not always able to recall
even recent incidents. I wanted to conceal it from my caregivers
and friends. My pride was also still intact, and I would hate to be
treated as the unfortunate mentally deficient subject laying helplessly
around. So, my plan was to present myself to the caregivers as a fully
capable intellectual human. I would devise schemes to mask any per-
ceivable hint of cognitive impairment. For starters, to demonstrate
how intact my memory was, I would try to memorize and preemptively yell out the names of my caregivers as soon as they entered the
room. The genius I was; their nametags were clearly on display, Mr.
Obvious would receive no award for such brilliance. Maybe I had

unravel. The impact of the juggernaut on my being was so
ming and beyond my control, it was distorting my thought
r-   And my pretense and denials were so transparent, anyone
could tell I was not firing on all cylinders.

In retrospect, I imagine I must have made quite a fool of myself
with my delusional antics. Pity the unfortunate caregivers who were
saddled with providing for my care in my confused state. The former talkative and opinionated me was languishing helplessly in a
place of uncertainty and information deprivation with my wild and
uncontrolled thoughts. I perceived everyone as being so motivated
to extract information from me, yet no one was telling me what was
wrong with me. What was puzzling to me at the time was the necessity for my caregivers' repeated questions about the same things. "Of
course it's my name and birthdate on the wristband. I have been
wearing it since one of your peers tagged me with it when I checked
in and I wouldn't have the strength to rip it off and replace it if I
wanted to," I would gripe to myself every time they asked me to
verify my personal identifiable information. I needed answers about
my condition—everyone was questioning me, but no one seemed
capable of filling me in on what was going on. In frustration, I was
often tempted to go into information-lockdown mode.

I guess this was an automatic self-defense strategy that kicked
in to protect me from bad news. The caregivers understood that
I was a Christian because I regularly alluded to the fact that God
would heal me and maybe mentioned a thing or two about my
faith. However, I met my match and was subsequently subdued
whenever a particular caregiver administered care to me. Served me
right! She had a Christian perspective on which she pedantically
lectured me. As I recall, her view did not totally align with mine.
Hers was highly academic and majored on minor details that, in
the grand scheme of things, did little to influence any change in
my understandings. To her credit, she was always in charge of the
monologues, lecturing me to her heart's content and giving me little
opportunity for rebuttal.

I imagined her delight each shift as she waited to give me a
dose of her dogma while I pretended to be ingesting it. As for the

rest of the team, I would give anything to have some of those discussions rehearsed to me. I developed a great relationship with most of the staff, predicated on wit, wry humor, and self-deprecation. When taken from the hospital each morning for radiation, I was usually strapped to a gurney. The EMTs elevated it to the highest level, so everyone had to look up to see me. Adorned in my neck brace and a hospital gown, I would be wheeled out for my half-hour ride for radiation. While passing by the nurses' stations, I would make some silly remarks, such as, "Behold, here comes your king, highly elevated," or some such garbage.

In my deluded mind, that charade had the desired effect: it evoked laughter, or at least positive responses, from my captive audience, and I relished their daily participation in my ridiculous act. In those days, I somehow craved the responses, as they assured me that I was still of some worth. Any gesture of positive acknowledgment made my confounding journey a bit more pleasant, and the attention helped to allay my fears.

Speaking of attention, I relished the initial feedback I received from my earlier Facebook postings. Shocked by the awareness of my deteriorating state, I made other preliminary posts, one of which I now reflect upon as conveying self-guilt. It was a follow-up to the previous precept that warned about the uncertainty of life. I was now advocating the need for right living, a remorseful voice too far gone to correct any past misdeeds. It advocated the need to do good things always, as we had no idea of when we would be called to give account for our work on earth. I felt like the biblical rich man in the Lazarus parable. Condemned after death, the rich man pleaded that Lazarus the poor man be sent back to the living to warn his family to do good deeds so that they would avoid a terrifying afterlife. From my hospital bed, I wrote down the following childhood precept, which reflected my perceived end-of-life appeal to everyone to do good to each other.

Do all the good you can / In all the ways
you can / To all the people you can / For
as long as you can. (John Wesley)

From my position of despair in that hospital room, confronted by the unknown, I wanted to make sure that if I departed from the current reality, others who read the posting would be inspired to do their best to please God and not wait until it was too late.

The mention of radiation earlier might have hinted to the fact that I was being treated for some form of a tumor. I was vaguely aware that, from time to time, there were various practitioners and specialists communicating with me. They were obviously not aware that I could not grasp most of what they were talking about. I was becoming more cognitively diminished, and my memory and comprehension capabilities were all but gone. Up to that point, I don't think anyone had presented us with a complete diagnosis, although I had many imaging tests done, including X-ray scans, MRIs, and bone biopsy.

They had identified a tumor in my cervical spine, and the object of five or six days of radiation was to eliminate it. That wretched mass had nestled and grown in my spine. As I later learned, one of the characteristics of the disease is to attack the skeletal system and (in my language) eat at your bones, then deposit tumors to infest the skeletal system. The clinical term is plasmacytoma, which is a tumor made up of cancerous cells. My cervical spine was one casualty of this phenomenon and my entire skeletal structure was affected.

All this time, the pains in my spine and bones were intensifying by the minute. The prescribed opioids only alleviated the misery for a while, and I had to be prescribed additional as needed dosages along with regularly scheduled ones. Opioids are medications that are commonly prescribed for intense pains, such as those associated with cancer. They are usually marketed as fentanyl, hydrocodone, tramadol, morphine, and oxycodone. My cervical spine C2-C4 was impacted. It was fractured and collapsed in that region. The pains associated with the fractured bones bearing down on my central nervous system were oppressive and intolerable. My fractured ribs and lytic bones throughout my body were riddled with excruciating pains, such as I have never experienced before. I was concerned that my privileged guest status at the hospital would soon end, and I would not have the host of round-the-clock professionals attending to my needs.

After seven days, I was discharged from the hospital. I knew I was in bad shape and did not need the confirmation the labs results would later provide. I was hypercalcemic (critically high levels of calcium in my blood). I had clear indications of plasmacytoma (the accumulation of plasma tumors in my spine), which necessitated the radiation. My white and red blood cell counts were low, as were the immunoglobulins (antibodies that help fight diseases). No wonder I had unusual shortness of breath, fatigue, and felt delirious and confused at times. My blood pressure was high, and I had lost more than twenty additional pounds. I was taking so many medications, I lost track of my daily consumption and the purpose for which each was intended. Such were some of the precursory indicators that signaled my eventual diagnosis.

By the time I left the hospital, I was speculating that I had some form of cancer. The doctors later confirmed that I had the most advanced stage of multiple myeloma a type of blood cancer—it was stage 3. The prognosis placed me in a survival rate category of months. I had to come to terms with the statistical possibility that I had less than a 50 percent chance of enjoying my retirement, seeing a grandchild, or fulfilling many of my dreams. I could predecease my mother and other older relatives; I could die without adequate preparation for the future of my loved ones.

No matter how I analyzed it, or whatever platitudes were used, I could not begin to accept an outcome framed by casualty and be a part of the death statistic. There was just too much left for me to do in this life. I assured myself that I was not ready to die.

I desperately needed to cancel any reservation on that swinging low sweet chariot; it certainly shouldn't be coming for to carry me home, at least not yet. I was not ready for angels to bear me away on their snowy wings to my celestial home. If my home is immortal in glory, it will still be there up to the time I would be ready for occupancy, having completed my God-given assignment. Those who had gone before me wouldn't consume all the milk and honey. The streets of gold did not have the allure or appeal to me just then. God created me perfectly in His image; I did not want to return as a broken vessel with my report card showing "assignment incomplete." My place was here on earth then. Yes, I am bound for the Promised Land, but that glory bound train must leave without me this trip. The earth was my home, and I had no plans to move at that time.

The only Rock that I needed to cleave for me was Christ because in Him I could hide. God placed me here for His purpose, and I would not want to leave until I had accomplished whatever tasks He had set for me, so that He would be pleased with me. Of course, someday, I will go where Jesus is. I will be there when the roll is called up yonder, and I am entirely convinced that my Father will receive me and say, "Well done, my child." Explicitly and emphatically *no!* I won't die, but I shall live so that I will be able to fulfill my assignments from the Lord and then declare with confidence, "Lord, I am coming home." I was committed to leaving the hospital, exercising my faith to its maximum, and living. My journey had just begun.

Many episodes of what transpired during my hospitalization remain cloudy for me. During those times, I was barely conscious, unable to grasp much of the things that were said in my presence, or I was unaware of many events that had occurred, even of things I was later told I was an active participant in. When they were rehearsed to me, I still had either a vague recollection or none at all.

As I improved over the months, friends and well-wishers attempted to recount incidents that took place and conversations we shared during their visit with me, but I couldn't recall them. I could not even remember them being present at the hospital. No prompting or jogging of my memory provided any clarity to those lost memories. A significant event such as my son running out of gas on the busy and dangerous interstate while returning home from taking me to the hospital would otherwise be a cause for me to worry. When I was reminded that I was party to a discussion advising him on what to do, I had no recollection. The American Cancer Society notes that confusion and trouble thinking are two of the effects of multiple myeloma.

After receiving my diagnosis, I often pondered about how much my initial denial about what I clearly could decipher and interpret from the MRI results helped me cope with the eventual diagnosis.

Would I have been better off just facing the facts that *metastasize* meant "cancer that had spread"? In retrospect, it was clearly spelled out in the MRI report. Did it bring me comfort to keep my head buried in the sand of perpetual ignorance, hoping something else would have been the diagnosis? Was ignorance bliss in this case, or was it even worth the unquantifiable hope that maybe I did not have the disease? Prudence dictated that I explore all the alternatives before I went down the oncology route; in fact, those were the doctor's orders. For me, it was the scariest option, to believe that my speculative interpretation of the doctor's comments could be confirmed. My level of medical ignorance was no excuse; I could have asked my primary care physician to provide clarity. I could have done a better job of educating myself to interpret the cryptic, unfathomable medical morphology in the report, but it was not the comfortable option.

How many among us would be able to decipher terms such as "bowing of the posterior cortices," "abnormality within the inferior anterior aspect of the C2 vertebral body," "suspicious of neoplastic marrow replacement," "spinal stenosis," and "foraminal stenosis"? I did eventually Google most of the terms many months later. But in my state of mind, should I have tortured myself beyond what the physical impact of the disease was doing to me by taking a course in medical science? There is no denying that I did have some sense of the implication of "severe disc degeneration of C3-C4" and "osseous metastatic disease," which were the phrases in the report that terrified me. I figured out that my cervical disc C3-C4 was severely damaged and that *metastatic* meant the "spreading of something like cancer."

Nonetheless, I took comfort and clung desperately to a brief part of the summary notes that stated, "Findings are most likely related to metastatic disease—strictly speaking, TB." Just that possibility of tuberculosis, although a very dangerous disease, was the lesser of the two evils. That TB could be the eventual diagnosis gave me the slimmest scintilla of hope, to which I had been desperately clinging.

CHAPTER 3

Documenting My Journey

*Then the LORD replied: "Write down the revelation and make
it plain on tablets so that a herald may run with it."*

—Habakkuk 2:2 (NIV)

M y sudden hospitalization was an unexpected turn of events.
I went for evaluation only to be told by the oncologist that I
would not be returning home that day and was admitted there and
then. Most of my friends and people in my circle were not aware
that I had an issue; I was plugging away at my usual activities up to
a few days before. The question of how I would mass-communicate
to keep everyone informed in real time initially posed a challenge.
It would undoubtedly be a cumbersome task to man my phone and
maintain a consistent narrative to everyone.

As stated earlier, I used the technology that Facebook provided
to mass-communicate with friends and control the dissemination
of information about my evolving status in real time. Several people in my circle were active subscribers, and I could interact and
receive immediate feedback from them. I had initially intended that
medium to be my bulletin board for posting my status reports, but
it evolved. The interactions were beyond anything I imagined; they
were cathartic. Facebook provided a medium where I could share my
current experiences, and receive immediate feedback, comfort, and

encouragement, so that even in isolation, I felt like I was physically close to friends. This experience ranked high among the positive benefits received from choosing this medium. People responded with assurances of their continuous advocacy to God through prayers on my behalf; others always had inspiring words for me to sustain the battle in faith. Still, others recounted testimonies of how their lives were being impacted by what I was sharing, to the extent that some committed to initiating life-changing actions in their relationships with others and, most profoundly, their relationship with God. I could also tell that others were awakening to their mortality and the need to make personal spiritual changes because of what their unpredictable future could portend.

It was not long before my posts began to transform in content to reflect my Christian perspective and my conviction that I would receive healing through faith. They had evolved from being mere status updates of a scared and bewildered soul on his deathbed, to a rigid declaration of my stance in faith. I will confess that in my weakened state and position of surrender, some of what I wrote was incomprehensible, filled with grammatical errors, and had the most awkward sentence structure.

Many people may still not be able to come to grips with one or two of the postings in which I related the unusual spiritual experiences I had. Some considered them to be paranormal; I prefer to refer to them as transcendental spiritual exposures. When I use the term transcend or any derivative of that word, it should be understood as that which is beyond this universe and is unexplainable with physics, mathematics, reason, or any natural science. I firmly believe that the composition of those posts was beyond me. I was grossly cognitively impaired and barely able to think or stay awake; these writings were spiritually led. I believe that my hands and my thoughts were guided.

God took charge and empowered me to write the accounts that I did. I had no difficulty in pouring out what I was moved to write in each post. Regardless of the torturous pains, the influences of the medications, and the terror of the "Evil One," I felt compelled to persevere and share what was happening to me each day. What I wrote were my truths, uninhibited, unfiltered, and written with unbridled enthusiasm. When I wrote, I did not consider if it would be embarrassing for me at the time or even later. I put aside my pride and spoke from my soul, with the hope that others would gain something from what I was going through. I had no intention of revisiting the postings, and, in fact, I never did until I was urged to put them together for this book.

As I documented my story on Facebook, I was encouraged by many people to publish a book so that others from a broader audience would benefit. Eventually, I felt the urging of the Spirit in me to do it and secretly began to review all the postings, then later started writing expanded comments to them to provide a more contextual perspective to each post.

The event that profoundly changed my approach and convinced me to write this book occurred on May 20, 2018. After the main Sunday message, our bishop generally presents the congregation with the option for him to pray for specific needs as the Spirit urged him to. When he issued his call for prayers, I was not initially inspired to be among those who responded. After his customary prayer, and in an unusual move, he made a second call to pray for other needs. Something about what he stated in that second offer made me respond, and I proceeded to the altar along with other members of the congregation.

After praying, he turned his attention to me and gave a prophetic utterance. He declared that I would write a publication that would be widely read and that it would have a significant impact not only on the general readers but also on other communities of interest. I was taken aback by this prophecy because I was at page 53 in my review and updates, and it was only a few days before that I had revealed to my wife my intention to do something with the posts that I was feverishly working on.

Now, my wife is someone who can keep a secret even from herself, so I was sure she had not revealed my plans to anyone. Saying it was a surreal insight to hear God's prophetic revelation for me is a gross understatement. A project that I had shrouded in secrecy, ambivalent about whether to make a book of it, had now been publicly revealed by our bishop.

I was overcome with emotion and shock. Observing how God had moved miraculously, to empower his minister to see my secret assignment and publicly reveal it, meant that I was on divine duty to complete the job. That prophetic endorsement gave me the confidence that God would guide me to achieve my testimony that would give Him glory. If I equivocated, it would be a sign of unbelief, and that could lead to disobedience. Disobeying God is sinful.

I redoubled my efforts, with the commitment that regardless of how it would be received, I would make every effort to document my journey in this book. Cancer is a miserable, scary demon. God is omnipotent, loving, and merciful. By His love, I live, and He gave me a testimony for the ages. Since it was prophesied that I would not die but live, I can hold up this book as a part of the fulfillment of that prophecy—all glory and worship to God our merciful Father.

CHAPTER 4

New Realities

Dear friends, do not be surprised at the fiery ordeal that has come on you to test you, as though something strange were happening to you. But rejoice inasmuch as you participate in the sufferings of Christ, so that you may be overjoyed when his glory is revealed.

—1 Peter 4:12-13 (NIV)

In biblical numerology, the number 7 is significant. It is the number for spiritual perfection. Creation was completed in seven days, so 7 is said to be the number of spiritual completeness. It has been calculated that 7 can be found 287 times in the Bible, which is itself a multiple of 7. Even in the physical world, where physics and chemistry are the backbones of science and technology, 7 is significant. When white light is passed through a prism, it splits into seven different colors or wavelengths. The periodic table is a hierarchical structure comprised of seven levels. I was discharged from the hospital after seven days. Why shouldn't I believe the number seven bears some significance for me too? Could spiritual completeness also refer to the completeness of my healing, even if it has not yet manifested for all to see?

Returning home was the most joyous moment of my recent life. I could sleep in my own bed again, and that meant a lot to me. I could now appreciate the relative peace one enjoys in his castle. No more pushing and poking or abominable needles equipped with a heat-seeking missile to find me and pierce my withering skin at the most forbidden hours. Sleep filled most of my days and nights. I was fatigued and weak, continuously beset by light-headedness and dizzy spells. Every movement impacted my spine, producing unspeakable pain. But I knew I had to keep my body from atrophying, and there was always the threat of developing blood clots and even bed sores if I stayed stationary. I had to do some form of physical activity. Just getting out of bed, however, took minutes. Imagine my struggle trying to descend the stairs with a walking stick. Just a few short months ago I was able to run for miles. Now, I was practically an invalid, immobile and helpless. And the medications brought their own challenges, with a multitude of side effects, including breathing issues and various stomach complications.

I was out of breath easily, and there was no relief from the excruciating pain I endured when I moved. Every joint was a pain point. My ribs would jab at me, as though I was being speared with a sword. It felt as though all moving parts were depleted of lubrication, and bones were raging war with other bones in my body. The biggest offender remained my persistent, pesky cervical spine pain. It felt like there was severe tearing of flesh with even the slightest turn of my head. The neck brace I had been prescribed to wear 24/7 by my first orthopedic doctor was ill-fitting and uncomfortable. I was glad when my daughter got me one made from foam at the local pharmacy; it felt much more comfortable, so I cheated by wearing it quite often.

Each day, with my nose pressed against the window looking out at one of my favorite hobbies, the now prohibited and unreachable backyard garden, I would delight in the flourishing display of plant growth. I yearned to be outside and wondered how long it would be before I would once again be able to feel the wind blowing across my face or even enjoy the hot, humid weather outside. In my solitude, my thoughts would race wildly, as I was incapable of focusing on anything for any extended period of time.

The physical borders of my existence had shrunk from limit-less global possibilities to the four corners of my bedroom. I could hobble around with the aid of a walking stick or by holding on to someone, but even that had to be limited. A mobile tray was within arm's reach of my bed and served as my main point of access for everything—my medicine, food, TV remote control, and phone. Is it any wonder my emotions at times spiraled out of control? For my listening pleasure, I favored the old-time religious songs—the ones my grandmother used to sing to me as she tucked me in. They evoked memories and deep emotional responses, to the point that I wanted to cry out as the Psalmist David did, when he said, "How long, LORD? Will You forget me forever? How long will You hide Your face from me?" (Psalm 13:1, NIV).

Ironically, I did appreciate the alone times, if for nothing more than to melt myself in my sorrow and grieve about my sad state. "Wasn't I a strong, ambitious man a few days ago, bubbling with hope, aspirations, and dreams of conquests?" I would muse in humble self-indulgence. "How could such misfortune have befallen me without any warning or any conscious act on my part?" "Was there something I could have done to prevent this?" "Could my doctors have foreseen warning signs before I hit stage 3 cancer?" "What of the future and those who value me?" "Is this how it will really end for me?"

These were the questions that jolted me into my new reality as I contemplated what it meant to have that cataclysmic rock landing on me without warning. It was targeted to crush not just my body, but my very spirit and soul. A spiritual novice would not be able to endure the onslaught. I was forced to quickly mature in faith, since my toddling baby faith walk would be inadequate for this attack on my total being. I had to prepare for a long hike in my faith journey, where I could stumble and fall during my time of testing and tribulation. I desperately needed to lean on Jesus and have Him pick me up to prevent me getting lost while on this journey.

Meanwhile, I was very anxious to re-establish some form of normalcy by reconnecting with friends. Thank God for the age of the smartphone, which enabled me to post my first status update on social media from home. Looking now at the post that follows, it reveals a state of mind reeling from shock. I had accepted the grim possibility I could die. I was, however, hopeful that even if the omnipotent, all-powerful God allowed it, some good could come from it.

> There comes the point when you STOP, LISTEN, and WAIT for God. He is neither deaf nor uncompassionate. God did not hang the moon on your timeline or mine. He is omniscient (yes, the OMNISCIENTIST) A thousand years is but a day in the Lord's sight. Sincere prayers have been offered, testimonies have been received, and lives have been touched. I have had my unique experiences. Now I wait on the Lord.
>
> Is cancer bad? Yes. However, if it is approved by God, then it is for a definite purpose. Everything can give God glory. Do we have a choice in the matter then, to receive and accept? I did not choose this, my Nineveh assignment in the belly of cancer. Difficult as it is for me to say this in my state, death sometimes produces a harvest. A single dead seed can germinate when planted and bring huge recurring harvests. Can you imagine being chosen to demonstrate even a small part of God's magnificence as an active participant? To be elected requires that I should be thankful to God. Does God not know beforehand that what he orders will be executed? Last time I checked, He did not need blind side mirrors.
>
> Thank you for your prayers and thoughts. It is now time for thanksgiving and praises. The sacrifices have been made; your sincere prayers have been heard. God will demonstrate His pleasure in your faithfulness. Please rejoice with me as I move through the next phase, whatever it may be. Whatever Phase II is, be it such unto the Glory of God the Almighty.

Reading this post, it is easy to assume I was coming to terms with my situation. It was as though I was already in the acceptance phase of my grieving process. But I was still in shock and hoping through faith I was where I was because God had allowed it. I decided to believe that my state was a privileged appointment by God to accomplish certain things for His useful purpose.

This was a tremendous spiritual premise for hope; physically, however, I was in bad shape. The members of my body refused to work in harmony as designed. I could find no peace because it felt like a civil war had started among each member. Individually, they had taken leave of their designed functions and now refused to cooperate with each other. My skin, the body's largest organ, would burn like a flame to the touch. I would be viciously stabbed in the neck each time I turned my head beyond the limited radius my fractured spine allowed. My legs could not bear my weight without assistance and would rebel painfully whenever I stood or moved.

Imagine being terrified of getting close to solid objects because of incidental contact. My fear was the insufferable pain I knew I would experience should any of my bony protuberances accidentally make contact with any material object. I had similar concerns when walking close to people. There would be the constant fear and panic of bumping into or tripping over them. Worse, I could not trust my brain to direct my actions, as it had now become unwired and was inclined to react rather badly to the incalculable pain signals being sent from each rebellious faction of my body. Was my condition really that bad to cause such symptoms? The answer would be provided a few years later when I quizzed a multiple myeloma specialist about the severity of my illness and he stressed that it was relatively bad. How bad? My numbers were not the highest he had ever seen but, according to him, "they were right up there."

God permits me to activate and use the power that works in me according to my faith. He tells me in Romans 4:16 that, based on faith, I will be able to inherit His promise through grace. I am saved by grace, according to Ephesians 2:5. Although grace provided my salvation, I needed to use faith as my key to access it. My healing and all that I need have already been provisioned for me by God through

Jesus Christ. God provides grace that includes healing; I am responsible for believing it and accessing it through faith. Exercising my faith is a process. I need to apply it continuously to develop my spiritual muscles. The more I use it, the stronger I become spiritually. When I have demonstrated the power of faith in little things, I develop the confidence to overcome more significant challenges through my faith. Jesus says if we have enough faith, we can move mountains. These were essential concepts I decided to use to empower me to achieve my healing.

CHAPTER 5

Where Is God in This?

The LORD is my rock, my fortress and my deliverer;
my God is my rock, in whom I take refuge, my shield
and the horn of my salvation, my stronghold.

—Psalm 18:2 (NIV)

The doctors had spoken, the die was cast, and I had a problem so big, rational human solutions could not solve it. With a diagnosis such as mine, the objective is to treat the disease so that the patient can maintain some improved quality of life. I would be on various plans of care, taking medications indefinitely. Each line of care would inevitably fail, and I would relapse as my body adapted to them. I would then be prescribed other treatment until all the known drugs were exhausted, following which I would succumb to the disease. Modern science could not provide the ultimate hope I sought, which was a cure.

I had witnessed a family member die, age 36, from the same condition, multiple myeloma, within a few weeks of diagnosis. The excellent knowledge and skills of the medical team could not save her. Pharmacology only offered her temporary relief from excruciating pain. Her moaning and groaning were incessant. The flesh from her bones had been sucked away so fast, she was unrecognizable in days. She became cognitively impaired and delusional, only being able to hold brief, incoherent conversations periodically. At the onset of her diagnosis, she clearly articulated her optimism and conviction of how the miracles of current advanced science would cure her. Being a nurse, she had every reason to be confident. She had done her research based on what the science availed. Although she fought bravely, I wept for her as she was quickly referred to hospice care and passed away in short order.

Now here I was, less than a decade later, confronting a similar devastating beast. It was the same disease, the killer that was staring me down with vicious intent. Our natural tendency when faced with crisis is to react with fear and push the panic button. However, this never results in proper solutions as it sets in motion actions to defeat ideal results attainable by faith. Fear works to overcome anything that faith strives to accomplish. Jesus Christ Himself, having had the human experience, understands human reactions. But He desires that we believe in Him and His promises, so that we may adopt and maintain a faith posture, to achieve that which He has empowered us to attain through grace.

The arresting news of my diagnosis was eviscerating. It was as though my internals were continually being ripped apart and pulled through my throat; just thinking of which would make anyone feel like vomiting constantly. I no longer had a sense of wholeness and could no longer lay claims to wholesomeness. It was as though I was a ship with a dysfunctional rudder cut loose from its moorings. My imperative was to find a place to drop and secure my anchor, lest I drifted and be tossed onto dangerous rocks of death. With the waves of peril crashing against my crumbling boat, was it inconceivable that I might ask, "Where is God in this?"

What makes me of stronger faith than the disciples who, when they were caught up in the storm, perceived Jesus as being asleep and cried out to him in fear and panic, as we read in Mark 4:38 (KJV)? "And he was in the hinder part of the ship, asleep on a pillow: and they awake him, and say unto him, Master, carest thou not that we perish? And he arose, and rebuked the wind, and said unto the sea, Peace, be still. And the wind ceased, and there was a great calm."

What was important was who was in my shaking boat with me. If Jesus is in the boat of my circumstances with me, regardless of how precarious, I can rest assured that I will not perish, not that my boat won't be rocked and tossed violently. Would I hear Jesus saying peace, be still in my situation? How could I be in doubt when He spoke to me in Isaiah 49:16 (NIV), saying, "See, I have engraved you on the palms of my hands; your walls are ever before me"? Fortunately, my God, who is the immovable Rock, held the beacon of hope. He was with me, and I did not have to go searching for Him.

My trouble therefore was not as a result of the absence of God. He would calm my seas and provide me the solid rock on which my anchor would hold, regardless of the severity of the storms ahead. He had the sufficiency for my needs, the assurance of security and comfort, and would be ever-present in all my times of desperation. I could rest in the confidence that my preexisting relationship with Him provided me access to His grace. Therein was the bastion of my hope. Jesus the Christ was my Savior and Lord. If I was not in good standing with God, I prayed that He would judge and forgive me, because there with my affliction, and in my distress, whom else could I call?

With a heavy heart of contrition and repentance, I prayed as I usually do in times like these. The prayer below may not be exactly as I prayed then; however, it is along the same basic lines. It is a prayer I would rather never have to pray again as it reflects the confession of my negligence. I had read something like this somewhere during my illness and made notes which I modified.

Heavenly Father, I confess that I haven't put You first above other things that occupied my days, because you are so reliable and do not make pressing demands on me. I frequently forget that You are with me guiding my success and preventing bad things from happening to my family and me. Please forgive me when I neglect to carve out time for You. As a Christian, I ought to know better. Times with You only make me a better person. I should have appreciated the pleasure I would have derived from studying Your Word more, compared with the vain things I did instead. Had I spent more times dutifully and passionately in your Word, I could better understand how to please You and how to more effectively know Your promises for me and be able to claim them in times like now.

I pray that You will remind me every moment to put You first in all areas of my life from now on. Keep me from being overly concerned with the mysteries of tomorrow, trusting that You are in control so that I can live one day at a time. I desire to have the faith to rely completely on Your promises. Only you are caring and close enough to understand my current and future needs, spiritual and physical. And only You are loving and capable enough to provide for them. You understand my current health requirements, my emotional state, material and relational needs, and most of all, the need for a strong and resilient faith to persist and endure through whatever confronts me. Guide me to do good to others, but most of all, to do whatever pleases You. Teach me how to trust You more regardless of how many challenges may arise to cause doubt, fear, and unbelief. Help me to see the positive possibilities through You so that I will not worry. I pray in the name of Jesus Christ. Amen.

I was thankful to God that I still had life, for however long He would mercifully extend it to me, so then I had the good fortune of being able to work out my own salvation with fear and trembling. The privilege of access to my eternal Father was critical, but the confidence in knowing that He would accept me and not say, "Depart from me because I never knew you," was even more comforting. I seized upon the words of Jesus in Matthew 28:20, where He said He would be with His disciples even to the end of age, which became my personal affirmation, regardless of the circumstances foreshadowing my situation.

I had to accept that it was not God's will for me to die then, so succumbing to brokenness was out of the question. Biblically sourced affirmations formed the foundation that encouraged my faith. The knowledge that I could influence what happened to me through Jesus Christ because the same Spirit that raised Him from the dead is a part of me was empowering (Romans 8:11). I pledged to use the authority He gave me to petition Him for my healing. Guided by that knowledge, I had to abandon indecisiveness, stay rooted, and remain in obedience, then await my healing. Compliance would also have the element of perseverance, since it was inevitable that during an extended period of being vulnerable various trickeries of the devil would emerge, attempting to lead me astray. I chose to pattern myself after Job, who in all his adversity did not curse God and die to rid himself of his torment. Even when my faith would eventually be tested, I had to remember that if I disrobed myself of the armor of God, I would be exposed to the attacks of the devil. As 1 Peter 5:8 reminds us, "Your adversary walks about, seeking whom he may devour." And any disobedience on my part would give the devil permission to have his way with me. "He comes to steal and kill" (John 10:10) because, according to Hebrews 2:14, "he has the power of death."

God assures me that no weapon formed against me will prosper. Yet by allowing fear to overcome my faith, I would allow entrance to the devil. With the gloomy forecast about my life, it was imperative that I believed Psalm 112:7 that if my heart is steadfast, trusting in the Lord, I should not be afraid. The great number of promises I found in the Bible was encouraging and, because I had no idea of the length of the journey I was on, I needed to remember these promises in case things got worse.

Science provides us so much these days, and it would have been foolish of me to question the integrity of provable facts such as my diagnosis. In my critical situation, I needed what transcended scientific boundaries. Understandably, in my weakness, I was not totally fortified against temptations, fear, and doubt; my challenge was to acknowledge my present reality, while always being mindful that everything could be changed by the omnipotent God.

I knew that every little avenue of fear I allowed was a vast thoroughfare for the devil to enter and attempt to counter my faith, which would lead to my eventual destruction. The Bible documents evidence of the devil's devious, cunning, and subliminal modes of operation. Peter often came to mind at times when I was most vulnerable and on the brink of involuntarily yielding power to the devil. As a close disciple of Jesus, he was a chief witness to God and His glory. He had the privilege of first-hand teachings, and had witnessed countless miracles by Jesus Christ and, the ultimate, Jesus' transfiguration and His resurrected being.

Those were unique and unprecedented privileges, but with all that, even Peter displayed his fear on many occasions. He walked on water in faith when Jesus called him, but started to drown when he allowed fear

MY GOD, IT'S CANCER

to overpower his faith. With all those years of closeness with Jesus, he went back to his regular job after denying Jesus three times, rather than continuing the ministry Jesus had instructed him to. After His resurrection, Jesus Christ had to reiterate Peter's assignment and advise him of the works of the devil to infiltrate and sift him. I thought about how the life of Peter impacted me not very long after I accepted Jesus the Christ as my Lord, and I was so profoundly moved by the interaction between Jesus the resurrected Lord, perfect in all ways, and Peter, a vulnerable, impetuous human, like me. I was so moved by Jesus' love and forgiving actions, even to one who had doubted His promises and denied Him. It was not difficult for me then to find comfort and assurance in the lyrics of the little song I composed years ago when I tried to empathize with Peter. At the time of writing it, I felt akin to Peter and how he might have responded to our Lord in repentance.

The Song of Simon Peter
Written by Courtney A. Mullings
02-07-2009

When you called me, I knew I was unworthy
When you called me, I knew I was unclean
Yet you told me that I could be someone
A winner of souls; yes me.
Chorus
More than three times, Lord I denied YOU
More than three times, I've lied in shame
More than three times, Lord, you I've forsaken
Who am I to call you friend?
Then you told me that I'd be sifted
And of Satan's desires for me
And you told me that I am a sinner
Lacking in faith but in fear
Chorus
But you showed me your love and forgiveness
With your prayers to strengthen my faith
That if I should repent and then serve you

A great leader you'd then make of me.
Chorus
Feed my sheep now; Lord, you did ask me
Feed my sheep now, you asked as you left
Feed my sheep and all of my lambs then
If you love me much more than these.

If by commission or omission, I had inadvertently given room to the workings of the devil as Peter did, the manner in which Jesus dealt with him, as a friend, dining with him, trusting him to be in charge of spreading the Gospel to His proverbial "sheep and lamb," I was assured that I served a merciful God. Unlike a vengeful, ruthless, emotionally codependent human monitoring my misdeeds, God does not sit around with a giant hammer ready to play whack-a-mole by smothering me every time I fall out of line. He sees my heart and, in His judgment, does not mete out punishment commensurate with my sins as a fleshly man would. He knows my flaws and my inherent frailties. He is merciful and forgiving. God gives life, and He desires that I continue living and have an abundance of His goodness.

I know that truth and the truth of God will set me free, even from what ails me, as John 8:32 teaches. God's purpose will be accomplished through me, as it was with Peter after the come-to-Jesus meeting. The current facts were presented to me. With my natural eyes, I read the reports of facts from the doctors and understood what was implied. Based on the Word of God, I had to attire myself like a Roman soldier, fully armored, but instead of fighting mortals, my preparation was for spiritual warfare, as Paul instructed in Ephesians 6:11. With Jesus Christ as my Savior, I would be adequately protected. My helmet of salvation would prevent contravening thoughts of fear from entering my brain. The breastplate of righteousness protected my heart so that it would retain what God had placed in it. Using my shield of faith, I could ward off the attacks of fear. Then armed with the sword of the Spirit, which is sharpened by God's truth, I could mince the scientific facts to shred and supplant them with God's truth. Finally, with feet rooted in God's gospel of peace, I would be mobilized to fight in faith whatever omen was foreboding.

CHAPTER 6

Back Home

For I know the plans I have for you, declares the LORD,
plans for welfare and not for evil, to give you a future and a hope.

—Jeremiah 29:11 (ESV)

I didn't believe that God caused me to be sick and desired to destroy me. Not that I was discounting His sovereignty and authority to cause sickness or death for His good purpose. However, I felt compelled to assure myself of the need to be in right standing. I accepted that God is beyond moodiness, intemperance, and revenge. In fact, Ephesians 1:3 states that God has blessed us in the heavenly realms with every spiritual blessing. And 2 Peter 3:9 declares that God is patient with me, not wanting me to perish. Would I have to go through an extended period of suffering, or would God intervene as a result of prayers on my behalf and provide instantaneous healing for me?

With all I had come to learn about my physical illness, I was hoping that God would deliver me from the dreadful future that I was envisioning. So far, my faith practice had not triggered an instantaneous, tangible response to change my state of illness. I knew that miraculous healing was possible. But was it in God's plans for me? The Bible records several incidences of instant healing because of the individuals' belief. Others were required to take some action. God is omniscient and knows what is in my best interest—ultimately, He decides for how long this season of impairment will last. He is sovereign and omnipotent and has my healing. My duty was to believe and demonstrate my belief. God chooses when and how He wants to show His power for His glory. If it is His will, much good could result from my journey. My prayer, therefore, is that God will not allow a scintilla of unbelief to cheat me out of His designated purpose for me.

The post that follows was not only my update upon returning home but also my attempt to grapple with the gravity of my situation and concerns about my righteousness and worthiness to receive God's mercies. I was rambling across the confluence of different ideas that were emerging and causing me concerns. I felt the need to pour it all out publicly to satisfy my fleshly desire to purge myself of the guilt of past sins.

> The love of the Almighty God is universal and consistent. It appears to be new and exciting as I wake to new experiences each day. The key is I awoke, alive to see a new day. The simple pleasure of sleeping in my bed again last night and waking up to what seems to be a whole new world is exhilarating. Of what consequence or impact is my existence in this world, I pondered. It appears that the world never missed a beat while I was out. The vegetables that I planted before my illness have all grown, duded out, blossomed, and producing of their kinds. Weeds have grown, things of nature are still as orderly as God designed them, and even the corporation for which I work is still providing services to its customers and continue to be profitable without any contribution from me. Bummer! The world really does not need me in order to turn on its axis, it continues unaided by me. I pray that God, my Father, will find usefulness in me.

Otherwise, He has the power to terminate me in an instant.

Update: After five radiation treatments, they are now observing its effectiveness on a tumor that was lodged in my cervical spine and was severely impacting my neck movements. The cancer has eaten away at my cervical spine, causing it to collapse. Imagine the bony structure of my spinal column now scraping against my nerve center. To be more graphic, this is the sensitive area of my body that houses my central nervous system, that aggregates and carries signals from all over my body to my brain. The collapsed bony structure, I imagine, is resting on my central nervous system, scraping and grating against it with every movement. This is what I feel. Imagine two strips of raw bacon suspending my head. With the slightest movement of my head, it feels as though a sharp object is resting on the strips and viciously shearing and tearing at each fiber.

Every movement of any part of my body is harrowing. What is the probability that, under normal conditions, I would be able to move any part of my body without moving my head and neck? I've tested it, and it is literally impossible. As such, every move that I make is sheer torture. So, while the radiated area of the tumor heals, it is still raw, and the collapsed bones of my spine cannot be lifted from this sensitive area anytime soon. I must be heavily medicated to help nullify the pains. Although this is real, I use this as a reason to ask that you excuse any rubbish I may write here from time to time.

As mentioned earlier, the tumor is a direct consequence of the metastatic multiple myeloma. No longer is the letter "C" only significant as the first letter in my name, it further defines me at this stage as a victim of a deadly form of cancer. I can't back away from that reality now; it is the doctors' diagnosis. It is not, however, my destiny. From what we have all agreed, invoking the help of God is what will heal me. You, my friends, have urged me to fight because I have much work to do. In my compromised state, I am committed to fighting in faith, flawed and weak as I am.

I am so blessed by my recent life experiences through these postings. They have allowed so many people to express positive thoughts to me. People I have not spoken with in more than thirty years have reached out to me. They bear messages of hope through God the Almighty. Do you know what's encouraging for me to discover? Arrogant and prideful men like me are really God's little babies. There are situations that bring that truth to the fore. I am so encouraged when I get even the faintest hint of folks, who I never heard mention God, expressing hope and prayers for God's intervention in my situation. There are so many of my male friends who know of God's goodness, but to be associated with those hypocritical Christians is like the fear of a leper's curse.

The name of God is apparently quite potent as a curse word, as it can be used to damn anything and anyone, while equally, in times of desperation, it can be an impulsive cry for help— for example, "Jesus Christ!" or "Oh God help me!" Some men see being a Christian as a sign of weakness and relinquishing control to some unknown, intangible entity. Mostly, they are the self-proclaimed self-made types. The mandate to strive to do good to everyone inclusively is also another deterrent. To be moved by the brotherly love, human equality and oneness that Christianity demands seems to go against some unrelinquishable prejudices acquired over time, that to me, is incomprehensible. Even worse, the Christian way of life exposes the protected sensitive child within us men. It reveals our vulnerabilities and yearnings to seek the comfort and protection of a higher power in our times of weakness. Whatever the case is, I get excited when I can demonstrate how God's love has changed me for the better, especially to those who have not yet accepted salvation through Christ.

When trouble comes, and fear grips us, we take flight of the falsehoods that we are conditioned to believe. Society decries grown men publicly displaying emotional weakness; so we men are accustomed to parading ourselves as tough and invincible, to hide from the world that helpless, fearful, and desperate voice that cries within us. I confess that I am a child, and if for no one else, a child of God, who sees past my façade and pride to my very soul. Yes! I plead guilty. When I changed my life to follow Christ more than two decades ago, I boldly paraded an entourage of friends to witness my surrender to a greater power, in the form of baptism. It was my public display of my non-equivocation about my decision for a new life in humble surrender to God, on whom I now depend.

For clarity, I have made some corrections to the original Facebook post above, omitting or rephrasing parts that were mostly senseless ramblings. However, it is evident that I wanted to share my physical hurt as graphically as I could, while reinforcing my sense of humility with respect to God. Although not articulated in that post, my feelings of guilt and shortcomings as a "good Christian" were now emerging. I was obsessed with pouring out my inner emotions publicly, but could not immediately discern why at that stage in my illness. As rationalized and seen in later posts, this was just the beginning of my attempt at self-distillation during the initial phases of my journey. Amid the pain, confusion, and loneliness, there was a more intense hurt that went to the depths of my soul. Feedback from my friends was empathetic and comforting. In retrospect, I was somehow apparently at the initial stages of a cathartic process toward spiritual cleansing, ridding myself of the burdens of my soul. It was my effort to reinstate myself in right standing with God, so that He would show mercy on me and grant my request for healing. Did God require that of me, or was the Evil One influencing my thought process to make me feel unworthy of what God would do for me if I believed?

My feelings were that I had fallen short in the area of public witnessing and testifying. As a Christian, Paul instructed Timothy not to be ashamed of his testimony about the Lord when he told him in 2 Timothy 1:8 (ESV), "Therefore do not be ashamed of the testimony about our Lord." That, after all, is what Christ expects, as Luke records Jesus saying in Luke 12:8 (ESV), "And I tell you, everyone who acknowledges me before men, the Son of Man also will acknowledge before the angels of God."

CHAPTER 7

Angry With?

Do not let the sun go down while you are still angry.

—Ephesians 4:26 (NIV)

This was a very challenging chapter for me to write. I wrote the contents of it in my journal but did not make a Facebook post. I felt ashamed that I had allowed my emotions to supersede my Christian beliefs and general decency. At this juncture, I not only confronted my inherent frailties as a man, I also found it difficult to prevent some of my unresolved personal demons from surfacing and adding to my tribulations.

The initial feelings of shock and denial, brought on by my diagnosis, had turned to annoyance, then anger, and it was now on display, with my wife gradually becoming a casualty of its expressions. The psychotherapists, behavioral analysts, and experts might rationalize it to be a part of my process. The chemists may find some attributions to a side effect of certain medications that I was taking. However, the truth is, I believe, most of us have latent anger waiting for the appropriate trigger. Some people have a higher tolerance, a longer rope, or a softer trigger than others. Anger is a natural human emotional response. In the Old Testament of the Bible, Moses acted out of rage, contrary to how God would want him to, and lost the privilege of entering the Promised Land. To guide Christians who

71

may experience anger, Ephesians 4:26 reminds us that if we do get angry, we should not sin, or let the sun go down upon our wrath. Watching my life suddenly spiral out of my control to the point of possible extinction, and realizing I had not yet truly lived, was a contributory trigger. But as sobering as these thoughts are, there really is no justification for uncontrolled anger.

The unfortunate truth is, my anger was often misplaced. My faithful caregiver and dear wife became the object of my rage—who else did I have? I had been in isolation for a while, and she was the only person with whom I had any meaningful interaction. The strangest thing about my uncontrolled anger during that phase of my illness was that I would be conscious of a potential angry outburst or response in my head, try to resist the urge to give voice to it, and yet I could not restrain myself. Imagine you know that you are about to say something unpleasant, yet cannot resist the urge to blurt it out. I recalled watching people on TV with a condition that compels them to make impulsive, uncontrollable, profane utterances. I found it woefully unbelievable at the time. Profanity was not part of my usual means of communication, so I never used it during spurts of anger. It was incredible how I would say things that were mean, ungrateful, and hurtful without "biting my tongue" instead, as I would before I was sick. My wife had every justifiable reason to abandon me to a personal care home, so she would not be subjected to my mean-spiritedness, but she patiently tolerated my lunacy with dignified grace and patience.

While in the patients' waiting area one day, I overheard two senior gentlemen discussing similar challenges. I was relieved that this behavior might not have been unique to me but was shared by two other cancer patients. I could not help myself from rudely barging in on their conversation, and yes, I discovered that my experiences were not unique. They, too, were experiencing similar negative impulses they could not avoid acting out. Those negative impulses were either attributable to the disease or medicine. It would be interesting to understand which is the root cause. I felt somewhat relieved by my discovery and reassured that I was not a victim of a Tourette-like syndrome. I was aware that such behaviors are the basis for break-ups and separations. Months later, I saw on a reality show the struggles one couple was enduring because the husband was stricken with cancer. The wife had reached her breaking point and they were contemplating separation. She alleged that her husband had become unbearably mean and intolerable. His anger and demanding nature had become too much for her, such that their long-standing marriage was threatened. If only I could reach through the television and implore her to be patient, to explain that the poor man had little control over his apparent meanness and reassure her that the intolerable behavior would pass.

My spinal injury was a source of some of my most significant pain; it was also the trigger for some of my most vitriolic eruptions. I had limited range of motion in my neck, and every bounce, bump, or slight movement resulted in nerve-stabbing pain. As such, I did not trust myself to drive a 4,000-pound motor vehicle. That could be a lethal weapon, endangering both myself and others. My faithful wife would transport me on short trips. Over the years, at a minimum, I could tolerate her driving when I was healthy. During my angry periods, I became hypersensitive to the extent that I could almost sense every pebble she drove over, every time she made a sudden acceleration, turned a corner, or made any decision that was not in line with my prescribed driving standards. I would yell in fear, anticipating a move that would cause me pain, freaking her out and driving her to the point of becoming a nervous wreck. My complaints were incessant and biting. I was in a state of perpetual panic and anxiety. I had become a giant, irreverent pain in this poor woman's neck.

In other cases, my behavior was flagrantly insane, as I would regurgitate every conceivable inconsequential issue that I could find to criticize my wife and be cantankerous. Ever since returning from the hospital, caring sympathizers and family members, with the best of intentions, wanted to visit me. That is what good people do when illness befalls one of their own. But I was aggressively dismissive of any suggestions to have visitors, for various reasons. The pain was relentless and constant, and I was most ornery and irritable; added to that, I had lost the strength and ability to stay awake for longer than a couple of minutes.

Moreover, I was not thrilled to put my emaciated, disfigured physical frame on display for anyone to pity or criticize. Plus, my immune system was so severely compromised by the disease and treatment, I was instructed to limit contact with people, plants, and animals. So, my wife was my designated sentry, adding to the millions of other tasks she dutifully performed. My explicit instruction to her was to stave off all visitors (the audacity of me).

There was one particular night when I recklessly placed my irascible behavior on display by unleashing an unrelenting tirade at my wife. In my anger, I delivered my deluded "Genesis to Revelation" monologue that detailed every negative incidence of imperfection or mistake I had perceived since my illness. I started by accusing her of deserting me at the hospital, then of irresponsibly allowing visitors to invade the home when I wanted no visitors, and then I chided her for the substandard level of care I received from her as a qualified professional caregiver. In my incensed state, I recounted every instance when I needed her to attend to some whining of mine and she was absent. The only thing I fell short of declaring to her was my "Personal Bill of Rights."

I was clearly past unreasonableness, snapping at anything in sight like a deranged, rabid wild beast. My tirade was such that the ordinarily genteel, calm-natured woman of God had to stand her ground in her defense. She instructed me that my perception framed my comments. That line only served to infuriate my deranged mind because it went to the core of my fears and insecurities. Was she implying that I was going crazy, losing my sense of reasonable and rational sober thinking and behavior? How could she be so insensitive? I was just a poor hapless sufferer, who was fearful, but too proud to admit that he was being confronted with grave desperation and was panicking.

My compelling urge was to paint myself as the unfortunate victim lying in bed, while portraying her as my empowered, merciless prison guard who was insensitive to my needs—all in an attempt to manipulate her into pampering me. That approach did not garner the intended response, so I tried the pitiful charm offensive. I played the victim card, by petitioning my case for mercy, with the hope of appealing to her nurturing side. After thirty years of marriage, shouldn't she instinctively recognize my needs and soothe me, now more than ever? "I HAVE CANCER!" I eventually yelled as vociferously as my feeble, helpless voice could. "How much worse do I have to get for you to see that all I am doing is seeking a little compassion and care, some sensitivity, just a little extra attention?" I pleaded.

Although that route was deliberately manipulative, it was the truth from my pleading, terrified soul—and it worked. I could see that she was broken emotionally; she was so profoundly affected and immediately relented, confessing that my illness had significantly impacted her. She spared me the details, but I deduced that even the weird chemical odors of the medicines and the effects of radiation therapy oozing from my pores, and associating them with me, might have affected her psychologically. I never even gave thought to such things. "Oh my god! That was not my fault," I thought, but it provided some clarity and was comforting to know. She offered to pray with me before heading to church, but I was still fuming in my heart. It felt awkward, so I pridefully refused. With ungracious, self-righteous indifference, I arrogantly directed her to go to God and pray about her stewardship and the privilege of being entrusted with my care. Imagine that!

As soon as my wife left for evening service, I wrapped myself in an avalanche of misery and was consumed by a flood of gut-wrenching tears. I was grieving because I had declined into an unprecedented state of deep reflection.

My unrealized dreams and cherished ideas of the future were unreachable mirages, taunting me with episodes of a potentially unattainable future. The beautiful life I had idealized sharing with my wife and children might never be realized. The lifelong sacrifices we had made, with me promising her that such investments would be worth it and would yield an abundance of the good life in the future, now seemed futile or, at best, elusive. I was gravely ill in all respects. The prognosis for that type of illness was just months to live. Even if I received treatment and survived for a while, I had a medically incurable disease and, at best, my quality of life could be severely negatively impacted. I attempted to see the "blue sky" with an endless horizon, but my rose-colored glasses were of a dull gray. Unrealizable dreams, low expectations of life, and the pursuit of making final preparations to ease the pain of those who would be left behind plagued my thoughts.

As self-centered as I had become, I was oblivious of the mental and physical strain that my illness had placed on my wife. I had failed to appreciate the restraint she had been exercising to spare me from the sound tongue-lashings I deserved. She selflessly absorbed the torrents of undeserving criticisms I had been unleashing at her and tolerated my erratic behavior, so that she could mercifully administer care to me. Driven by her natural compulsion to reflect God's love, she was tolerant of my missteps, and I was the beneficiary of her kindness. Such was the personal sacrifices of my dear wife in extending angelic acts of love and mercies to me. I was so consumed with self-pity, I did not even realize the visible physical changes she had recently undergone as a result of my illness.

When I finally managed to redirect my focus from myself and on to her, I realized she, too, had lost several pounds; her beautiful face was distraught and appeared to have aged overnight from what was now months of stress. Sometimes she seemed to be wandering aimlessly about, consumed by unfathomable thoughts. I surmised that she was also trying to get a grip of her natural fears, while faithfully advocating God for me with every breath she took. That impacted me so profoundly, and it made me even more distressed. I had made her the object of my anger, demanding of her more than she could give, yet she maintained her faithful devotion to me while hiding her sufferings. Even when I spouted venomously at her in my testy, cranky states, she was sacrificing, fasting, and praying in faith, believing that God would heal and restore me.

Naturally, I was ashamed of my behavior. I wished that I had found a more civil way to engage my wife and discuss the burden and the fears I was carrying, yet I allowed myself to lose my temper, stretched the truth to the limits, violated the boundaries of decency and, even worse, betrayed the tenets of my Christianity. Not that we have never had disagreements before, but I was genuinely insensitive and behaved like a brute this time.

Cancer was about to rob us of that blissful autumn of our lives, and the great beyond beckoned. In grief, I wrestled with a myriad of unanswerable questions, such as, "Was there something I had done to deserve this sentence?" and "Where might I ascribe blame?" I didn't think that all my sinning and wrongdoings merited such a severe sentence. I truly believed that I had been a relatively good person. In all my dealings, I tried to be fair and treated people with love and respect. Like all humans, I have caused a few offenses, but I have never envied or robbed any individual, or wished evil on anyone. I took care of my physical body and fed my spirit with the Word of God. What had I done wrong to reap this devastation as my reward? I was miserable and unhappy.

Fearing the worst, I continued to play the story of my life in review, focusing on some assumed entitlements based on my selfish good. I had always tried to be the best at whatever I dedicated myself to do. In general, I usually do a pretty good job, because, with pride, I tried to do extra in striving toward the elusive concept of perfection. I was generally in control of whatever I was put in charge of, but now, there I was, losing control, and I could do nothing about it. To be caught sweating over a challenge demonstrated weakness, I had been taught, yet there I was sobbing like a baby.

My wife and I had done our best to raise our two children to become productive adults, representing our proud fruits. It was only fair then that we should now expect the rewards of a good life. However, there I laid alone, overcome with a deep sense of loss and loneliness, and fearing that my useful life was slipping away. All my worldly pursuits, the things I had built with much effort and diligence, were but vanity, and they were slipping out of my grasp and were of no value to me. I was experiencing what I can only describe as indigency of the soul, destitute of what I most desired, the presence of my family. I questioned even the soundness of my thought process. What rights did I have to want my wife and children to be fussing over me? Yet, I needed their affection then.

Flowers on my coffin would be good for the eyes of those who would see them; I would not appreciate them in death. I was selfish and self-involved. I found it difficult to rationalize and release my family to attend to their individual personal responsibilities during those days. What irony. Our children were doing what we raised them to do, asserting their independence from us, yet at that critical juncture, I wanted to change that paradigm; I needed them right by my side at that time. Unfortunately, there was no all-powerful switch I could flip and summon them to my bedside. My peevishness was beyond pitiful, and I knew it, but I felt entitled to be irritable, grumpy, and demanding. I was angry.

That was not the time to be told to toughen up and be a man. I was a man, just one that was broken and lying there wallowing in my anguish. My brain was incapable of producing any resolution to my crisis, so what I needed was someone who could help me navigate through my dilemma and direct me to a place of hope for the future. I wanted the great oracle, the counselor and comforter, as my brain was swirling in an emotional whirlwind.

What could I have done on my own from where I lay? I reverted to my place of comfort by cuddling myself in the fetal position, and returned to my childhood safe place. The sense of being a child with an outstretched arm, waiting for that strong arm to provide me guidance, was haunting me. That thought was emerging from somewhere in the depths of my discarded archives. The need for an assuring voice to say, "Hold my hand, son, I will lead you out of this torture," plagued me. I cannot fathom why, at almost sixty years old, I was allowing my mind to reflect on the insecurities of my distant past.

The needs and hurts for which I thought I had long ago developed the necessary survival skills were dominating my thoughts. Years ago, I accepted my lot in life and dealt with the deficiencies, absenteeism, and neglect that framed my childhood. I had done well with the hand I was dealt. Now there I was, in my lonesomeness, allowing this state of emptiness to unmask the child in me. Was there some eternal, unfilled void surfacing? Did it have anything to do with the lack of a father's love? A father whom I have never met or known anything about, except that I bore his name. Did it come surfacing in my time of anger and reckoning because I still had vestiges of rage from his abandonment that I needed to confront as the last act of closure on earth? Was I supposed to finally rehearse and fill every lifelong gap since my childhood so that I could rid myself of all anger triggers and go home to my God in peace?

I was so out of control and desperate that I was hopelessly searching for something to lean on, someone to blame. I couldn't just die here in my loneliness; there was still so much for me to do. My masterpiece was not yet painted. I had not truly lived. I had not yet accumulated the vast amounts of wealth that I had promised myself since I was younger. Yes, I was angry about my condition, but I was more annoyed that I was alone with myself and my destructive thoughts. My brain could not wrap itself around the truth that what had befallen me had nothing to do with an earthly soul or thing. Not every experience has a rationale or can be resolved to a logical conclusion in the present. My thoughts and emotions were not aligned with the ways of good Christianly behavior; I was not focusing on what God's grace avails. How soon in the face of a crisis had I forgotten the unchanging hand of God, the Rock that I should be leaning on, the enduring Comforter and eternal Father?

Thank God that He is forgiving and embraces me even when I am seeking solutions elsewhere. He allows me to have my own will so I can appreciate Him more when I find my way back home, or He gently guides my way from the path of self-destruction and eternal peril. He always provides a source of comfort and peace.

God led me to a sanctuary of peace, by allowing me to reflect on my life as a child growing up with my grandmother. She was the only person who would turn a blind eye when I would fake illnesses, with continuous sobbing, to cover some sadness or grief. I guess she understood that I craved affection and she would in turn pacify me with pampering. Sometimes she would calm my soul with a selection from one of those old songs from the church hymnal. In other instances, whenever I tried to hide my sobbing out of embarrassment because I was crying for something silly, she would hear and be there for me. When she inquired about the reason for my crying, I would fabricate some illness to justify her attention. Nothing felt better than her taking me in her arms, soothing the area of my alleged pain or administering some form of home remedy. Now that I think of it, many times what I thought were medicines might have just been some form of placebo, but they worked. They would bring me comfort, and I would magically float off into blissfulness and sweet dreams. So perhaps the child in me never grew up. The perceived death monster of my childhood that stole my grandmother could be lurking on my doorstep. But big boys don't cry. "Grandmama can't comfort you anymore."

I was supposed to be the comforter of many, so I needed to pull up my big boy's pants, dry my tears, arise from that bed, and go fix something. "Ah!" But I couldn't; my feeble body did not have the strength, and the pains worsened with every movement. It was becoming clear that I needed to cede control, even of my very thoughts, and be totally dependent on others. That meant letting go of my enormous ego and being submissive to God, my wife, and my caregivers. I needed to fall like a sick child in God's arms, which were stronger than those of my grandmother. Those arms that death cannot reach, arms that go beyond administering placebo and dispenses the eternal panacea of His mercy and grace. "Thank God, my Holy Father, that You are the earthly father whom I never had, the inspiration for my grandmother, even as You are still with me now."

I asked God to please remake me, mold me the way He wanted me to be so that I could be used for His good pleasure. Having made that request, I relished the peace and comfort it brought, knowing that God would make me whole again. I then engulfed myself in streaming some of the beautiful old-time religious gospel music that had filled the environment most of my nights as they ushered me to a peaceful sleep.

Having expressed this profound personal truth with utmost sincerity, I feel no shame. My wife is the greatest woman; I burdened her with way too much, yet she never seemed to get flustered or ever complained, but always rose to the occasion of meeting my unreasonable needs. I was both physically and emotionally needy. I know God will reward her with the desires of her faith.

As I reviewed the preceding account, I was shocked at how much I had documented and was revealing. Hopefully, it will be for someone's gain. The desperate, sick body and mind can be destructive, as in its weakened state Satan and his demons can invade and inhabit our thoughts. Recall in Matthew 4:7, that it was after forty days of fasting, when Jesus was in a weakened state, that Satan transported Him to the pinnacle of the temple and told Him to throw himself down. Clearly Satan had invaded Jesus thoughts, tempting Him to the extent of daring the Christ to commit suicide. As I shall relate in a later chapter, Satan invaded my dreams in my weakened state, with inducements that would have led to my death. His tactics are so familiar because they are rethreads—old, rehashed, and reused.

CHAPTER 8

Learning to Adjust

GOD said to Satan, "Have you noticed my friend Job? There's no one quite like him—honest and true to his word, totally devoted to God and hating evil." Satan retorted, "So do you think Job does all that out of the sheer goodness of his heart? Why, no one ever had it so good! You pamper him like a pet, make sure nothing bad ever happens to him or his family or his possessions, bless everything he does—he can't lose! But what do you think would happen if you reached down and took away everything that is his? He'd curse you right to your face, that's what." GOD replied, "We'll see. Go ahead—do what you want with all that is his. Just don't hurt him." Then Satan left the presence of GOD.

—Job 1:8-12 (MSG)

One of the most noticeable changes I observed was the dramatic volume of mass that I lost within a couple of weeks. I was lying in bed and happened to pinch my leg, only to realize I could grab a whole handful of loose flesh. It was a shocking sight when I eventually saw myself in the mirror. Staring back at me in amazement was a skeletal frame draped in droopy rags. My appearance and movement were uncharacteristic and unrecognizable even to me. I felt like a different person. I had been significantly transformed since I started the downhill sledding. I was nothing but a bony mass, a collapsed emaciated frame over which a loose draping of flesh hung.

The strange creature of mere skin and bones was the remnant of what I used to be. Sagging flaps of flesh drooped lifelessly over my arms where muscles once bulged. The once bulging pectorals that I used to proudly flex had now been replaced by two sagging mounds that tenaciously clung to my little deformed bird's chest as though they were tattooed on.

My skin had become ashy and scaly, and my eyes were so so deepset it was as if they were reaching for the back of my head. The tenuous structure that held me together was like a delicate filigree, so frail that it seemed breakable to the touch. Even without make-up, I had a good chance of successfully auditioning for a role as a zombie. I couldn't help frequently whining about my appearance. I wondered how anyone could stand the sight of the scary, pitiful image that represented me. Yet it seemed my dear wife still cared for me. I was a ghost of the man she married thirty years earlier. A rather sad anecdote to relate to our relationship was that we spent our thirtieth wedding anniversary in the hospital, with me barely able to greet her.

Submerged in the depths of fear, the face of my wife was the periscope I hoped would provide me reality checks. Mentally, I was unable to understand what was happening to me. I was drowning in doubt because of the perilous tides that were dragging me to depths of uncertainty. Like a young, helpless child, in desperation and seeking guidance, I would curiously scan for any changes in her expression and bearing, even in the lines of her face. I needed to confirm my worst fears or be provided with evidences of hope that our combined faith would produce, but she was unyielding.

It was difficult for me to read beyond what she wanted me to see. Her purposeful, stoic expression masked whatever emotional reactions she would otherwise freely display. Her commitment was to sustain every scintilla of hope that she could invest in me. She would not satisfy my cravings for expressions that would feed my negative emotions. I sensed that she knew that doing otherwise would be a disservice to me as they could counter my faith purpose. So whatever negative reports she received, or conclusion she had made about the negative prognostications, were stockpiled and secured behind hermetically sealed lips and covered with expressions of hope.

My customary dietary habits were in disarray, not only because of how painful it was to chew and swallow but also because of my overall distaste for everything edible. Normal foods tasted and smelled disgusting. Anything that went into my mouth produced either salty, sour, or acidic tastes. It was difficult to distinguish between flavors, sweetness, and bitterness, while seasoning and spices were absolutely sickening. Mostly everything edible made me nauseous, so I had to take counteracting medications before I could eat anything. Imagine being repulsed by the taste of pure water and my own saliva.

During the radiation of the spinal tumor, some of the intense rays had found their ways into my mouth and throat, causing damage to the receptors that would normally detect the different flavors. The doctors advised me that my taste buds would return at some point; months, years—no one could say for sure. It was ridiculous that I had a voracious appetite with no palatable options to satisfy it. Starvation would soon set in if I did not eat, so I resorted to consuming the prescribed nausea medications with great frequency so that I could forage all hours, day and night. Maintaining a proper diet was impossible as I would then devour the weirdest conceivable concoctions. I had the most bizarre craving for the strangest foods, including stewed pig's and cow's feet, chicken cooked in milk and cheese sauce, and stewed chicken liver.

Some of the prescribed drugs started to produce significant side effects, altering my moods, temperament, and emotions; simultaneously, I was becoming high-maintenance and maladjusted. The side effects of the drugs were plaguing me with a range of symptoms, such as constipation, sleepiness, confusion, periods of alternation between partial consciousness, and brain fogs. Sleeping became the best part of my life those days.

Admittedly, there were desirable effects of the medications, such as mental calmness, tranquility, and reduced pain. I often experienced periods that I characterized as blissful euphoria. I really enjoyed the peaceful euphoric quietness that some of the medications produced. My thoughts and dreams would be most pleasant, and it was as if my miseries would temporarily disappear. It is a mystery to me how these powerful medications are capable of totally swaying one's mind away from the reality of physical torture and mental anguish to delight and bliss. I would strongly discourage everyone from taking these medications without a prescription and to do so only under strict doctor's supervision.

The fear of addiction was real for me. I did not wait for my pains to subside before weaning myself off those prescriptions, long before the doctors thought I should. I was very aware of the addictive dopaminergic effects of certain prescribed medications and did not want to become a casualty of drug addiction. My little dopamine was not going to dictate my future. Incidentally, here is my layman's explanation of how the pleasing little dopamine works to trap the individual into becoming a dopehead. Remember, this is not a clinical definition, but it helped with my understanding. Dopamine is that part of the brain, a neurotransmitter, that sends signals to other parts of the brain to indicate how much they like a particular sensation, similar to the euphoria produced by opioids. The brain then starts craving more. By satisfying those cravings of the brain with more opioids continuously, one can become hooked, because it's hard to resist the compulsion to provide the brain with what it determines is good for it. However, by continuously yielding to the dictates of the dopamine, one opens the door to addiction.

During the daylight hours, I was usually drained, fatigued, and dizzy; sometimes I felt irritable, and I just wanted to be left alone. I was becoming a social misfit, as I had to make adjustments that profoundly impacted my friends and family. As my range of mobility decreased, and motivation gave way to listlessness, the interactions with my family and friends diminished. One of the issues I was forced to confront was how to honestly convey to this close group of people, who wanted the best for me, that I was physically and mentally drained and did not want to be seen by, or even talk to, anyone at that time. These were people who genuinely cared about me and tried to bring me comfort and their personal offerings of prayers and blessings, but I shuddered at the thought of having guests and socializing.

Admittedly, vanity influenced my decision. I did not want to be pitied or to watch the faces of visitors as they marveled at the remnant that was then me. I was a scaly, scrawny, bony, ugly fragment of my former self. Being almost totally physically incapacitated, I would also be challenged to move from our upstairs bedroom to meet with the guests downstairs. Imagine doing this at the whim of every drop-in. Mentally, I didn't trust myself to maintain any level of reasonable dialogue. I feared I would not be able to formulate any rational thought or maintain interesting conversations. Worse, I might say stupid, ridiculous, and delusional things to my detriment. I actually did on a few occasions, much to my embarrassment. Even if I could mentally and physically make a showing for my guests, I was unable to sustain any state of awakened consciousness. My neck would hurt when I sat upright for more than a few minutes, and I would have to support my chin between my palms.

Additionally, it would be unconscionable to put any more strain on my wife, my sole caregiver. To maintain care for me while playing host to the unpredictable stream of well-intended guests would be unreasonable. Fortunately, the doctor provided me with the soundest escape route. My immunoglobulins, the antibodies that protect me from harm, were extremely low. I was advised to limit interactions with things that could harm me, which was just about everything and everyone. It was so comforting to know how much people cared for me and wanted to share with me personally, but not endangering myself was paramount. It took every fiber of bravery that I could muster to maintain an attitude of snobbishness to avoid my friends, who could compromise my recovery.

Even as I tried to keep everyone updated with my postings on Facebook, there were those who insisted on speaking to me personally. In the rare cases where I accepted or returned calls, I would generally preface my monologue with the fact that I could only talk briefly and did not want to answer many questions. I likened my new existence to that of a trapped and isolated creature, encaged in a defined perimeter, isolated from the rest of the world, only allowing my fingers to do the talking through my postings. I searched for hope in the Bible, and the Book of Job provided me with a sense of purpose. Inspired by Job's journey and emergence from tribulation,

I was eager to share with others the basis for my renewed sense of confidence in the post below.

> I want to illustrate that even the pains and sufferings we endure in this world may be for God's glory. Even in my situation, I am drawing strength from the Bible, to show that not everything that appears to befall us will necessarily lead to our demise. If God allows it, He will provide for our needs, and if we persevere, we could be greatly rewarded.
>
> My faith-based perspective draws upon the account of Job, as related in the Bible. Job 2:2-6 records that God asked the devil where he had been. The devil responded that he had been roaming the earth. Even though God is omniscient, he further questioned the devil if he had taken note of Job. Job was a diligent and faithful child of God, who also went beyond what was required for his righteousness and proxy for righteousness on behalf of his children. In an attempt to undermine Job's genuine faithfulness to God, the devil asserted that Job's faithfulness was only sustained because of the hedge of protection God had placed around him, and if removed, he would not be able to maintain his loyalty to God, based on what the devil would subject him to.
>
> Confident in Job's faithfulness, God removed His protection from Job but charged the devil not to kill him. Essentially, God placed a high level of trust in Job, knowing the intent of his heart. The omniscient God saw beyond the logical devil, that Job's spirit was right and that he would remain faithful regardless of what the devil would put him through. Job subsequently lost all his wealth and children. He was subjected

to extreme torture, and torment, even from his three closest friends, who alleged that he must have sinned against God and became unrighteous based on the spate of suffering he was experiencing. Job's circumstances became so intolerable that even his wife advised him to curse God and die. But he was steadfast and resolute in his faithfulness to God, even considering all that he was enduring. In the end, Job prevailed over the works of the devil and validated God's infinite wisdom. After God counseled Job, He rewarded him with more than he had before.

When we are taken through tribulations, God expects us to rely on Him, no matter how extreme the circumstances become. He instructs us to call on Him, trust Him with all our hearts. He knows of our past deeds and knows our hearts, and He elects who He wants for specific assignments. The journey may not be comfortable, but God is mindful of that too, and He knows the end stages and outcomes.

As the ailment tries to assail me, I have chosen to reread the complete book of Job; maybe this is the third time. This time I am focusing on Chapter 38 as my point of reference for my eventual recovery. There God counseled the self-righteous Job before He delivered him from his torment, but indeed blessed him. As I struggle in my sufferings, I appreciate my helplessness and dependency on God, and the need to be grateful for mercies, even in my current state. God will continue to sustain me. The holiest I could ever be had no comparison to the lowest level of Job's righteousness. Nothing of my doing has earned me even the most minuscule element of mercy, but for Jesus the Christ and

His mercies at the cross. My healing is through my High Priest Jesus the Christ who has paid my sin debt with His blood, wherein also is my healing. This experience has been measuring me, sizing me up and reclassifying me. I have a new appreciation of humility as I become more aware of my mortality. I can't even imagine how insignificant I am when placed in the context of The Almighty eternal God, to whose pleasure I commit myself to serve.

Finally, after consultation with my oncologist yesterday, I will start chemotherapy next week, on Friday. I will be rid of multiple myeloma as it is known today, I will be rid of the bad monoclonal cells, have an abundance of functional immunoglobulins and whatever I need to be well. The lytic bones, collapsed spine, ribs, and all my infirmities will be healed. Sprouts of new bone growth will emerge, and I will become perfectly well. It is the will of God that it should be so. Healing and reconstruction are what I am expecting in faith, that is the substance of my hope, and I so pray, through Jesus Christ, that this shall be done. I love you, my friends, and I also pray God's blessings for you.

CHAPTER 9

With My Mouth

The mouth of the righteous is a fountain of life, but the mouth of the wicked conceals violence.

—Proverbs 10:11 (NIV)

The good person out of the good treasure of the heart produces good, and the evil person out of evil treasure produces evil; for it is out of the abundance of the heart that the mouth speaks.

—Luke 6:45 (NRSV)

There was a time during the journey when I pondered about the potency of my tongue to influence my demise. Although relatively small, the tongue has incredible powers. I used it in my appeals to God for healing and in expressing my hope to others, but could its actions also have led to my trauma and distress? Before I elaborate on what I call my "poison tongue utterances," I will cite a few scriptural references about the tongue. How many believe that the tongue can speak one's destiny into being? The Bible contains many accounts of the spoken word bringing things into being—from abating raging storms, to healing the sick, to restoring lives. Most of us use our tongue when we pray in faith, calling things that are not as though they were in reality and waiting in the hope of seeing them become real. But with the same tongue, we curse and cause hurt to others. Here are a few references from the Bible relating to the power of the tongue:

- "The mouths of fools are their undoing, and their lips are a snare to their very lives." (Proverbs 18:7, NIV)
- "The tongue also is a fire, a world of evil among the parts of the body. It corrupts the whole body, sets the whole course of one's life on fire, and is itself set on fire by hell." (James 3:6, NIV)
- "Those who guard their mouths and their tongues keep themselves from calamity." (Proverbs 21:23, NIV)
- "Death and life are in the power of the tongue." (Proverbs 18:21, NKJV)

Imagine that! Proverbs says that we can actually speak death into reality. Now, about my recurrent "poison tongue" pronouncements. I frequently told my wife that as soon as our children graduated from college, I might as well be finished with this world and go to my Creator, as I lived vicariously through them. In ignorance, I surmised that to be my life's accomplishment. I would have far outdone "the donor"—my absentee father. Maybe it was because, from childhood, I passionately nurtured the idea of one day becoming a great father and having the good fortune of raising my children to become decent, productive human beings. My wife would actively discourage me from making that cataclysmic statement. Nonetheless, I persisted. My daughter had received her advanced degrees several years ago, and my son had graduated just two weeks before I was diagnosed with the cancer.

Another careless loose tongue utterance of mine would occur when I sought to gorge on a favorite food—ice cream. My wife would counsel me to limit my consumption. With objection, I would unwisely remark, "Go ahead, you just wait until I get cancer, I am going to eat all the ice cream and steak I want." Who is the bold cancer infested person with the guarded tongue now? I have lived to see the profusion of ice cream and steak in all their glory, as though taunting me, and rather than being able to eat them, I was overwhelmed with nausea and disgust just looking at them. How pathetic. Was I the victim of my unguarded tongue, speaking the cancer affliction into being? Draw your own conclusion about the effects of a poison tongue on my dilemma. I have not taken a position on that. Yet I have lived to pray for God's forgiveness for every loose, destructive, or sinful word my tongue had ever uttered. What I concluded was that I needed to guard my tongue and speak encouragement with blessings to all of God's creation, while trusting that future words of my mouth and the meditations of my heart will be pleasing to the Lord our God.

As far as my earthly reality was concerned, I was declared a cancer patient by the medical community, and I had to deal with it. Not that I needed to remind myself of it, but I would find myself many times, quite loudly at times, with tears flowing, reciting my diagnosis to myself in disbelief, "I am a cancer sufferer." Maybe I did it because I considered how incredulous and highly unlikely it was that I could have been beset with that terrible scourge. My wonderfully made body from God couldn't be the carriage of such a vicious curse. The act of even enunciating the word *cancer* was not something most people in my circle commonly tossed about lightly; it was almost taboo and scary. Cancer was generally whispered and disguised in vague and ambiguous terms, such as: "the big C" or "the killer C"; it was an old person's disease.

Just thinking about it would plunge me into emotional chaos. Being saddled with the haunting knowledge of me bearing that vicious deadly plague was frightful. I was faced with a future of uncertainty, where at best, there would be periods of remission, which would be temporary until the inevitable relapse. Every relapse could be a step closer to death, since my body could become smarter and develop its own unique evasive mechanism to each progressive line of therapy. Eventually the lines of therapy would be exhausted, and medicine would offer me no more hope. Surely, I am encouraged by reports from those who tell me about people who have been living with the disease for years. However, my current reality was that I had a marked-for-death disease, and I had to confront its realities even as I pressed on in faith, believing that I would be healed.

With our children now on their own, my wife and I were looking forward to retirement, taking long vacations, and to finally begin living "the good life" as we had planned. With some regrets, I reflected on how we had sacrificed by living very modestly. The deprivations we endured, the holidays we did not take, the fancy vehicles we never bought, and all the trappings of life that we had postponed to build up a nest egg for an enjoyable early retirement after the corporate check payments had ceased.

Life is such a folly. The Good Book has parallels for everything. Luke's Gospel tells the parable of "the rich fool." His crops had produced in abundance, and he decided to accumulate the fruit of his labor by tearing down his existing storage barn and build a greater one, where he would store all his goods and crops. The man asserted that once he had done that, he would say, "Soul, you have many goods laid up for many years; take your ease; eat, drink, and be merry." But God said to him, "Fool! This night your soul will be required of you; then whose will those things be which you have provided?" (Luke 12:18-20, NKJV). That is a rather sad commentary as there was such a close similarity to my current situation.

The human mind cannot help but ponder the question of the flesh, and my mind launched a series of questions. What then should I plan for? Would there inevitably be new boundaries and restrictions on my life as a result of the disease? How would they impact my lifestyle? What would guide my planning framework now? What would emerge as my new priorities, possibilities, and limitations? Would we have financial sustainability? I saw one of my hospital bills and the string of digits before the decimal point was beyond the limitations of my abacus. Merely contemplating all new, unpredictable variables spawned increased stressors. What then of faith over fear? Would I allow myself to be a hostage to my fears? I knew it was imperative to bolster my faith, believing God would always be my source and all would be well, regardless of how long the journey took.

My battle was to prevent my logical, fleshly mind from overruling the works of the Holy Spirit through faith. Was it irony or divine assurance that while writing this account the track playing was "He's Got the Whole World in His Hands"? Ephesians 1:3-6 gave me authority, declaring that in love I was adopted into the sonship of God. My infinitely wealthy Father then would not disinherit me now. My bills and physical welfare are all covered because, in Matthew 6:25-28, Jesus reassures me that even the flowers and the birds are beautifully adorned and cared for by my Father. Without them giving a thought for their sustenance, God takes care of them.

How much more should I, with sonship status of God, need to be consumed with worry? God had always taken care of my needs, even my future healing has He determined. At least I was basking in the relief from the daily grind and pressures of my former everyday work life. Should I not then be joyous and write a post to my friends, reflecting on the positive alternative that the current sojourn had brought me versus the stress and pressures of what it could have otherwise been? Even as I was ailing from the harmful effects of the disease, I found assurance in the fact that there were positive upshots from my affliction. Such was the motivation for me to write the short post below on Facebook.

> So that I am not considered schizophrenic, I exercise restraints on publicly gloating and rejoicing about what I believe is my new good feeling. Considering my present experiences of constant pains and anxiety spells, I am learning how to sustain my faith through self-assurance that I am on divine assignment. Immersing myself in God's Word each night has become the core sustenance for my faith—the knowledge that, as I lay disabled, I am sheltered from the perennial annoyances and demands of the everyday grind of yesterday. There is no alarm clock to silence today. I do not have to respond to ceaseless deadlines and the myriad of things it takes to satisfy the insatiable job-cow. For now, I don't have to be on redundancy watch, constantly wondering

if my number will be the next called to turn in my badge, ready or not, because my services were no longer required.

In contrast, here I am, at peace, while being transformed by the Word, humbling me, calming me, teaching me as though I am being prepared for great work in the future. "Dear God, please keep me humble, I pray, as I feel so blessed, thank You." More than anything else, the Lord has provided me with the most excellent support group on Facebook; they pour so much into me with more positivity than I can pour out. Can you understand my joy in torment? It is good for me, so if I stop now, I may have withdrawal symptoms. I hope you, my friends, will bear with me. You don't have to comment, please hear me, and if you are so moved, I have the time on my hands to read your responses. I have been under the corporate work compressor for more than forty years, and this phase of decompression is absolutely exhilarating. So, if there is indeed joy in suffering, Why Not CANCER if it's God's will?

CHAPTER 10

I Called It Cancer

Let no one deceive you with empty words,
for because of these things the wrath of God comes upon the sons
of disobedience. Therefore do not be partakers with them.

—Ephesians 5:6-7 (NKJV)

In my journey through this illness, I was confronted with many routes to determining a cure for the disease. I was presented with more remedies than a traditional dispenser could prescribe, and more rules than a Pharisaic scroll could contain. Several well-intentioned Christians floated a notion of not naming the affliction. Some even asserted that admitting to the presence of cancer in me was contrary to the faith doctrine. Calling the disease by its name and associating it with me was forbidden, even though I was the one experiencing the calamitous symptoms. There were observable and experiential effects on my body that had me in the place I was. There, theology dictated that I dissociate myself from the experiential condition known as cancer. They believed actively voicing that I had the disease demonstrated my lack of faith, which was ostensibly claiming or prolonging the curse of cancer. It was as though the devastating menace was not already ravaging my body and was still somewhere "out there" waiting to consume me because of my unwitting utterance about what was plaguing me. I already had the disease, and it was not because I had commanded it upon my being.

The basis of my faith healing necessitated that I specify the affliction to be healed with my mouth. In the Gospel, Paul called his affliction a thorn in the flesh. So, I constantly prayed in faith to be healed from the type of cancer called multiple myeloma, believing that God would heal me through His grace. I accepted that the hope in my prayers was aligned with God's will for me to be healed, and when God decided, my healing would be manifested in the physical realm. However, denying the physical manifestation of the physical affliction, in my physical body, in the physical world, while I had the physical evidence, would not truly represent God's desire of me. There are physical laws regulating and governing the physical earth that we all must observe and obey in order to survive.

Pretending that gravity does not exist won't stop the earth's natural pull on my body and cause me to crash to my death if I were foolish enough to jump from a skyscraper in denial.

When I prayed, I called out the affliction by its name, even though, in His omniscience, God has foreknowledge about it. My ears, however, would hear me speak my truth as an earnest request to eradicate the disease. My soul would register what my mouth spoke and record it in evidence so that I could later recall it and bear witness to my faith becoming substance. And even as we walk in faith, we live in a world where testimony is not entirely credible unless it is demonstrable by sight. If I hobbled around bearing an expression of agony, while professing physical healing, that would not only be confusing, it would be laughable to those of little or no faith. Such people can establish a basis for their own faith or others might have theirs reinforced by the true testimonies of those healed to the glory of God. In Luke 5:32 (KJV), Jesus said, "I came not to call the righteous, but sinners to repentance." The righteous may not always need to be convinced about faith healing, but sinners may be convinced when I am healed, and God will have glory by their belief in Him. God does not need me to be an apologist or tell untruths to glorify Him, He will heal me in His time. His plans are timely and divinely advised.

I remained convinced it was necessary to enunciate the specific affliction, so I could likewise speak to what I was healed from. I collected adequate evidence of the damage done to my body by the cancer in the form of scans and images. Those are my proof of the marvelous works of God for doubters in the future. My faith rests in God's provisions through grace, and regardless of what I call the disease, it presents no barriers to the power of God. My conviction was, of course, that my healing would be done in the spiritual realm and progressively become apparent in the physical realm. Then the miraculous works of God would be self-evident and supportive of my testimony.

The Bible records that the general populace in the days of Lazarus pronounced him as dead. There was ample evidence for the natural man to declare him so. Only Jesus as Lord, operating beyond the physical realm, had the spiritual visibility to see him otherwise and the authority to declare that He was just asleep. When Jesus raised him from the dead, God was glorified. Certainly, Jesus understood that natural human had called Lazarus dead, but He had the power to pronounce the condition otherwise. Humans now had the evidence to declare Lazarus alive, after having called him dead initially.

So will it be for me. Whatever I call the disease will have no consequence on what Jesus says it will be. God is the only Omnipotent; He has unlimited potential to overrule anything that man in ignorance and folly characterizes by name. Calling the disease by the name humans ascribed to it serves merely for human identification. If I didn't name the evil disease that had invaded me, how then would I identify and distinguish it from my other ailments? I maintain that I needed to call it out by name. I chose to call it by the name the doctors had communicated to me. Calling cancer for what science had named it legitimized its existence, but in no way did it diminish the power of God when I called on Him in faith to completely eradicate it. I declared that the disease was existential, but only for a season. Cancer had affected me, and I was experiencing the reality of its existence. If God allowed it to be with me, it would only be for the time that He needed it to accomplish His purpose.

The doctors called the condition multiple myeloma. I took it to God in faith for His merciful action. The purpose, course, and consequences of the affliction would be the prerogative of God. God has allowed various hardships on humankind ever since the ostracization from Eden. Paul wrote that God told him that His grace was sufficient for him after he had prayed for the thorn in his flesh to be removed. Undoubtedly, the sufficiency of God's grace overpowered Paul's infirmities, such that it kept him humble, so that he could focus on the revelations of God and evangelize countless numbers of people to become Christians.

We are misguided when we get caught up in every wind of new doctrine and elevate unfounded utterances over God's truths. Such utterances are what sometimes grow to become theologies but are mere traditions of men. If not contained, they become legalistic terms that define the levels of righteousness and create rules for the self-righteous to execute judgment and condemnation of others.

CHAPTER 11

Which Spirits Do I Hear?

Today I have given you the choice between life and death,
between blessings and curses. Now I call on heaven and
earth to witness the choice you make. Oh, that you would
choose life, so that you and your descendants might live!

—Deuteronomy 30:19 (NLT)

My condition prognosticated death as a highly likely outcome of the affliction. Why shouldn't I accept and succumb to the destruction of the cancer? When the pains became so severe that my body was its own torture chamber, shouldn't I have opted for the apparent relief that death would bring and be over with it? If God saw and knew about my misery, what is the point of turning to Him in this unfathomable concept of faith, believing I could access healing through His grace? What good is faith to me if it is an intangible, indeterminable concept that I cannot predict, measure, or time?

I needed help right then. In that state of acute agony, what would sustain my tormented mind to stay assured that the Almighty God understood my sufferings, heard my earnest pleas, and would be moved with mercy to change my pathetic state? What qualifies me above all of God's magnificent creation to make Him more inclined to hear me and be merciful to me?

Well, why Abram? Maybe that's an excellent place to start. He is noted as the first man of faith. Abram (Abraham, as he was later called) endured the pain and inconveniences of separation from his roots, dislocation from the known and familiar, on an unsubstantiated promise from God at the time, in faith believing for a promise of generational blessings. God delivered on His promise to him. During Christ's time on earth, many were held captive by evil spirits, physical disabilities, and life-threatening circumstances. In faith, they just believed that Jesus had the power and authority to heal them; that He would, and He did.

It became my turn to demonstrate that I dared to believe likewise. That same Jesus said, through faith, we could move mountains. I felt like a mountain was on me; it was the crushing mountain of a critical illness that threatened me with death. Dare I believe that Christ had included me among those to whom He had spoken of as being vested with such power? By exercising my faith, would I have the distinction of being restored to a level of wholeness, such that I could achieve a level of restoration that would authenticate and validate the reality of the effectual faith of which Jesus spoke, and that it is as real, effective, and demonstrable these days as it was in His times?

There are certain revelations I had that affected me profoundly during the darkest days of my illness. I am not sure how many people believe in dreams. We have them, so there must be stimuli for them. These stimuli must come from someplace beyond our natural realm, even though they incorporate familiar things so that the dreams make sense and we can relate to them. The question of the source of the stimulus for a particular dream was one I thought was worthy of exploring. For me, dreams are infrequent occurrences. When they occurred, I generally would not remember them. Whether or not we believe in their substance or meaning, when they are as dramatic and under the circumstances as I experienced during my sickness, it is too difficult to ignore them. Since I did not document in real time either of the two situations below, I cannot precisely date when they occurred. I believe they were just before I commenced chemotherapy.

What if the voice in your dream presented death as your best and mildest option for relief from misery, pain, and confusion? How would you be able to distinguish between the divine guidance of the Holy Spirit and the compelling logical appeal of the devil's deception? During those times of severe physical torment, when the brain's response dictates that relief, at whatever cost, is the logical and correct choice, how does one repudiate the inducement of the Deceiver in preference for the belief that faith holds God's assurance of an eventual better outcome? I could not produce a reliable, logical faith formula, but I believe John 10:27-28 (KJV), which says, "My sheep hear my voice, and I know them, and they follow me: And I give unto them eternal life; and they shall never perish, neither shall any man pluck them out of my hand."

I vaguely remembered the first dream after the chemo fog had cleared, until my wife, to whom I had told it at the time, refreshed my memory. I mentioned earlier how much affection I had for my now departed grandmother, who raised me until my early teens. For years after she died, I cried secretly, because I missed her tremendously. However, as loving and kind as she was, I hardly ever dreamt of her. Her face was never clearly visible to me, and she would always be angry with me in the rare instances she appeared in my dreams. In that recent dream, I could clearly see her face. It was glowing with radiance and bore a warm smile. She was happily beckoning me to come to her. In that dream, I did not just shun her, but I adamantly drove her away with a stout rebuke and utter disrespect; something I would not have even dared think to do in real life. Although I agonized over my action, I felt justified. Had I yielded to her beckoning and followed her, I surmised that it would have meant my death.

In the second dream, I may have just fallen asleep and was in pain. As clear as a bell, I heard a voice telling me that I had two options: I could choose to live or die. If I chose to live, I would have much suffering and great difficulties. If my choice was to die, it would be relatively easy and would occur within a few days. I would be free of pains and the cancer, and be liberated. I was terrified because it all appeared so real. In that moment, I reflected on how I had wasted so many years in sin and had added so little value to the kingdom of God. Despite that, God had continued to bless me, and had not withdrawn from me all the talents, potential and capabilities He had bestowed on me. My life would be such a waste if I had to die at that time. It is said that, "To whom much is given, much is expected." I was supposed to be a good steward for the Lord. He had entrusted me with much, but I had done a poor job in managing all He had vested in me. How would I account to God if I died then?

I felt the need to revoke every utterance of ungratefulness, displeasure or complaint about life. My existence on earth was glorious, and I craved to remain and enjoy even the things I was previously disgusted with. I needed an Isaiah-type to bring me the good message from God that my life would be extended as he had done for King Hezekiah in Isaiah 38. I was appreciating the value and joy of life even as I was dreaming and dreading the thought of death. I had begun to relish every future moment that God would grant me to continue living, despite any suffering in the future.

Although my dreams never amounted to anything in reality before, those two were as real as they could be. Does Satan have the power to influence our dreams? Well, if he can influence our thoughts while we are awake and conscious, why would he not seek to steal our joy by infiltrating our dreams when we are impaired, weakened, vulnerable, and least capable of resisting him? Is it not his character to use the things and people we love and cherish to deceive us and cause death? That is exactly what he intended with the illusion of my dear grandmother, knowing how much I loved and cherished being with her.

Is there biblical support for my belief that he uses dreams as a channel for his deception and trickery? In Job 7:13-15 (NIV), there is a monologue of Job falsely accusing God of terrifying him in his dreams, in which he states, "When I think my bed will comfort me and my couch will ease my complaint, even then you frighten me with dreams and terrify me with visions, so that I prefer strangling and death, rather than this body of mine."

Job was obviously blaming God for his tormenting dreams. We know that God was not the one influencing his destructive dreams. God had already given Satan permission to torment him, as shown in Job 2:6. Satan was using Job's dream to achieve his objective. In my impaired state, the ruler of darkness had also entered the subconscious realms of my dreams, as he did with Job, to trick me into a destiny other than that willed for me by God. Had I surrendered to either of his lies in those dreams, I would have certainly died shortly afterwards and be his captive.

For I am convinced that neither death nor life,
neither angels nor demons, neither the present nor the future,
nor any powers, neither height nor depth, nor anything else in
all creation, will be able to separate us from the love of God
that is in Christ Jesus our Lord. (Romans 8:38-39, NIV)

CHAPTER 12

Called to a Place of Privilege

As you do not know what is the way of the wind, or how the bones grow in the womb of her who is with child, so you do not know the works of God who makes everything.

—Ecclesiastes 11:5 (NKJV)

God chose the lowly things of this world and the despised things—and the things that are not—to nullify the things that are, so that no one may boast before him.

—1 Corinthians 1:28-29 (NIV)

Considering the degree of my illness, and the fact that I was on several medications, I cannot blame anyone if, after reading my account below, they concluded that I had gone over the edge. The post was not an expository biblical lesson, inspirational thought, or another episode of my usual moaning and complaining about my pains and inconveniences; instead, it sought to transcend the reader beyond the natural with me and share in my bimodal supernatural journey. I was hesitant to post it, to have my sanity questioned and to be exposed to every cynicism and ridicule. After pondering my concerns for a while, I concluded that my hesitancy was rooted in fear and was being influenced by the devil. It was his attempt to destroy the magnificent revelation God had given me so that I would not share it.

My reasonable expectation was that most people would not be able to comprehend the experience as it was beyond logic. It was fair to expect that some would attribute my experience to delusion, drug-induced stimulation, or sheer madness, but how many would accept that God, indeed, gave me a window into a truly spiritual reality; a revelation of his mystery? I needed spiritual guidance on how to deal with such perplexity, and it would be ill-advised to seek it from just anyone off the street. I was still gravely ill, and I was concerned about opening this channel and allowing someone who might be manipulated by the devil to feed into my vulnerable soul.

I needed the counsel of trusted spiritual advisers whom I believe were God-anointed. It was not a difficult choice for me. I am fortunate enough to have two shepherds who care for my spiritual well-being: my bishop and my pastor. They listened intently to my account, fresh and unrehearsed. They did not find my revelation preposterous; in fact, they were very supportive, accepted my truth, and cited for my encouragement the testimonies of others who likewise had had transcendental encounters. Their counsel gave me the confidence I needed to share my story with the world. I was then prepared to face whatever confusing, skeptical or critical feedback my posting garnered. Regardless of the responses, I hoped people would realize that it was an authentic experience, and one I was incapable of fabricating.

In the account, it will be seen that I toggled between physical and spiritual states of consciousness. If possible, when you read my account, please try to see the supernatural power of God at work in me, His imperfect child. Disregard for a while my physiologi-cal or psychological states, so that you may experience through my encounter the mysterious actions that God allowed me. Remember that, being sovereign and omnipotent, God can confuse even the wisest among us with His mysteries as He pleases. He chooses to whom and when to reveal the secrets of the unknown, even from time immemorial. We are spirits first, clothed in flesh. To exist in the physical dimension, the flesh requires active senses, emotions, and intellectual abilities. The Spirit transcends the earthly domain; it is our connection to God. "God is Spirit, and those who worship Him must worship in spirit and truth," as John 4:24 (NKJV) states. Naturally, at that level I had to experience such works of God in spirit; I had to travel beyond the earthly domain for this divine encounter. I had a spiritual journey. Remember this preamble as you try to relate to my journey below.

Lonely, dreary, and timeless understate the state of the derelict and desolate place to which my spirit had recently transcended. I felt as though I was living between two states. I functioned between states of consciousness, experiencing and presenting a dual persona. I was conflicted as to whether I was dreaming or drifting between states of realities. The reason is that even as I was in that place of horror, I was somewhat conscious of interacting with the outside world in what I regarded as a depersonalized existence. Hence the confusion that led me to conclude that I was experiencing episodic transcendental dispositions. Apparently, I was switching between the natural and the spiritual in a fugue state. I was in a place of unfathomable isolation and desolation. Imagine a place where peacefulness was way too peaceful. Where deafening silence is not a cliché, but where the absence of sound is like loud noise in reverse. Such was the quietness of this place. It was so quiet that my audible sensory system went berserk, as though my brain was scrambled, causing me to have an uncontrollable headache.

It was so terrifyingly silent that it was unhealthy for human survival. The place was devoid of familiar things. Nothing moved, I sensed nothing, nothing spoke, nothing was heard, nothing called, and nothing answered.

There was no activity, so to me, there seemed to be no element of sensibility or intelligence. Time seemed to have never visited that place, and there was no life form. That dismal place was so stark, I likened it to what it must have been like in the beginning, just after the Spirit of God moved and creation began but then went no further. It is the domain of nothingness, devoid of God's later creation, existing in isolation and desolation. That is a place to be avoided at all costs. It, unfortunately, became my sporadic dwelling place, long enough to experience the reign of sheer terror on my soul. I felt trapped and confined to that place because I could not leave at will, but my consciousness would periodically transcend that supernatural realm back to the physical reality, with my soul still trapped there.

I was keenly aware of everything that was happening there, which was absolutely nothing. From my vantage point above, my disembodied spirit could see my natural physical body. It seemed as if it was frozen in place, as though it was completely dead, a carcass that had been vacated by both spirit and soul. My head was perfectly still and lay limp, and my legs were curled in the fetal position. I was somehow aware this position mimicked the way my natural body was then lying on the bed, I was motionless. I was lying on top of a collection of what looked like rolled scrolls with writings and other relics. There were forms of iconic religious symbols, all dusty and aged, stacked throughout the space; it was like an old, dusty cellar that had never been exposed to light. I reasoned that I was in an old archive of religious artifacts. At times I thought I was floating rather than lying. There may have been other forms of matter surrounding me, but I couldn't accurately describe them because of the poor visibility. Everything, if viewed in natural light, would be the color of tanned brown leather. It was as though I was having an out of body experience. There was, however, one remarkable element that stood out and was indelibly etched in my consciousness; it was a dull, misty blue light, which I called the Blue Haze. It was a hazy blue illumination, as though filtered through a fog or mist. The blue haze was the only thing that gave visibility to the place. It presented as a soft, still glow of low luminosity and translucency. So unique was this color of blue that I doubt any man-made or natural pigment could replicate it in either quality or essence. I sensed that the blue haze was connected to an infinite external source beyond the visible realm and was dispersed via an object of some geometric shape in front of me. The way that I sensed the presence of the objects around me was a result of how the dim blue light bounced off them, which was barely at all, otherwise, I was unable to detect anything with definitive shapes or forms.

Feeding from that light source was the thinnest of membranes. The membrane was my connection to the source of the blue haze. At some point, I became aware that something was not quite right. The membrane appeared to be getting dry; it was stiff, not soft and flexible as I imagined it should be. There was evidence of dark patches and kinks along the length of this membrane, indicating deterioration. I liken it to the deteriorating stages of the detached umbilical cord from a mother and baby after a few days. It occurred to me that in its normal functional state, there should have been a form of green liquid flowing through it. I am not sure how I knew that. I was continually trying to use my saliva to moisten it (at least I thought I was), but I couldn't tell if it was effective since I was frozen in place and couldn't reach the length of the membrane. I feared that if the membrane became totally dry, I would be cut off from the source of the blue haze and I would die. It was imperative that I remained connected to sustain my life. If the liquid stopped flowing or I became detached, I knew that I would die. It is rather uncanny how I was aware of those things, considering the place and state I was in.

What was I waiting there for, frozen in silence? I could not comprehend my purpose there. It was puzzling to me how I got to that place and for how long I was lying in that position. Time seemed to be inconsequential. Apparently, that was how things worked in that realm. I knew that I had not physically died because I was aware of certain physical occurrences. Seemingly, I slipped back into physical reality occasionally. I knew that because of certain natural activities of which I became mindful. The feeling of hunger, then later feeling full; maybe I ate something. Inexplicably, I was also interacting with friends on Facebook during that horrible sojourn. I believe my proof is provided in the post below. My Facebook friends were assuring me that they were praying for my healing. I thought I was also reading get-well cards. With some consciousness, I could also account for the objects in my immediate physical environment close to me, such as my phone, which I knew was muted. It became increasingly confusing to distinguish between my places and states and how and when I transitioned.

The place of desolation was becoming more unbearable and terrifying. I was alone and miserable. I tried to cry, but made no sound; I tried to speak, but my mouth was shut, and I got no reactions from anything or anyone, not even my own body. I saw myself as just "a stiff," but contrarily, I was alive. I had lost all control over my person and felt entombed in an abstract existence.

Nothing moved, nothing quaked, and nothing was there to break the eerie stillness. The place lacked all stimuli for emotion and motivation; everything was suspended in time, stillness and quietude. My best description of my environment would be passively hostile. It's a place where I believe all sinful souls are destined for final disposition. I was consumed with thoughts of fear as I contemplated my fate. Would I be suspended in that infinite, eternal, timeless domain forever? To whom should I have appealed for deliverance? If I shouted, would my voice carry from my vocal cords to my lips so that I could pray? Could my lips even move? If I could cry passionately, would God hear me from that place of desolation? Did I even have tears? Because I kept briefly drifting back to physical reality, I felt assured that I was not dead.

I needed my Savior. Where was my God? How could I reach Him to remind Him that I was there waiting for His deliverance? Did I call on Him too late? Did my pleas and those of my army of friends not reach Him before I was placed in this state of doom, isolation, and damnation? Were the prayers of my friends in the physical still finding favor with God Almighty to save me? Could anyone hear me from there? Was I lost? Did the membrane completely dry out and decay? I felt as though I no longer had a soul; but how could it be, if I still experienced emotions such as grief and fear? What if I lost my soul? Who could access and retrieve it from that place of horror where no one else but me seemed to exist? Was I spiritually cut off from God and doomed there for eternity?

It was like the unfathomable thought of being lost in space, sucked in by a black hole that has no bottom and nothing to grasp on to but perpetually sinking infinitely into nothingness forever. I needed to sense some form of emotion in that place, even angry or negative ones. If I was to be tossed into the place of weeping and gnashing of teeth, might it not be better than the calamitous place where I was? At the very least, there, I would experience some form of familiar emotions, regardless of how gruesome they were. If there is such a place as the bottomless pit, might it not be better than the chamber of death that was my current situation? At least I would hear sounds, even if they were blood-curdling shrieks of tortured voices from hell. I could not imagine a more perilous place, even in the absence of physical torture. "O my Lord God Almighty, please rescue me from this place," I prayed. "I seek your presence, Oh Lord," I lamented from the depths of my heart.

While still agonizing in that desolate place, I had a spiritual revelation; it truly did not make sense to me. The revelation was: "The spirit is a vast sustaining force, but it has no emotion." I was vigorously seeking to be released from the tormenting struggle. It occurred to me that, if

I could transition to the realm of consciousness and reach another Christian, who had authority in the Word and could validate that statement as revealed to me, I would be released.

I somehow mustered the presence of mind to post the revelation I had just received about the spirit on Facebook, hardly expecting anyone to comprehend it, let alone comment on it; a confirmation response was what I desperately needed as my ticket out. I knew it was my last desperate hope to get out of the place of desolation where spiritual death occurs. In faith, I hoped that the right person would see the posting with the urgency it contained; that it was my desperate plea for help and not just another glib or delusional comment. I needed a response to validate and confirm that what I had written was true.

I could hardly keep my eyes open as I waited for a response. I was fatigued and drifting between states of consciousness. At some point, a miracle happened. Just before my eyes fell shut and I drifted off into that next dimension, Pastor Mike Cronin, of my church, responded, "Yes." And that was all it took. I didn't even bother to read the extended comments he posted. All I cared about was a "yes" for validation. I needed this as a ticket for my deliverance from the place that I thought was devoid of God's presence. That simple "yes" validated what I learned in the spirit. I did not know how much time had elapsed between when I reached out and when he responded. I know that after his response, I felt the weight of the place of desolation being lifted. Without warning, everything went to a state of even more silence, if that were possible; it was even more deafening. Then I had a sense of a presence in the room, it made no sound. There was a click, a loud bang, what sounded like a door slam, the place shook, a switch clicked and then the blue haze was extinguished. There was intense darkness everywhere. I could no longer see anything in that realm. I felt a sense of great relief. I was alive; I did not die. I would not die. I did not suffer the ultimate, spiritual separation from God Almighty. The relief and joy were immeasurable. I was once again in the presence of God. His favor was with me. This feeling of deliverance, restoration, or whatever goodness of God you may describe it as, was the sweetest, most comforting, joyous event I could ever imagine. I knew then that I had a new life with purpose; cancer would have to go in God's time, and all I cared to do was crave for God to do His will, and by faith I wanted my living to please Him.

Post-Experience Comments

That the God of our Lord Jesus Christ, the Father of glory, may give to you the spirit of wisdom and revelation in the knowledge of Him, the eyes of your understanding being enlightened; that you may know what is the hope of His calling, what are the riches of the glory of His inheritance in the saints, and what is the exceeding greatness of His power toward us who believe, according to the working of His mighty power.

—Ephesians 1:17-19 (NKJV)

Many people are convinced that there is an impenetrable barrier that separates our physical reality from the spiritual. And that to transcend to the spiritual domain means that we must physically die. However, could it be that there is just a thin veil-like vapor that separates the two realms? Do we overcomplicate the matter and limit our capabilities by the constraints of the logical mindset, based on science and reasoning, such that it inhibits us from entering the spiritual realm? In 2 Corinthians 12:2-4 (NIV), Paul spoke of his transcendence into the spiritual/heavenly domain as follows:

"I know a man in Christ who, fourteen years ago, was caught up to the third heaven. Whether it was in the body or out of the body I do not know—God knows. And I know that this man—whether in the body or apart from the body I do not know, but God knows—was caught up to paradise and heard inexpressible things, things that no one is permitted to tell."

Sure, death releases us from the constraints of our logical mind so that we can inhabit the spiritual, as 2 Corinthians 5:8 (KJV) advises, "We are confident, I say, and willing rather to be absent from the body, and to be present with the Lord." Being spirits, we are empowered to breach the human imposed barrier and enter the spiritual realm. I am convinced I did just that. Obviously, I did not die, but was able to have that unique otherworldly encounter. My carnal, logical, rational human mind had to be temporarily disabled, so that I would not reason myself out of the spiritual reality that I experienced. An active mind would contend with and defeat my spiritual attainments. As we learn from Romans 8:7, the carnal mind is enmity against God. God is Spirit and of the spiritual realm.

I thank our Father God Almighty for the privilege of the experience, the ability to recall it, and His authorization to share it for His glory. When I compiled the post a few days after the occurrence, I was amazed that God had given me such clarity and vivid recollection, as though I was reliving it. For anyone who thought I was deranged or delusional, I take no offence. Let me assure you that, to the best of my knowledge, I wrote the post with absolute clarity of mind—I was not delusional or hallucinating. I believe God allowed me that extraordinary experience for good. It might have been my least favored post, however. The "likes" were relatively sparse, and there were relatively few comments. Of the responses, only a few gave any indication of what I would characterize as convincing endorsements. I was nonetheless convinced that God Almighty had approved and led me through the journey. Everything in creation is for God's good pleasure, and I hope and pray that by sharing with you my recollection of the events, it will support someone in some way and please God.

After posting this account, I continued to sense the skepticism surrounding my revelation. Some feedback was received from direct interactions; others were from inferences and innuendos. It was not hard for me to recognize the skepticism. It was difficult for most people to dissociate what was my real experience, unnatural as it may seem, from some form of neurotic and delusional expression. The assertions were that I had been affected by the medications, which had induced some type of hallucinogenic reaction. I chose not to argue that truism. It is a plausible and logical conclusion.

Research shows that some of the medications I was taking could produce hallucinogenic side effects. But I counter the assertion of a medication-induced reaction by asking: How is it that I never had a similar recurrence, even though I did not cease taking the prescribed medications after the experience? Why was this a onetime occurrence? Isn't it logical that with continued use of the drugs I would have similar or other hallucinogenic experiences? On the contrary, I slept so often and for so long in the most tranquil bliss without any similar recurrence or dreams that I can recall. I have transparently listed most of those medications and their side effects in Appendix I, "My Prescriptions."

Let's say I was chemically affected by the medicines. That does not incapacitate or limit the power of the omnipotent God in any way. Being sovereign, God needs no direction or authorization to use whomever, or whatever method or vessel, He chooses to accomplish His will. If the effects of the medicines placed me in an altered mental state to receive His direction, who am I to question the sovereign Lord? Does anyone truly know the mind of God, the extent of His power and how He makes a decision? Whatever led me there for those ephemeral slots of time is not critical to me; neither does it invalidate my experience. In my own life, because of my nature, I sometimes need a little prodding to incline myself to what generally produces my best outcome. Whatever was my mental state, it might have just presented the ideal opportunity for God to take me where He desired.

I am not qualified to dispute any conclusion arrived at in the natural realm of science and logic. But who among us can deny the legitimacy of my spiritual revelations and understandings as given by God the omniscient Father? In Acts 2:17-18 (NIV), the Bible tells us, "Your sons and daughters will prophesy, your young men will see visions, your old men will dream dreams. Even on my servants, both men and women, I will pour out my Spirit in those days, and they will prophesy." Further, the Bible teaches about the inability of the natural man to discern and accept the legitimacy of spiritual mysteries. In 1 Corinthians 2:14 (NKJV), we are told, "The natural man does not receive the things of the Spirit of God, for they are foolishness to him; nor can he know them, because they are spiritually discerned."

God calls whomever He elects to reveal mysteries, at the time and in situations that He judges as suitable for His divine purpose. Could God have possibly revealed a mystery to someone like me? Our Bible is a guidebook of revelations from God to the natural man. We revere the biblical prophets, having read accounts of the fulfillment of their spoken words as they heard from God. But before their divine appointments, who would have given them any regard as legitimate purveyors of God's words?

Moses had become a humble shepherd in a foreign land, filled with self-doubt, when God manifested His essence to him in the mystery of the burning bush, as detailed in Exodus 3. He eventually led the most significant emancipation from slavery in his time.

Samuel was just a boy, not even knowing the Lord, according to 1 Samuel 3, yet God called him while he was sleeping and gave him a revelation of His future deeds. As Revelation 1:9 shows, John was going through tribulation being exiled on the Isle of Patmos when the Lord gave him the great revelation of things to come. When God offers spiritual revelations, they are not given to be kept as secrets. Several of the Old Testament prophets were charged to "speak the Word," as in Jeremiah 1:9 when God told him that He had put the words in his mouth.

In Ezekiel 2:7, Ezekiel was instructed to "speak my words" to the people, even though they were rebellious. Some have suggested that Ezekiel was schizophrenic, because of what could have been regarded as the bizarre symbolism contained in his prophecies. I chose to elevate my conclusion above logic and reasoning to the spiritual level, believing that my unique revelations are unexplainable in the realm of science and logic and can only be appreciated and understood spiritually.

Even though many months have now passed since the experience, I continue to receive revelations about the mysteries of my encounter and what I should draw from it. I am continuously provided with more clarity. I believe that the Spirit sustains life, but it can exist independent of the physical being as we know it. Our spirit connects us with the spiritual God. Spiritual separation from God leads to eternal damnation. My encounter was merely a tiny glimpse of the horror that spiritual impairment with God can produce. Had I fully experienced spiritual severance from God, I would not physically live to give the account that I did.

But think through what I related. I could see my own body lying as though dead in a place of relics and darkness, yet I still had some awareness of reality from time to time. There was no physical pain, but the experience was painful. How do I explain that? Through my struggle in the place of desolation, I was privileged to sense the anguish and suffering, none of which was physical, but I could not bear to dwell there. Shouldn't that confirm that the spirit and soul can survive the body after physical death? We can draw from 2 Corinthians 5:1-8 that our essential self, the spirit, dwells in the body; however, the spirit and soul can survive without the physical body, but we'd better be connected to our Lord God.

I surmised that the blue haze represented our eternal Source, God the Almighty. The membrane represented my spiritual connection to God, my Source. The deteriorating state of the membrane represented the state of my faith. As my faith waned, my spiritual connection deteriorated. God apportions gifts to believers, such as the Word of knowledge, which I believe his ministers should possess. To be liberated from the dreadful place, I needed the sustaining

Word of God to feed my faith and sustain my spirit. My pastor, led by the Holy Spirit, possibly without even realizing it, confirmed the Word of revelation I had posted on Facebook that liberated me from destruction.

God allowed me to participate in a mystery, to which I have ascribed my personal interpretation. I know I am not the first to have the death/life or near-death experience in some form. Most people, as I understand, do not come back from such an experience to testify about it for the enlightenment of others. I am convinced that spiritual death, which I regard as separation from God, is the worst thing that can happen to a created being. I have since pondered these questions: Did Jesus the Christ experience spiritual death on our behalf for a while? Is that what made Him cry out, "My God, my God, why have You forsaken Me?"

Consider this: Jesus had earlier endured every scourging, torture, torment, and punishment that humankind could inflict on Him without a murmur. After all that had ceased, He was there hanging on the cross. At the time of His passionate appeal, in such a very personal way to our Father, there is nothing that we read to suggest that any physical torture was in progress. So that means He was not crying out from ensuing human-inflicted pain. Evidently, His pain at the time was not physical and was likely way beyond even a visceral experience.

When David used those same words hundreds of years before in Psalm 22:1, he too was in a place of desolation and felt abandoned by God. But that was just a foreshadowing of when the Christ would use them in the capstone event, which was God as man taking on the sins of the world so He could later return to His triune existence as God, our Lord. By virtue of Jesus' sacrifice, we have been given the right to a life beyond what we know.

When I allow myself to rely exclusively on the power of reasoning and rationality, where doubts reside, I discount the power of my divine nature that gives me privileges beyond my current reality. But I had long moved beyond such limitations, having enthusiastically accepted the privileged invitation from Hebrews 4:16 to go boldly to the throne of grace. There, I became a part of a covenant relationship and could openly embrace things of the Holy Spirit in the cosmic realm. Why then should I allow any doubt over my power to transcend from the natural to the spiritual domain? Remember that Jesus became human for a time. He later gave up His flesh by dying, then transcended to the spiritual realm. After His resurrection, He then returned to earth so that doubtful earthly humans would have proof of the compelling spiritual reality that is beyond our reasoning capabilities. We have a choice to believe and accept it for our empowerment or reject it, which would be our greatest loss.

God has spared me, extended my life, and given me this opportunity to express what I do not even fully comprehend. The best way I can explain it is, I was made to have an empathetic experience, without suffering the real consequences, one that I could not possibly bear. I am purpose-built for God's use. He heard the lamentation of my soul while I waited in the mire of desolation, even as my spirit was passive but still connected to Him. In the place of spiritual death, there are no emotions. What is life without emotions? There is no joy, no love, no passion, and no activity of the senses. Pray that you never enter this place.

Because of the journey, I became even more convinced of my position of privilege and my eventual healing. As I noted earlier, I never read the complete response of my pastor beyond the "yes". Now that I am preparing this material for a wider audience, I reviewed the original post and realized that what seemed to have been an eternity was only eighteen minutes between my outreach and the response from my pastor. If after reading this account, anyone still thinks that it is some mythical tirade of a delusional and deranged individual, I present physical evidence of the interaction between the pastor and me in real time.

I dug through the archives of Facebook to recover the original post and response I mentioned earlier (and which I have included). Now it's up to you to search your soul and come to your own conclusion as to the authenticity of what I related in this chapter. I believe that God still interacts with us lowly beings through the Holy Spirit. I need no convincing that the omnipotent God chose me to have a small glimpse of his impressive and extensive mysteries.

I crumble in humility in His presence for this. I fear His awesomeness and power, but cherish the fact that I am continually gaining from His benevolence and love. I am praising and honoring Him in humility that I was privileged to have such an unusual experience, complicated and challenging as it is to relate and be understood. Someday, it will all make sense when we fully transcend this reality, in our glorified selves.

The actual Facebook extract of the interaction with my pastor follows:

> *[Monday, July 4, 2016, at 5:58 pm EDT]*
> *The SPIRIT is a vast sustaining entity, completely devoid of emotions.*
> *[Monday, July 4, 2016, at 6:16 pm EDT]*
> *Mike Cronin: Yes! And of logic, reason or any of our senses!*

So, I have learned that God works in what appears to us humans in mysterious ways. He is no respecter of persons and appoints those to whom He reveals mysteries, not based on any classification that humans ascribe. God sees the true heart of the individual and determines among the multitudes whom to call to places of privilege. He also places us among other humans so that we can be beneficial to each other because of our mutual interdependencies. Some people, such as pastors and ministers, are apportioned specific gifts to cater to our various spiritual needs, while others cater to our physical needs with generosity and love.

I am a spirit, and my very existence necessitates that I am spiritually connected to the eternal Source. God Almighty is the vast, infinite Source. Someday, I will no longer struggle to comprehend the full meaning of God's revelation to me. "The Spirit is a vast, sustaining entity, completely devoid of emotions, logic, and reason." We are spirit and are indwelled by the Holy Spirit. Imagine the scope of our capabilities if we would potentiate our faith to stay connected to and draw from the vast, eternal spiritual source. We are created in the "image of God," which I interpret to mean being superior to other creatures and vested with spiritual empowerment. Yet we use emotions such as fear to impose limitations on our God-given spirit-potential to oppose or underutilize the power of the Holy Spirit that God has vested in us.

That state or place of desolation was agonizing and excruciating. There wasn't an eternal fire in the place; I did not smell the burning of flesh. How is it then that I expressed a preference to be tossed into the place of weeping and gnashing of teeth as a comparatively less punitive and torturous experience? That indicates the magnitude of the misery in that place.

While in our mortal existence, we are linked to the vast spiritual source of God that sustains us in this life and, hopefully, hereafter. Spiritual separation from God, I must conclude, is the ultimate of all suffering and beyond what humans can tolerate. I know I have woefully understated the gravity and intensity of my encounter. It was momentous, unimaginably painful, miserable, and unbearable beyond any physical tolerance. However, there was no eternal fire, bottomless pit, or an identifiable torturer. Could the pangs of hell be any worse? Or could I have had a preview and experience of hell itself?

CHAPTER 13

Rationalizing the Cancer

Oh, the depth of the riches and wisdom and knowledge of God!
How unsearchable are his judgments and how inscrutable
his ways! "For who has known the mind of the Lord, or who
has been his counselor?" "Or who has given a gift to him that
he might be repaid?" For from him and through him and
to him are all things. To him be glory forever. Amen.

—Romans 11:33-36 (ESV)

What would it take for me to fully come to terms with the fact that I was stricken with cancer? I was uncertain, but I knew I would eventually have to. There was no logical reason or scientific fact identifying me as a prime candidate. I didn't precisely match the typical profile of one predisposed to cancer. I made a deliberate effort not to dwell on analyzing why I had been chosen to be afflicted with such a disease. Not that these thoughts did not arise continuously, but it was difficult to associate myself with this terrible predicament.

With that mental commitment, I have no recollection of asking specifically, "Why me?" Who knows, I may have slipped once in a while, but my wife recounts that one of the reasons it was such a pleasure to care for me during my suffering was my general attitude. According to her, I never complained about the misfortune of being ill, but rather, that I was always thankful to God in my prayers. I demonstrated, she said, an attitude of hope and encouragement.

As the shock of my potential demise started to diminish, I began rationalizing the new dynamic that was cancer and me. It would be grossly dishonest of me to act as though there was an instantaneous epiphany that God could be using my illness for excellent work. No, it took me some time to understand whether I had a predisposition to cancer, or if by some willful or unintentional act, I had somehow done something to cause the deadly and mysterious calamity to invade my body, but without success. I reflected on what I believed was my relatively clean living, favorable environment, and active lifestyle. I then factored in whatever scientific attribution I could find qualifying me as a logical candidate. But that did not add up either. In my opinion, I was not a prime candidate for cancer. The fact is, I had a sickness of unknown origins.

I hadn't been all righteous and faith perfect in the struggle. At times my mind would drift to wrestle with this dilemma, when the reality of my condition would hit me like a ton of bricks. Regardless of what I was doing, my consciousness would be abruptly disturbed by the glaring fact that cancer was wreaking extensive devastation on my body. To hear the voice in my head saying, "O God, it's cancer," then to accept that it was in reference to me being afflicted with the condition, was unbelievably surreal.

There would be a momentary, subliminal perception of my body being associated with cancer. I would literally hear it, as though spoken out loud, "Courtney, you have cancer." My heart would skip a beat, then I would be jolted back to reality. This would trigger an inevitable emotional response. I would tremble, sometimes even tear up, before quickly reminding myself I had control over every emotional response because God had invested His peace in me. It was unhealthy for me to dwell in grief because He had knowledge of my current state, way back from my premortal existence. Being omniscient, He knew the exact time the cancer would invade my body and the precise moment it would be completely eradicated. He understood how much of its torture I could bear before my joy would be multiplied.

With confidence, God allowed my condition because I was special to Him and could be counted on to give Him glory through it all. Those were comforting thoughts that reinforced my positive attitude. The belief that God Himself had such confidence in me, among millions, to designate me for this mission was tremendously assuring. If I faithfully did what He expected of me, I was assured of a glorious postmortal existence.

So, although logic and reasoning had failed to produce a rational answer as to why I was afflicted, my faith in God comforted me that we are all privileged with our current existence to realize His purpose. And it is for His pleasure we are chosen to demonstrate faith. The concept of faith belief is, of course, illogical and irrational, but that is the enigma of faith. Faith does not reside in the realm of the logical. I chose the path of faith, believing that everything concerning my affliction was shrouded in mysteries to be revealed as God willed it.

The following post illustrates my struggles while trying to rationalize why I was afflicted with the disease. It was my outlet for the debate raging in my mind, helping me come to terms with my inability to figure out the root cause of my illness but believing that God had all the answers.

> Mine was not the hand that was raised as a show of candidates likely to have cancer, based on evidentiary materials profiling typical potential cancer candidates. My behavior would be the opposite of what is popularly ascribed to risky cancer behavior. As a family, we rarely eat out. Period. Almost 100% of what I eat is home prepared, and we generally maintain a healthy backyard garden of vegetables and fruits to supplement what we must purchase. My wife rigorously scrutinizes every ingredient that goes into each meal, and we tend to buy non-GMO and whatever "natural/organic foods" purport to be. I work in a low cancer risk area, frequent the gym, don't

smoke, never did drugs, and only occasionally, indulge in the extravagant treat of a single glass of wine or beer with dinner. So, my behavior is not of the stereotypical cancer risk type.

Can we genuinely profile someone and their behavior as at risk for cancer? I have become cynical about that. The scientific data I have seen is not compelling enough for me to conclude what are risks factors for cancer, particularly multiple myeloma. Since there are many different cancer types that are manifested differently, and are treated in different ways, are the behaviors that make one prone to tumorous cancers similar to those for blood-related cancers? I believe that much of what I may have been told about behavioral risk factors that contribute to developing cancers like multiple myeloma is speculative conjecture, and based on inconclusive findings.

I am open-minded about whether genetic attributes and exposure to certain chemicals such as weed/insect poison and genetically modified organisms precipitate the onset of this disease. I, for one, always believed that every edible thing that exists should be eaten because all foods contain nutrients as well as poisons. The caveat is eating just enough of any one thing to derive adequate nutrients and provide enough poison to act as an antidote for the poison in the others. I have concluded that there are still innumerable unknowns about cancer. While on the question of the unknown, what is known is that the unknown has always mystified humans and we are at our highest form of our godliness when we solve for the unknown. Creativity generally emerges and rises to its highest. In God resides the solution to all that is unknown. He reveals mysteries to humankind that uncovers answers to the unknown. As I journey through my sickness, I will try to content myself with what I know. I don't have the answer to the recurring question, "Why me?" Maybe I should accept that since God knows, it is not a part of His will for me to know. When pain and disappointment emerge, I need to perceive them positively and not as yokes. Again, I reference Job, who had no choice in his divine assignment. Unbeknownst to him, he was divinely selected among all living earthly beings by God with high confidence. In ignorance, some of us must be drafted into God's service by drastic means.

Paul, one of the greatest Apostles of Christ, was first physically afflicted and then drafted into the service of Jesus Christ to do His will. His calling was opposed to the fundamental tenets of his previous religious beliefs and traditions. Once he realized he was under divine calling, he made spreading the Gospel his life's work. No threat of death, beatings, or other persecution could stop him; he was a formidable force with which to be reckoned.

So, what is my profile today? A man living with symptoms caused by an affliction of unknown origins that manifests in torture and torment on my human flesh? Will I realize my true calling through this illness? Struck down as I am, will I rise to the privilege of my calling according to God's will? Will the outcome of my calling glorify God? Could my life's works hereafter be symbolic of one who held firm in faith knowing that this was all a part of God's marvelous work? As things that are presently unknown evolve, I shall endeavor to do my best by giving God praises, worship, and honor, and seek His guidance. If it pleases God, this situation may move me from the position of the relatively unknown person to that of the privileged servant of God who, through faith, accomplished His glorious will and purpose.

We classify things that are unknown to us as mysteries. Today the cure for multiple myeloma is one such mystery. It baffles the domain of science and challenges all logical thought. Our impulses make us view things as impossible when a solution or a satisfactory outcome defies logic or has never been accomplished. Because we live in the human dimension, our abilities are limited by the attributes of the soul. Our souls enable us to intellectualize and use our natural senses to find solutions. But what about current impossibilities? They are the mysteries of God and exist in the spiritual dimension. In that domain, our intellect and senses are useless and confounded; things don't make sense. In order to derive benefits from that dimension, we must act in faith, which is beyond the body and soul domain.

For example, saying I have been completely healed is ridiculous from a human perspective, because the facts do not support that declaration. It would get a better reception were I to say I believe I will be healed. The faith perspective acknowledges what is not yet evidenced, believing that an act has been accomplished and will be manifested as though it has already been done in this dimension. Spiritual healing, which today is cloaked in mystery, will be revealed by God through miracles or scientific discovery. Think about not long ago when finding an effective treatment for a disease like HIV/AIDS seemed nigh on impossible, until God revealed several treatment options to us—options now regarded as mainstream therapy. Well, did we create some new elements, or did we use naturally occurring substances to synthesize medicines that worked?

When I go to the Lord in faith, I am asking Him to perform my healing so that it will be evidenced in our natural dimension and my physical body will experience it. It would be such an awesome thing if I could predict the time and place of my healing. However, I am aware that God's will supersedes my desire, and I am on His clock. But what a privilege it is to know that God, the awesome, infinite Alpha and Omega, even considers my request made in faith. Isn't it beyond privilege to know that God has selected me to do whatever He desires of me?

I had to put aside rational thinking, prostrate myself in His presence and, with humble supplication, acknowledge the Almighty as Jehovah Rapha, my healer, trusting that through His benevolence and mercies His perfect will would be accomplished. Since God honors His Word, I shall be healed, as declared in Jeremiah 30:17 (ESV), "For I will restore health to you, and your wounds I will heal, declares the LORD."

In retrospect, it is clear from the post above that I was transitioning from shock and anger to the rationalizing stage. But where normal avenues failed to provide an answer, then the ultimate, all-knowing God, the Omniscient, was my source of knowledge.

Knowing He had allowed this to happen to me, for there is nothing in creation that He is unable to prevent or remediate, I rested on that, believing I was taking the next step in the healing process, which was the acceptance phase. My peace would have to come from the recognition that God knows about my condition and had divinely selected me to go through this, so I could rest on Him to see me through whatever would arise. My attitude then needed to be transformed from the woeful state of self-pity to the new positive maxim of thanking the Lord for choosing me and asking Him to help me to be obedient to His instructions.

The ways of God are mysterious; why He does what He does in His time is inexplicable and unfathomable. Isn't God sovereign? The dictionary explains that it means He possesses supreme or ultimate power that is unlimited and infinite. That being the case, God either willed that I would have the disease or permitted it; otherwise, He would have prevented it. It would serve me best then to be still and be surprised by the ultimate revelation of God's mysteries through me. Adopting that stance gave me a sense of distinct privilege; it was as though I was hearing from God even through my suffering. It allowed me to begin coming to terms with the notion that if God allowed my misery, it had to be for a reason. Ultimately then, I needed to be spiritually transformed from victim to sanctified champion, chosen and placed on a divine assignment with trium-phant expectations of a glorious outcome.

CHAPTER 14

Bless His Heart

*For You, O LORD, have made me glad by what You have
done, I will sing for joy at the works of Your hands.*

—Psalm 92:4 (NASB)

The little things that delighted me during the early periods of
my tribulation were relatively insignificant in the usual course
of life. Being able to use parking spaces close to elevators, doorways,
and business entrances meant I did not have to walk to too far to get
to an appointment or access places of business. The first time I was
able to confidently secure a parking spot close to the doctor's office
and a restaurant, I was overwhelmed with relief and delight. Just
shortening the distances in the midday sun and not having to cross
lines of traffic, twisting my neck from side to side to avoid being hit
by oncoming vehicles, while I crawled from the parking places in
the summer heat, meant less pain and anxiety. Those enviable blue
parking spaces were now options available to me. For the first time, I
could use the handicapped parking space without suffering any consequences. I was thrilled; it felt like an actual accomplishment. I had
been issued an authorized handicap permit, and I was ecstatic to use
it. How drastic priorities change based on needs, and the unremark-
able emerges as a great thing. Perhaps that's what happens when a

formerly overactive mind is laid to waste; trivial things become significant accomplishments.

Surprisingly though, every time I used those handicap spaces, I found myself cautiously looking around with guilt, as though I was violating some rule. My thinking was that there was someone else more deserving of the space than I was and should have it. So much so that we have used that permit maybe, at most, four times in more than three years. Was getting a handicap permit anything to crow about? Not really. But, given my state of mind, that minuscule bit of privilege represented such an elevation in status, I had to share it with my Facebook friends, picture and all, with a jocular comment that would have had ordinary folk thinking it was time I was committed to a mental institution. In retrospect, it would have been justified. What would you have thought at first glance if you read the following lines, only to later realize I was simply referring to a mere piece of paper—my newly issued handicap parking permit?

DON'T MAKE ME!!! I am fully trained in the use of this device and reserve the option to activate it in an instant, so DON'T tempt me now!!!

Truly, as the saying goes, "A mind is a terrible thing to waste."

CHAPTER 15

May I Help Me?

*"Let not the wise boast of their wisdom or the strong boast of
their strength or the rich boast of their riches, but let the one who
boasts boast about this: that they have the understanding to know
me, that I am the LORD, who exercises kindness, justice and
righteousness on earth, for in these I delight," declares the LORD.*

—Jeremiah 9:23-24 (NIV)

My postings were generating an overwhelming number of positive responses with assurances of support and prayers. I could not yet provide any verifiable evidence of miraculous healing at that stage. It was a time to accept that God had heard the prayers and that my healing was already secured in the spiritual realm. I assured myself that since God never makes mistakes, it was a time for me to dwell in seclusion with Him. It was a wonderful occasion for me to spend time in this place and rest—resting not in the sense of respite and physical repose, but spiritually laying all my burdens, distractions, and destructive behaviors on the Lord, confident in His promises to me. It was an excellent place to become more aware of the presence of God and be more intimate with my spiritual self so that I could focus on hearing from the Lord. In faith, I believed that I could better discern my true calling and receive divine revelations. It was remarkable how my perspective was evolving to the extent that I could view the sickness as a sanctuary and not an oppressive rehearsal for my death.

Divine wisdom abounded in the place of rest. If I took the time to listen and not complain about my misfortune, I believed I could hear the revelations of the Holy Spirit and be led in avenues of wisdom and discernment. Think of Paul after God called him; he did not go to Jerusalem to understudy the church elders. Instead, he went into isolation in Arabia for a time, where God could minister to him, equipping him for his unique ministry. He says in Galatians 1:17 (NIV), "I did not go up to Jerusalem to see those who were apostles before I was, but I went into Arabia. Later I returned to Damascus."

In faith, I accepted my spiritual healing, believing its ultimate manifestation was in the physical plane. My expectation of being able to instantaneously jump from my bed one day and be back to normal was being tempered. It was becoming apparent this would not be the route for my healing. A process of gradual reconstruction and restoration would be the path for me. I believed, however, that I needed to proactively prepare my body to receive my healing. So, ignoring my disabilities and bodily pains, I gradually began trying to do simple physical exercises and forced myself to eat sensibly in preparation for the new me.

I was now coming to terms with the fact that since my healing would be via a process, clinicians would have a role to play. If the Lord required me to wait in their care, albeit with compromised health, so that I would demonstrate His good work through my faith, then I was obliged to listen. Accordingly, I prayed God's guidance for those He elected to administer my care. These professionals, although highly educated, are mere humans—fallible—so, I prayed for God's wisdom to understand any deviation from His blueprint for me. Believing that God had my healing in control, I was prepared to appropriately insert myself in the process of my care as God instructed me. I was ready to be confounded with medical jargon and cryptic terminologies to convince me of my ignorance, but I owed it to myself to resist any tendency toward despair or discouragement.

My duty was to be as prepared as could be by doing my research, questioning the options presented to me, and in faith depending on

God to instruct me on what would best align with His will for me. I believed that the Holy Spirit would reveal all truths to me and guide me, as stated in John 16:13. I would later confirm that my obedience in faith was duly rewarded. The post below reflected the newly empowered me, emerging from woeful solitude, reinvigorated and preparing myself for God's process for my healing, armed with the knowledge that any perceived delay in my healing from God did not mean denial. God would be on time, His time, and that would be the right time for me to emerge from "time-out"; perfectly healed.

Most cancers are treated with a reduction approach to reduce the levels or sizes of disease-causing substances. Among the more modern methods are targeted therapy and immune therapies, which seek to halt further growth of cancer cells by interfering with the receptors and proteins to starve the cancer. I cannot say definitively at this time how my care providers will manage mine, but I hope to do whatever I can by inserting myself in the process so that with God's guidance I may influence my care as best I can.

During my first visit to the oncologist, I plan to demonstrate that I am capable of being an active part of my care decision. I can only imagine how they will be taken aback when I launch out in ignorance saying, "Do you mind if I tell you what I think my diagnosis, stage, and possible treatment are, and then you can correct me and fill in the blanks with your professional input?"

I expect the suddenly stiffened posture they will display will not precisely communicate, "Go ahead my well-trained peer, this is exactly what I spent years of training and thousands of dollars to do." However, I have learned it is necessary to actively insert myself in a non-confrontational way to ensure that my best interest becomes a mutual priority for my caregiver and me. I must read, listen, seek clarification on all that will impact me, and use my gut instincts, the voice of the spirit from God, to guide me. I always need to remain vigilant and actively involved to the extent that I can. Sometimes the caregivers try to dumb you down with generalizations, jargons, and euphemisms, as I have already experienced during this process. So, what if they get mad at me? What more dire consequences can they proclaim for me, tell me my attitude will give me cancer? I already have that.

So, here are some of the things I have been doing:

The combination of tasteless food and medicine at all hours has thrown my digestive system out of whack. Initially, I had been eating uncontrollably, non-stop throughout the nights. These days, I ingest fruit combinations to stimulate bowel movements and prevent the constipation some medicines cause. I force myself to consume vegetables, smoothies, and large amounts of protein-based foods, both animal and plants, to regain some body mass. I am now at the stage where I am regulating the intervals of my intake, but I do eat profusely larger quantities than I ever did before. The primary issue with food continues to be taste, and my fear is that I am consuming too much sugar. I am working on that. I must take medicine to avoid indigestion, based on how aggressive the other meds are on my stomach. Even water tastes unpalatable, but I force myself to drink it; I drink a lot to flush my system of the dangerous toxic drugs I take to survive.

Exercising: This is very challenging, but I try to push through. I could hardly move an eyelid when I got home. I have pains from the radiation in my neck, in addition to the ones that have now spread through my body, which make it a rather arduous task to move any part of my body. So, I started with a few toe taps, then graduated to a step or two aided by my walking stick, and now I am up to 5lb weights and ten minutes on the exercise machine at the slowest speed. I do about a half hour each day, most of which is spent just sitting and wishing, but I am preparing my body in faith believing for my healing.

Rest/Stay Busy: I could spend most of the day resting from fatigue because the meds wear me out. I am not sure if it is because I am such a disgusting perfectionist, or a control freak, why I have work-related withdrawal syndrome, and do certain unnecessary things. I built spreadsheets and scrap notes to document, track, and plan every single activity that could impact the minutes of my days, so that I can project-manage my life. Whatever home management, personal, and business task I observe to be outstanding, I try to indulge, but all my regular routines are challenging. By sleeping ninety percent of the day, it is not hard to imagine that I do not have a single minute of free time. Oh! Incidentally, even though I use Facebook in my attempt to communicate to as many friends and family as possible, my phone is constantly ringing. Very nice people, just wanting their little pound of flesh. They want to hear my voice (again and again), I guess so that they will be assured that I am still on the natural side of the gulf. Unfortunately, I am unable to answer all the phone calls and text messages, as many still expect me to. Indeed, I am at home just lying around, but that is the issue. They do not realize that I am sleeping most of the day, in pain and incoherent and unable to speak well. The feedback I keep receiving from those with whom I speak is that I sound different. Of course, I know that "different" is code for "like he is on death's bed." So, I am sorry friends; it's not happening, I will pass on the calls; with Love. Admittedly, it occurred to me to change the voice recording to one of me moaning, groaning, murmuring and whining; well, that would be mean-spirited and unchristianly, and I would not be present with the caller to enjoy the reaction. My best bet for now I guess is to unfriend my phone by turning it off. Maybe this sickness is turning me into a grumpy old man.

Other Stuff: Well if you are a country boy, raised as I was, you will understand that there was some bush/weed, a panacea, that always grows in the backyard. Granny would have me pick from it, steep it in some hot water, and sip some to cure anything that ailed me. I do have friends like me of similar heritage, and already, the only weed that I haven't been offered is the sure-fix panacea, marijuana. Between us, so far in my desperation, I think I have tried a little of everything I have been provided. This is not for my doctors' ears, so that's all I will say on that subject.

My grandma used to say, "If it does not kill you, it will fatten you." The fact is, even before chemo treatment, I am feeling better than I did a few months and weeks ago, moving around, regaining weight, but needing to go outside for air if my legs could hold me. Jesus gave us so many assurances that demonstrate the infinite capabilities of faith, and I choose to take him at his word. How do I go beyond lip service on this board? I work as though my healing was all done; I do, I act, I move to live in the manner of my tomorrow as if it is today. Whenever Jesus performed a miracle, someone had to show faith in Him for it to be effective. If the same Spirit that raised Jesus from the dead lives within me, it connects me to God, it empowers me, and so I too need to exercise faith in Jesus, being spiritually connected to Him. With that, I will awaken that spirit in me to demonstrate God in me to sustain my Faith in Him. Do you think God's promises will return to Him void? You are my witnesses. Watch me! I tell you that I am healed. God controls what we regard as time and process, and He will use them for his good pleasure; no matter how long it takes, His will must be done. I will ultimately celebrate victory over my situation. I ask that you, likewise, call your faith into action for your own needs. Exercise your faith to the max, believing for your result through grace.

As it later turned out, I did insert myself as an advocate in my care and refused to be ignored when it became apparent that I was deemed incompetent to relate and contribute. Although my ability to reason and comprehend was diminished, I was not deterred by the health-care professionals' perceptions of me. I felt they were obligated to treat me fairly, or at least communicate with me about my health and treatment plan options, and discuss the demerits of any objections I might raise.

There were times when I felt patronized and even condescended to, particularly if my nurse wife was in the room. When she was not with me, I would blatantly be asked where my wife was, or be dismissed with remarks such as, "Maybe we should discuss this with your wife." Because of this, when I could find alternatives, I would deliberately avoid having my wife with me on some doctor visits, just so I would be addressed directly and not be spoken about like a pathetic bump on a log. The insinuation was that I was too far gone to understand anything. It made me wonder at times if they thought me a mindless imbecile. Or was I a bit sensitive? Maybe. But I had my best interest at heart and, although cognitively impaired, I was sure that my disease was not gray matter leakage. Some caregivers should be sensitive to the fact that the devastation of cancer may impact the physical and sometimes the mental state. However, the patient does not necessarily lose pride or intelligence, or gain a new desire to be condescended to; the disease is enough of a burden.

CHAPTER 16

My Healing Brings

For in the gospel, the righteousness of God is revealed—a
righteousness that is by faith from first to last, just as
it is written: "The righteous will live by faith."

—Romans 1:17 (NIV)

I cannot remember where I heard it or the exact quote, but it is one of the most profound truths I believe I have ever heard. Essentially, it says adversity motivates us to be right with God because of our desire to see our misfortune changed. When we are enjoying prosperity, however, we rely on the things that make us prosperous, which are not necessarily things of God. In my case, I went back to the Bible. Before this illness, I could not fully appreciate how much of my acquired fleshly principles I had to strip away to experience the power of faith. Sure, I followed the church routines, studied a lot about God and Christianity, and tried to apply reason to things that are unfathomable with mere learning. During my tribulations, however, my need of God moved me to a higher level, where it was more about the quality of the relationship I had with Him than rituals, practice, or traditions I observed to show righteousness.

For a long time, I obsessed about applying logic to explain things I had read in the Bible. I spent more time intellectualizing what was written than trying to see through faith the mysteries of

God's actions. As one of my favorite pastors explained, we anthropomorphize God, framing Him with the characteristics and familiar behaviors of humans in an effort to understand Him. Thus, God is perceived as an emotionally unstable being, unhinged, and reacting with surprise to the unpredictable misdeeds that characterizes human behavior, as if anything we do or say could surprise the omniscient Alpha and Omega, who knows our every move. Instead, I believe that what we see as huge, unbelievable sins that spring surprises on God are but deviant little missteps for which He has already accounted.

In all realms of possibilities, there is nothing we can do that would shock or surprise God the Omniscient; He knows everything. He even knows our wrongdoings before we act. He is forgiving and should not be portrayed as easily enraged, reckless and emotional, with the tendency to punish our simplest misdeeds. If that were the case, who among us would escape His wrath? As our eternal Father, He corrects us, and not necessarily in destructive ways. His corrections are done in love and should motivate us toward good. God did not have to decide to love us. He is love and is predisposed to love us.

With all that said, I had to go through my own period of truly accepting the unconditionality of God's love. The post that follows provides an insight into the difficulty I had coming to terms with the fact that I needn't struggle with the burden of doing things to earn God's love, but believing in faith that His sacrifice afforded me all I needed for healing.

> As stated earlier, I started these unstructured and informal posts to control what would be communicated about my progress to the masses as a result of my illness. At some point, I knew word would get around that I was seriously ill, and I wanted to manage the narrative about me for consistency. I did not nor do I have any further agenda. I am not qualified to act as a conduit for scholarly knowledge of the science behind my sickness, neither do I have a good enough command of biblical teachings to be a Christian

theologian. If our omniscient Father selected the most eloquent and most qualified in the field, then the attribution for success could be given to the individual and God would be robbed of His due glory. Just look at the prophets He chose in the days of antiquity. Most were not worthy in the eyes of man. I read somewhere that God does not choose the qualified, but He qualifies those He chooses. God moves as He sees fit. Choosing this medium to go public was partly influenced by a friend whom I have never even met face-to-face, or even spoken with. I cannot precisely remember the content of a Facebook post he made about an encounter he had with some sickness, but he was very candid. I was moved by his blunt authenticity. Observing how he publicly opened up about his health situation encouraged me to do likewise.

The reactions to my postings have been overwhelmingly positive. I observed certain commonality in the responses to specific comments I made in my postings. Most have been with love, empathy, and compassion. I was gratified by many of the reactions that pointed to the power of God, who has the exclusive control and prerogative to heal me in His time and according to His will. My responsibility was to seek healing through faith, and the responses to each post bore support and assurance that by faith I would be healed. Your messages assured me that you were praying in faith, believing for my healing. It is inspirational words like these that led me to question my actions, particularly as they relate to making a public display of faith beyond my secret private expressions to God. "What was my initial hesitation to go public through social media, not realizing how much God could use that medium to accomplish His good will?" I often questioned myself. My disclosures, particularly the process I used, may one day serve as a guide for others seeking deliverance from God for whatever suffering they may be experiencing.

As soon as I became suspicious that something was rapidly headed downhill with my physical health, I did what the Bible teaches in James 5:14—"Is anyone among you sick? Let them call the elders of the church to pray over them and anoint them with oil in the name of the Lord." I was obedient and took my request to our bishop and our Senior Pastoral Team. Before I knew it, various prayer campaigns from diverse groups were proceeding; it kept me thinking that if heaven could be rocked, it would be done, on the strength of the many people who were petitioning The Lord God Almighty for me.

My next step was to seek comfort in evidence of suffering shared in the Bible. As most of us do, I ended up going to Job; the epitome of a good man who was suffering physical torture, judgment by his peers, fighting to defend his righteousness and God level setting him and then prospering him even more than he was before. This study gutted me and shrunk me to size. Job was a good man who had enough faith to do great works that he believed would honor and please God. He exceeded what was required of him to be at his best righteous self. If works justified anyone, Job would be chief among them. Job pleased God and was chosen by God to exemplify the faithfulness of humanity, notwithstanding torture and torment. Unlike Job, I had done nothing really of worth to have mercies stored up with God; my record was one of fear, unrighteous deeds, and unfaithfulness.

I felt a sense of uselessness; I had wasted my time on earth compared to Job and had no claim to God's mercies in my suffering. I craved an extension of my time on earth. I wanted to use whatever time God would spare me to live and be used to do good works to please Him. I hoped He would use me to accomplish His good will. Comfort came to me when I reflected that I was the righteousness of God through Christ Jesus and that I, too, had met the qualification of pleasing God. It took nothing more than accepting that Jesus Christ gave His physical life so that I could be justified by my faith in believing that such unprecedented action took care of all my needs, salvation, righteousness, healing, and the blessings of eternity.

Subsequently, revelations started to unfold. I could indeed have been chosen by the Almighty God as someone special. So, I too chose Facebook as the platform on which to stand and give my uninhibited voice to the truth about God's goodness in an unashamedly and fearless manner. I had come to a place where every trace of bashfulness, pride, and fear was almost gone from me. I was at rock bottom—a man dying of cancer. I had nothing to lose by yelling out to the world exactly what I felt God was laying on my heart. By doing so, I trusted that the Holy Spirit would guide my expressions to be of God's so that the messages I wrote would be from God. Here I am on Facebook; it may just be a conduit to tell my story of how God is working through my sickness. Just maybe someone out there, while checking on how I was doing, may see God's love through something I wrote or a comment from someone else's reaction to my posts. Maybe that someone may be impacted to the pleasure of the Almighty God as they witness the love and power of God through my sickness and my eventual healing through faith. So, as you have seen, it has been real, with grammatical errors, structural writing flaws, and other writing mistakes that I have left uncorrected, in the moments in time that God is allowing me.

I hope this review will set the stage for my next postings, which will undoubtedly reveal the progressive miracles that God has started in and through me. I am envisioning a process of the continuing miracles from God. Even as I write, I am experiencing progressive wonders. So please, walk with me in faith. Challenge your faith for your miracles, claim them in faith, and observe your outcomes.

What I did not reveal in the above post were the days of spiritual agony and torment I put myself through as I struggled with what I saw as my unworthiness and unrighteousness before God. I would engage in bouts of self-condemnation, contemplating my spirituality through the prism of Job's experience, as I strived to be considered worthy by God. It was audacious of me to believe I had been chosen, as Job had been, when I clearly did not measure up to his level of good works. I was making a doctrine of worthiness based on Job. Did I need to impute unrighteousness on myself by using Job as a comparison?

Harboring such doubts was naturally paving pathways to unbelief, the apparent tool of the devil and a ploy designed to keep me in condemnation. Yes, I had Romans 8:11 to inform me that the Spirit of Him who raised Jesus from the dead dwells in me and that He who raised Christ Jesus from the dead will also give life to my mortal body. If that was not powerful enough, there was Ephesians

3:20 to remind me of the magnitude of God's ability to do far more abundantly than all we could ever ask or think to ask for, according to the power at work within us. Shouldn't those scriptures adequately demonstrate the immensity and strength of the indwelling power I possessed through the Holy Spirit?

Rather than persistently trying to unravel the confounding mysteries of God, I needed to experience Jesus Christ through faith. It was becoming clear how much the humanization of God had occluded the transcendental potential of faith, over and above what my good works could produce. Obsessing over my worthiness using the gauge of religiosity and traditions could only hinder me from benefiting from all God had provided for me. To allow the proclamation of flawed human tradition to be the basis of my judgment would be a death sentence. Just believing in how God had empowered me through Jesus Christ was enough. Indeed, Job was the epitome of enduring faithfulness under torment, and I needn't try to measure up to his works. Through faith, I needed to believe that I, too, was privileged, called by God for His specific purpose.

God is no respecter of persons. He loves us all and chooses us for individual assignments. He is immutable, so He won't ever change. He loves us with such a love, it is beyond our comprehension. So much so that regardless of all our transgressions and failings, He made Jesus Christ a universal sacrifice. This is personal for me. I can choose to believe and have all it avails or perish in unbelief. It was time for me to grasp that concept in its fullest and not try to bring God down to the level of man in order for me to predict His behavior and die without utilizing the power of life itself, which He gave me through Christ. Of course, I craved the perseverance of Job to endure in faith regardless of the tribulations. James 1:2-4 provides me adequate motivation in saying to consider it all pure joy, knowing that the testing of my faith will produce perseverance. This in turn would help to make me more mature and complete, eventually lacking nothing. Matthew 24:13 adds even more incentives with the assurance that, "The one who endures to the end will be saved."

CHAPTER 17

Chemotherapy

Peace I leave with you; my peace I give you.
I do not give to you as the world gives. Do not let
your hearts be troubled and do not be afraid.

—John 14:27 (NIV)

Am I the only living soul who had no idea what chemotherapy involved? For years I'd heard cancer patients speak of this dreaded, mysterious thing, and imagined them being placed in some high-powered radioactive or electromagnetic contraption not dissimilar to a spaceship. The therapist would activate the machine, various waves and radioactive particles would penetrate the body and somehow target the cancer cells, then immobilize and destroy them. I believed it to be a painful process, as the body would be so traumatized by the cell destruction, and I knew it resulted in hair loss, fatigue, weakness, vomiting, constipation, and other adverse reactions. Some years ago, a friend who underwent chemo told me about the nausea and other undesirable side effects she had experienced. They were so severe, she swore she would never subject herself to another round of treatment and would rather die—she eventually did. So, I was totally wound up on the day of my first therapy.

Maybe, like me, there are others who have no clue what chemotherapy is, so let me lift the curtain and reveal what I have learned about this mysterious therapy. Chemotherapy uses various medications—in some cases, a combination of medicines (cocktails)—to attack, kill, or slow the growth of cancer cells. The most common method of administering the treatment is known as systemic therapy, meaning it uses the bloodstream to distribute drugs throughout the body to reach and treat cancer cells. The treatment is applied in various ways.

Chemotherapy.com describes these methods as follows:

- **Injection.** Types of injection include:
    o **Subcutaneous (SQ):** Chemo is given as a shot just under the skin.
    o **Intramuscular (IM):** Chemo is given as a shot directly into a muscle.
    o **Intravenous (IV):** Chemo is given as a shot directly into a vein.
- **IV infusion**: Chemo medications are dripped through a tube that is attached to a needle and put into a vein.
- **Oral:** Chemo is taken by mouth as a pill or liquid.
- **Topical:** A cream containing the chemo medication that is rubbed into the skin.
- **Intra-arterial (IA):** Chemo delivered into an artery that is connected to the tumor.
- **Intraperitoneal (IP):** Chemo given directly into the area that contains the intestines, stomach, liver, ovaries, etc. This area is called the peritoneal cavity.

Chemotherapy is often given several times over weeks or months in what is known as a course of treatment. This is made up of a series of treatment periods, called *cycles*. During a *cycle*, you may get chemo every day for one or more days. Since chemo also kills healthy cells, these chemo days are followed by periods of rest when you receive no treatment. This rest lets your body recover and produce new, healthy cells.

The night before my first chemotherapy, I can't recall if I had had much sleep. My mind was running wild, trying to imagine what this chemo thing was all about and how I would react to it. It was one of those nights of soliloquy, with me talking to myself without caring if anyone heard or chose to engage with me. Who knows what the chemo's response was at the time? We do, however, have the benefit of reading my side of the dialogue below, and it shows me coming to terms with the fact that I had to undergo the therapy.

I accepted that I would be healed, but it would be of God. I maintained that even if aided by the chemo and other treatments, my healing would be under the prescription and direction of God. The prescribed medicines were actual necessities, to bridge me over as my faith training progressed and the good works of God were accomplished in me. Maybe immediate healing would not achieve what God desired for one as dogmatic, obstinate, and prideful as I was. I needed sufficient time-out, the physical compromise, or subjection, of my flesh so that I could focus on my developmental curriculum from the Father, in preparation for the greater good He had prepared for me to do. It was a time for my rebirth and maturity in God's perfection. I would have the privilege of divine guidance and revelation like never before.

But, despite Philippians 4:6 advising me not to be anxious about anything, I was. My mind meandered the twist and turns of what could be next in my life. When reading the monologue below, which I posted on Facebook, you will get a glimpse of my state of mind as I contemplated the implications of chemotherapy as a possible tool of God in my healing process. Remember as you read it, this was a monologue going on in my head, with me anticipating the unknown—chemotherapy.

> Nice to make your acquaintance also, chemotherapy. Not really! I have no objections to you; it's our first date, remember you won't be around long enough for me to get comfortable with anyway. Of course, I understand you have your place here with me for a time. OK! Yes, you are here because you are thought to be a part of my overall solution; but I am not exactly sure about the

answer in this case. I am about *The Process,* not the solution. Yes! This cancer is one with a divine appointment and is set out to accomplish the ultimate, the will of God the Almighty.

You are called upon now, just as another instrument or tool that the Lord God allows for His good will. Well, know that in the grand scheme of things, not only you but all of God's selected tools, experts and the experiences of others will be used for a time to help in my healing. Mostly, however, it is the honest declaration and demonstration of my vested FAITH in God the Almighty, the acknowledgment of HIS DUE WILL, PROCESS and PURPOSE, and is for a calling such that I don't yet understand, only that it will indeed accomplish all for HIS PERFECT WILL and my benefit. Yes! In time, all will be revealed. I have the Conduit, the Faith that wells up with the spiritual evidence that are tomorrow's realities and testimonies yet to be revealed. All will come clear in God's own time, and I KNOW that. Great! So now that we are all in alignment with the WILL OF GOD, let's go get our chemo moves on.

When I later recovered the preceding notes, I was ecstatic and pleasantly surprised because it revealed an instant in my troubled mind I had managed to document. Although not the most coherent or of much substance, it was a soliloquy that brought me peace within, and I was thrilled I had recorded it. Personifying that unknown process allowed me to establish a relationship with it mentally. Maybe it gave me a sense of control over what could otherwise be a scary process. How often does one get an opportunity to capture and share the thoughts in one's head, particularly as mentally impaired as I was? I was actually excited to read and share it, to review the thinking of my confused and lonely mind at the time. The words may not exactly jump off the page with drama and excitement. However, we are not always privy to the inner dialog of another person's mind. In my case, it provided a fascinating insight of what happens when anxiety is added to an already stressed mind that is dealing with the complexities of a critical illness, and the coping mechanisms instinctively employed.

There I was, burdened with the anxieties of the future but comforting myself with the hope that whatever awaited me would be of God and, as such, I would face this unknown monster with bravery. I was trusting I would stay faithful and prevail over whatever loomed in my path, so that what I prayed for in faith and believed would be accomplished.

I am so blessed by the optimistic aspirations, simple truths, and my earnest desire to faithfully look to God for my deliverance. I was thankful to God for giving me the presence of mind to document my experience in real time. Since recording these posts many months ago, it is only now that I can read and truly reflect on how God helped me to focus on Him. He provided me various coping mechanisms to deal with the challenges and the many unknowns—not the least of which was the possibility of death. God had sustained me with His all-sufficient grace.

CHAPTER 18

My First Chemotherapy

Have I not commanded you? Be strong and courageous.
Do not be afraid; do not be discouraged, for the LORD
your God will be with you wherever you go.

—Joshua 1:9 (NIV)

It was day zero of my date with chemotherapy. I was quite anxious, but it was my inevitable date with destiny. It was time for me to be courageous because God would be with me. It was time to take the first step in my treatment and surrender my body to that mysterious demon called chemotherapy. As far as current science was concerned, for my type of cancer, this was the next step in the treatment protocol. Hereafter my body would be infused with dangerous, toxic substances. So much for all the years of healthy living. I can't deny that I pondered the question, "How come 'that guy' who lives recklessly, consumes everything in sight without any regard to health, and practices all that is termed 'bad habits' is still laughing and having cancer-free fun?" I also pondered vain things, such as losing the little hair I had left, and the majors, such as drug reactions, side effects from the therapy, and life after chemotherapy.

It was a lonely time for me because I had no one who had gone through chemotherapy and could give me comforting experiential assurances. Imagine then all the possibilities and fantasies that occupied my brain. I like to be directly confronted with what lies ahead; I always want to know everything beforehand—present me with the issues and let me deal with them. However, here I was, alone, with my active and adventurous imagination conjuring up the wildest eventualities.

The first day of chemotherapy was my second day outside the house since hospitalization. I saw hope in the flowers, plants, and trees. People were taking brisk morning walks in the name of health, and restaurants serving breakfast were all abuzz with patrons eager to have their hunger satisfied. I bet their thoughts were filled with wonderful Fourth of July plans, with no worries about cancer. The world was going about its business with great hope and expectancy, just as I had been a few months before. Life's rich tapestry, so beautiful and appealing on the display side, where it shows best, and a convoluted mess of disorganized threads on the reverse side. Our good Father shields us from the ugly reverse side of our lives' tapestry because it's hard to handle. This is one thing I would not have wanted anyone to reveal to me ten years ago—the reverse side of my life's tapestry. No! Not the possibility that I would have been a victim of cancer; it would have sucked the fuel out of my ambition and derailed many of my accomplishments.

Instead, my current situation gave me a glimpse into a part of my life's tapestry, and I was struggling with it. There I was, keenly observing and appreciating everything God had created and allowed me to see. But now my perspective had changed. Now, I admired every blade of grass and was enchanted by the beautiful wildflowers in bloom, dancing as if they would live forever, unconcerned that soon they would fade into oblivion. The attitude adjustment did me some good. I can't believe I was relishing the toxic fumes coming from the truck in front of us (that would have previously disgusted me), and had complained less than two hundred times about my wife's driving. All these activities helped subjugate the aches and pains plaguing me at the time. I was deep in thought, contemplating the myriad contradictions life was throwing at me. There were so many ironies being played out in my mind as it related to health, sickness, joy, the mysteries of life, and the eventuality of death.

Life's opportunities are fleeting. What's here today will be gone tomorrow. Save for the hundreds of time I rudely tried to school my wife on proper driving techniques, we drove in silence. I needed only a glance to see her tightly clenched jaws and laser-like focus on the road. I imagined her asking God to control her tongue so she would not have to inflict upon me some choice words to put me in my place for always objecting to every driving decision she made. I needed to be sensitive to the concerns that plagued her about me, the stress and burden of being a sole caregiver, and her efforts to get us to the doctor safely. She did not need me antagonizing her and, looking back, I thank the Lord for the Holy Spirit who comforted her.

Before we set off, I had taken a selfie so that I would be able to recognize the future cancer-free dude, should I get lost and have to identify myself, or happen upon a mirror, where I may be tempted to introduce myself to the stranger that would be looking back at me. But as it turned out, it was not going to be chocolate cakes and apple pies; things were not coming up roses on this my first day of chemotherapy. Being faithful to my promise of transparency with my followers, I wanted them to share in this my maiden voyage to Chemotherapy Land. What I wrote below were parts of my persistent monologue, as I remember it, at the time of posting it to Facebook. I will just let the post speak.

> I see nothing wrong with a pre-chemo selfie. OK, sweetie, you don't know how much I appreciate you and especially for taking me to meet with chemo today. Something is wrong with me, though. My eyes have been dehydrated over the past two days, I can't see well enough to read without straining, and now I can't make out the faces of people walking in the neighborhood—most things are blurred.
>
> Anyway, if we leave now, we should be there on time, chemo and I will be having our grand union and, according to the schedule, we will be back home by, say, noon.

It is Friday before the Fourth of July and the light Sunday-like traffic on the expressway is unusual. Maybe it is because I have my angel driving me for my chemo date.

The parking lot at the hospital is full but, fortunately, I am authorized to use the handicap space. Gee, honey, I wish you would come to help me cross the street; the sun is already piping hot. I am shaking; I can't move very well. The poor girl. After more than thirty years of watching me play "Tough Guy," "Mr. Fix-it-all" and "Mr. Independent," I bet she cannot intuitively reconcile my sudden physical debilitation. I am physically weak and unstable, and every inch of my body aches. I am aware that she is trying to process, in silence, the recent changes impacting our lives and what today's first meeting with the oncologist may bring. Here I am, leaning on her for support, and she has bravely defied all the odds to be here for me. God is good to me for blessing me with her.

Why can't I quench this insatiable thirst? I have been drinking everything in sight all day— something is wrong. I have had several bottles of water, many cans of soft drinks, and everything drinkable. I need to get to a bathroom quickly, and it is all the way in the lobby. I am light-headed and bloated. I desperately have "to go," and very soon. Thank you, Lord. What a relief! I almost spilled it on the restroom floor, all that liquid, that unusually high volume of fluid I have been consuming. We have been checked in for nearly an hour now and no one has even acknowledged us. Everyone else has moved on to see the doctor, and we are still waiting. Would you please say something to someone, please honey? Maybe we did not do something we were supposed to? Am I loud?

After nearly two hours, I am finally called to see the doctor. I am so happy, I could hug him. But can't you see something is wrong with me, doctor? I have had more than a gallon of water, soft drinks, coffee, and still crave more drinks. Why am I so unusually jittery and unstable? And my skin and throat are as dry as bone.

Now that the doctor has outlined his treatment plan, I lumber over to the infusion center. Goodness, they have reviewed my blood work and I am astounded—my glucose level is 645 mg/dL. This is what I call the killer range. My level should be about 100 mg/dL. Or less. The nurses are not panicking. After they consult with the doctor, I am given insulin, some tablets of various shapes and sizes, and hooked up to a drip. I am relieved this high sugar level was caught. Where is my faith? I can sense that the other part of the chemotherapy is coming; this is scary; the chemo drug must be hazardous. I think I counted maybe two or three pairs of gloves. And what of that plastic raincoat? All that for me? "Which side of your tummy do you want it?" asks the nurse. The right side today, I say. So much scrubbing to sterilize the site for the injection. I hate that needle!

OMG, IT'S LIKE FIREWORKS!!! Shooting, burning, itching, fanning out all over my body from the site of the injection. CHEMO, is that you? The initial experience is frightful. It is like a thousand scorpions stinging me, but it is soon over. Through ultimate FAITH and following the will of God the Almighty, may His excellent process continue to the final accomplishment of His divine will. I am blessed. I have survived my first chemotherapy. Side effects? I guess that's for later. I felt like I was being stung by thousands of scorpions as the medicine rapidly dispersed over the injection site, but nothing horrific yet. But where is the large spacecraft machine with all the dangerous waves and radioactive particles that I had envisioned? Is that all? Thank you, God.

If I remember correctly, I was also administered a unit of blood that day because my red blood count was very low. The thought that most people had exaggerated the effects of chemotherapy was short-lived. A few days later, I started to have some of my worse experiences to date. I started suffering from the most dreadful pains and fatigue. In my distress, I could not resist the urge to be blunt, as evidenced in the short post below.

Chemotherapy is no fun; it is an aggressive brute. Every bone in my body is now sensitive. I hurt, my head aches, sleep refuses to visit me, and confusion rules my life. Rashes are breaking out all over me, and my blood sugar/glucose level is out of control, even with the two different insulin medications I have been prescribed. I am sweeter than I ever was; my glucose is bouncing in the 300-400 range. Don't worry for me, though; I know it gets much better from here, through Jesus Christ.

Here is what a typical chemotherapy day routine looked like through my eyes. It started with registration, where I would be tagged with a secured armband that was encoded with personal identifiable information. The clinicians used scanners with near field communication (NFC) technology to scan the armband at every juncture they interacted with me. Then they performed double authentication by having me confirm personal identifiable information such as my name and date of birth. The next step was my least favorite, where my blood was drawn to fill more tubes than I dared to count.

Then there was the long waiting period to see the oncologist; that was the time of anxiety. Why do doctors make patients wait so long anyway? No matter how exalted you are, it is the most humbling time. This phase is where I meet my good news/bad news person. Some of that day's lab results are generally analyzed and available within an hour. Those results are basic "blood work" and, along with other metrics, such as my weight, would be used to determine the volume of certain medicines I would be administered that day. They would also help to determine if I needed blood products or supplemental medications before the chemotherapy treatment was administered. The oncologist would also review previous lab results with me, which were not available in real time on the previous visit.

Those days, some of the most disheartening words would be *aggressive*, *destructive*, and *spreading*. On the other hand, the oncologist would be my best friend when he spoke words like *improving* and *healthy*, and phrases such as "You are going to do well."

My next stop would be at the scheduling section to arrange my next appointment. The final stop would be the infusion center. I generally allotted around six hours, plus travel time, for my chemo days. Some less fortunate folks, I was told, could spend upwards of ten hours in the infusion center. Incidentally, that became my lot later in my journey.

My first line of chemotherapy treatment was a cocktail of three drugs. They comprised of Velcade (bortezomib), administered subcutaneously, and Revlimid and dexamethasone, taken orally. This cocktail is sometimes abbreviated as RVD. Accompanying this cocktail was some form of hydration. I think hydration is given because of the potential side effects of chemotherapy, such as sweating, diarrhea, and fever. When these occur, there can be an accelerated loss of electrolytes.

Remember the symptoms I was experiencing earlier on the day of my first chemotherapy, such as blurred vision? The preliminary lab tests revealed that my blood sugar was at a critical level of 645 mg/dL (the normal range is 75 mg/dL-110 mg/dL). Some of the symptoms I had had earlier that day indicated there was excessive sugar in my bloodstream, similar to someone suffering from diabetes. The symptoms included blurred vision (which caused me not to recognize the faces of my neighbors), unquenchable thirst, frequent urination, and dizziness. In the weeks prior to my chemo, I had started experiencing severe burning and tingling in my feet. It is noteworthy that before the cancer, I was not diabetic. With continued therapy, I was compelled to do daily blood tests to monitor my blood sugar levels. Self-administering insulin, sometimes two different types, also became a new routine for me.

My diet had to be drastically altered, both in type and quantity, particularly in carbohydrates and sugar intake. Some of the medicines I took played a major role in me having drug-induced diabetes. Research shows that some people develop type 2 diabetes or hyperglycemia due to glucocorticoid from certain medications. According to Diabetes.co.uk, "People on steroids who are already at a higher risk of type 2 diabetes, or those who need to take steroids for longer periods, are the most susceptible to developing steroid-induced diabetes." Appendix I highlights medicines with diabetes-causing side effects.

Before cancer, I had no real concern about being affected by diabetes. I was not aware of any family member with the condition, so I never considered myself at risk. It was quite an awakening for me to learn how severe the disease was. So much so that I am obliged to summarize some of what I have learned about it. High blood sugar can cause damage to blood vessels, which means every part of the body can be affected by too much sugar. Some of the more common problems are kidney disease, strokes, heart attacks, vision loss, a compromised immune system, erectile dysfunction, nerve damage, and poor circulation.

CHAPTER 19

My New Normal

Therefore, if anyone is in Christ, he is a new creation.
The old has passed away; behold, the new has come.

—2 Corinthians 5:17 (ESV)

One of the terms I hear being bandied about these days is "new normal." Before my journey, I considered it rather trite, as it was so grossly overused in very trivial ways. Eventually, I had to embrace the term as relevant and appropriate for me. My new normal was dynamic and evolving because, as I gradually discovered each day, my state of health imposed various limitations and restrictions on me from time to time. When any of the unwilling members of my body cooperated and performed as they were designed to, without inflicting torturous new pains, I would celebrate my redefined new normal. The slightest improvement, the briefest relief from pain, and the lifting of the dense chemo fog would give me a great sense of optimism and hope. I would feel compelled to lift my hands in prayer and shout for joy.

When I was able to rise from the bed and endure the agony of my feet touching the floor, causing my spine to respond as though it was set afire, I wanted to dance, even though my stubborn mass would not cooperate with my willing spirit. Nonetheless, I would feel justified because it was an indication of restoration. I cherished even the briefest moment of being able to move. Joy was redefined for me; every little sense of life in my body was a reason for celebration. My revised definition for a normal quality of life was significantly lowered. Even the things I hated before were now new aspirations. To rise at the once-dreaded early hours to get to work on time in miserable traffic would now be welcomed; cutting the grass, even in the heat of the day, would give me pleasure, and there would be no incomplete tasks on the "honey-do list"—if only I could.

Anything would have been better than me having my face pressed against the window staring grudgingly outside. Then I would reflect on the fact that God had allowed me to have a good life, and how much I had, in the past, frequently expressed a desire to serve Him more purposefully to show my appreciation. However, my preoccupation with life's other demands consumed most of my time. I had convinced myself that without me things would fall apart. Naturally, my focus determined my priorities. Mammon emerged as my key focus, relegating my spiritual nurturing to the "see you later" bucket. I was a negligent steward, starving my spirit man and feeding the insatiable, ever-demanding flesh man.

Much to my chagrin, the world continued to turn precisely without me. All the people I thought needed my indispensable contribution were doing maybe even better without my input. Imagine that! I wondered how many gave more than a fleeting thought to me. All the time in the world was now mine to fulfill commitments made in secret. In a testimony I once heard, someone said that from his knowledge and experience, one ought to be careful about promises made to God and not keep postponing them. If you get too busy with the things of life, which make you keep relegating such promises to the bottom of your priorities, God will give you the needed time-out so you can fulfill your vows to Him. Our God is a covenant keeper who does not renege on His promises, and we ought not to make covenants with God we cannot keep.

My sphere of influence had significantly diminished, as I was no longer in the position of trusted adviser who had a solution for everything or the durable man whose days did not have enough hours to complete the plethora of projects and tasks that once consumed his life. As my environment and circumstances changed, I endeavored that, even if I could not fully dictate what my new normal would be, I would influence it as best I could. Isolation, loneliness, longings, pain, and discomfort colored this new normal. Eventually, I made a choice: to view my alone times as periods of solitude versus isolation, since isolation had punitive connotations. With all the time in the world for a one-on-one audience with God, I could build and strengthen an incomparable Father-son relationship.

When alone with God, and with no one to impress, I have no hypocrisy or pretense. I am my truest self. It was during these times I started to develop a more positive attitude and appreciation toward the unique benefits of being in time-out with God. They were individual, close, personal, and exclusive. My relationship was moving beyond "Lord I want," to more like "Father, I worship, appreciate, and thank you." I could be confident my private attitude of gratitude would be rewarded openly with favors and blessings, as confirmed in Matthew 6:6-7. It was easier to indulge in the regrets of no longer being the life of the party, the butt of all jokes, the problem-solver, the persistent troublemaker. I was consumed with my predicament, lamenting how I had become a fraction of my former human self, impaired and disabled, stripped of my former competencies and yearning for periodic glimpses of my former life. I had to compel myself to acknowledge that I was in a place of privilege where I could truly devote my whole being to learn what God wanted to teach me.

Acknowledging God as my closest friend was easy then; with the absence of distractions, I yearned for the continuous presence of a close friend, and it was good to know that my LORD was always with me. It was comforting to perceive Him as my source of inspiration, refuge, and hope. I had nowhere else to go then but to God, my Lord. From my soul, I would cry out with lamentations, passionately seeking mercies. My prayers became more frequent, more pious, and more penitent, and I was more diligent, expecting in faith to have positive outcomes. Each day I would make physical checks for the slightest incremental sign of healing. Then I would offer prayers of thanksgiving and joyous praises, expressing to God my willingness to wait in faith for His will to be done in me.

Every day I was alive brought new privileges from the Lord Jesus and a closer relationship with Him. Even as God is beyond my ability to conceptualize and comprehend fully, I had to reorient my concept of Him as being distant, unearthly, and too celestial. I accepted the ambiguous as truth, that even as He is celestially remote, He is omnipresent and therefore close by because He is an intricate part of me. He is the purest form of love and infinitely merciful, and I could embrace Him as caring Father. That being my reality, I needed to fully surrender to His will and be attuned to His voice with constancy and diligence. With that attitude, there was no room for equivocation, fear, or doubt but the need to embrace the indisputable fact that, unlike humans, He is incapable of deception and lies.

God transcends the limits of how we define love, in the sense that He does not have to make an effort to love. Instead, He is love, where love is natural, an attribute of His divine essence, and it is unconditional and always accessible. He desires my honest, pure, and contrite heart with love. I should not allow distress and desperation to govern how and when I relate to Him, as those are the times I am likely to try bargaining, bribery and making promises and commitments I could fail to fulfill. God is divine, but He is also accessible and relatable. As the supreme Love, He is merciful, so He would never reject my prayers in faith.

Supporting this new attitude was a very appealing revelation, which came to me from Hebrews 4:14-15 (KJV). It makes it clear that I have Jesus as my high priest in heaven. Beyond that, according to my interpretation of verse 15, Jesus can be touched with the feelings of my infirmities, which to me means He is touched by my cancer. Because of those assurances, I needed to fully utilize the only true open door policy and step into my Hebrews 4:16, where I am instructed to come boldly to the throne of grace, that I may obtain mercy and find grace that would help in my time of need.

CHAPTER 20

By What Authority?

Truly I tell you, whatever you bind on earth will be bound in heaven, and whatever you loose on earth will be loosed in heaven. Again, truly I tell you that if two of you on earth agree about anything they ask for, it will be done for them by my Father in heaven. For where two or three gather in my name, there am I with them.

—Matthew 18:18-20 (NIV)

Upon reviewing the post that follows, it is clear that, at the time, I was facing apparent contradictions. With all the accolades I was receiving for my posts, I became emboldened and started to believe I was doing works inspired by God. People were asserting that they were inspired by them and I was encouraged. I took that as proof that God was using me, with all my impairments; that even as a physically broken vessel, I had been selected to be the bearer of hope and inspiration. However, I questioned my authority to sermonize to the world through my writings. I was at a fork in the road. I was struggling with an identity crisis, trying to resolve who I was in Christ and the authority that came with that identity as opposed to who the devil was trying to tell me I was. There was a prominent battlefield, not just in my mind, but for my mindshare.

Doubts and fears had even started to emerge about the solidity of my Christian foundation, to the extent that I felt a compulsion to purge myself through public confession. There was guilt urging me to open up about all my past sins, unpacking them publicly so that my readers could see I was not being hypocritical and approve of me as a worthy messenger of God.

The law of "not good enough" sought to impose barriers of unworthiness that would disqualify me from continuing to run this leg of the faith race. Oh, how easy it is to revert to our legalistic knowledge—the traditions of men. Although a Christian, I harbored doubts that I measured up to some self-defined "worthy Christian" status. This kind of thinking was not only robbing me of my blessings from God but also stifling what I could do for His purpose. At the core of this unworthiness was an overwhelming sense of being a poor steward before I became sick. Now, here I was, physically impaired but with this newfound boldness, as though awakened from spiritual slumber, writing like a man vested with authority from God.

By all indications from the feedback and interactions, my postings had become desired reading for my followers, and my circle of Facebook friends had increased dramatically because of them. People I had not interacted with for years assumed I had become a pastor. So, I used the post that follows to remind my friends I was just a sufferer crying out, trying to let others understand why I was posting—it was an attempt to utter what God had placed on my heart that day.

In the post, I candidly opened up about my inner contradictions, vying for some rite of passage to prove to myself I was a worthy minister of the Word. But there was still a prevailing tendency, fed by the taunts and deception of the devil, to correlate past sins with my current illness. It was like a magnet pulling me back to dark stages in my life to keep me trapped in the guilt of all that I had been liberated from through Christ. In the courtroom of my mind, I was on trial, assuming the roles of judge, jury, prosecutor, defendant, and plaintiff.

My self-declared guilt then ran the gamut of how much God had blessed me in many ways—talents, possessions, and a great family. He had provided me a relatively good life. Shamefully, though, my actions were not always those of the perfect Christian steward. Where were the public testimonies about God's goodness to me?

With my past countless sins, even as a Christian, what made me think I deserved healing? What gave me the right to spout off with such authority about how to live as a Christian? What gave me the right to publicly claim with such enthusiasm that I would be healed through faith? How could I write with such authority about what God would do, without proper credentials? I had no formal theological training. I was no preacher.

With admiration and praise for my healthy faith posture increasing, I felt a sense of guilt and would cringe from any feedback insinuating that my writings were inspired and that my faith was strong. Any comment implying I was preaching or ministering like a pastor drove me to a place of unworthiness. I believe the office of pastor should not be taken lightly and is deserving of the highest regard. The devil was at work here, "inna me," trying to plant doubts in my mind, and my first impulse was to tread cautiously over grounds he suggested I had no authority. I could sense his insinuations permeating the depths of my soul. However, I knew I should not give ear to them or allow his distractions to lead to disobedience and absolute destruction. I knew he could not force me to do anything I chose not to do and that he could only influence what I ultimately decided to do. I had no loyalty to him and was not bound to obey him; he hated me anyway. If I chose to follow the leading of the Holy Spirit and disallow the devil's influence, what more could he do to me? Inflict more disaster on me?

As a child of God, I can expect His protection and deliverance from the works of the devil if I am obedient to Him. Therefore, I could not allow the devil's deceptions to impact me; they were distractions from hell, seducing spirits of evil, all designed to thwart God's good purpose for me. Second Corinthians 10:5 (NIV) charges that, "We demolish arguments and every pretension that sets itself up against the knowledge of God, and we take captive every thought to make it obedient to Christ." There were numerous supporting scriptures authorizing me to speak my conviction from anywhere through any medium because it was approved by God. The indwelling of the Holy Spirit, for instance, makes me an able minister, according to 2 Corinthians 3:6 (NIV), which states, "He has made us competent as ministers of a new covenant—not of the letter but the Spirit; for the letter kills, but the Spirit gives life."

It was imperative then to stop feeding into the sources of my insecurities, which were breeding self-doubt and self-criticism. Instead, there was Romans 8:1 (ESV), which assures me, "There is therefore now no condemnation for those who are in Christ Jesus."

Lacking the confidence to assert my authority over what God had already declared was not in His will and would effectively defeat my faith objectives. When I needed answers to the "Who, me Lord?" question, I could always turn to the assuring Word of God.

In Exodus 4:10 (NIV), we see Moses using the defense of being inarticulate, lacking the abilities of a compelling speaker, saying to the Lord, "I have never been eloquent, neither in the past nor since you have spoken to your servant. I am slow of speech and tongue."

Similarly, the prophet Isaiah, in fear upon receiving his assignment from God, confesses his unworthiness because of the foul language he and his neighbors practice, as we read in Isaiah 6:5 (NIV), "I am ruined! For I am a man of unclean lips, and I live among a people of unclean lips, and my eyes have seen the King, the LORD Almighty."

Paul, too, coming to terms with his past wrongs as a zealous persecutor of Christians, confesses lowness. In Ephesians 3:8 (NIV), he makes it clear, "Although I am less than the least of all the Lord's people, this grace was given me: to preach to the Gentiles the boundless riches of Christ." Just imagine, Paul was called "a chosen vessel" of God in Acts 9:15-16.

Because my posts were now regarded as inspirational, the Evil One recognized their potential reach and effectiveness and mounted an intensified counteroffensive. My mind was a battlefield of intensified struggles. Through it all, God gave me the confidence to not be deterred. God instructs me, in Hebrews 10:23, to hold firmly to the profession of my faith without wavering, for He who promised is faithful. And what kind of empowerment is embodied by such faith? Luke 10:19 (NIV) illustrates the extent of the power God gives us, extending to the domain of the enemy in the spiritual realm. It declares, "I have given you authority to trample on snakes and scorpions and to overcome all the power of the enemy; nothing will harm you." This to me means I am authorized to trample on the mind games of the devil, exercise authority over his trickeries, and assert authority over the domain that God has appointed me. What greater honor could there be than that of being a child of God? John 1:12 (NKJV) reminds me, "But as many as received Him, to them He gave the right to become children of God, to those who believe in His name." My charge then was to reassert myself with confidence, by acting on God's instructions, and not allow myself to be swayed by the distractions of the devil because as Hebrews 10:35 (MEV) instructs me, "Therefore do not throw away your confidence, which will be greatly rewarded." So, as to who I am, that was already settled with Christ eons ago even before I was born, now it was for me to recognize, accept and appreciate it.

With such assurances, there was no reason to harbor doubts. God created me for His purpose, to be used at His will and pleasure. Criticizing and debasing myself, considering God's approval and His appointment, go against the core tenet of the new covenant. Unquestionably, God uses individuals just like me, regardless of prevailing physical and mental conditions. Cancer and the side effects of medications should not be a deterrent, neither should the job description of man. I became more assured and inspired. The contents for future posts would thereafter flow with unbridled confidence. The dominance and power of the Holy Spirit over the deception of the devil were compelling. Incorporating the Word of God in the updates then became imperative. I was grounded in the knowledge that it was up to the sovereign Father, not any authorization of man or the taunts in my mind, to determine who should give voice to His Word. Upon the Word of God, I had permission to liberate my mind.

There was also no requirement from God for me to bare my unrighteousness publicly to be eligible for His grace. Doing work for my healing that had already been done through Christ was unnecessary. Baring my soul, getting it all out there, might have been cathartic to the flesh, but it was not required by God. I was not under judgment or condemnation from our Father. My innate desire to act on what seemed right rather than what was required by God was not scoring me any righteousness points. Instead, it pleased the old Deceiver because any element of self-doubt was a breeding place for fear, which is the antithesis of faith and works to its destruction. What good then would my journey of faith accomplish dwelling in doubt and unbelief? My doubts about my righteousness are reflected in the post that follows. However, it was my vehicle at the time to justify my right standing with God in order to merit His favor.

> I would not be surprised if the question arose that, having claimed healing in faith, why am I writing as though I am still sick? My response would be framed around occurrences in the spirit as opposed to our reality. Although I claim and believe that my healing has already been accomplished in the Spirit, I live in the natural realm, and though in faith I know that it is done, I can still physically feel symptoms of my ailments. Hebrews 11:1 says, "Now faith is confidence in what we hope for and assurance about what we do not see."
>
> What has been done in the spiritual through faith will manifest itself in the natural in time. As for my actual mental state now, I am not so much focused on being able to do the things I could before the disease. I am more concerned about the accomplishment of God's will, mainly through me, however long it takes. So, to fake some bogus performance as a show of my complete healing at this time would belie what is real. God does not need me to cover or make up for what faithless humans see as His inability in the short term. His actions are process driven, orderly, timely and sure. He will heal me according to His plan. I should not make any feeble attempt to concoct explanations as to how and why God

does things, as that would be deceptive and may forfeit my deliverance. Any such act would be a product of my ego, motivated by an overzealous mindset to persuade the faithless about the trustworthiness of our benevolent God at any cost, and that would be wrong. I don't quite understand why God allowed me to have this journey. Since I did not set the course or the destination, I am surrendered and happy to be used for His purpose in His timeline.

Having fallen so many times from the truth and been forgiven through grace is my benefit of being a Christian. To have my illness used to impact lives for God is a privilege beyond words. Who am I that God would call me to a place of privilege in His service? I pray that with all my inadequacies, I shall prove to be a worthy steward. If my life story were reviewed, there would be so many flaws revealed; I am just another hypocrite. I was happy to build my Christian tabernacle that fitted me comfortably. I was my little church that was joined to "the Body" but not as I should be. My religion suited me, as it was my own best brand of Christianity. I chose scriptures that suited me; I listened to teachings that justified my belief. If challenged, I could be logically disputatious and be good at it.

In my pursuit to know of God, I did not honestly know God (to the extent that any human can). It is easy for anyone to speak of their walk in faith, but let them be put to the test to bear the fruits of faith. I am now journeying on the faith walk. The time has come for me to prove it. Will I yield to the temptation of reverting to my strengths and wisdom, or will I indeed demonstrate my faithfulness, regardless of whatever comes, by listening and yielding only to the true voice of God?

Our Lord requires obedience. The cornerstone of Christianity is faith, so if I am not walking in complete faith, I cannot be obedient. Disobedience to God is a sin. Certain things have been happening during these past few weeks, which have provided perspectives that have been transformative. Fortunately for me, I continue to believe that God the Almighty is merciful. He offers me access to grace. Everything that Christ ever died for is available through grace, and I can rest in peace that I am a worthy beneficiary. All I need is to believe that Christ has made them accessible, and I can lay claim to whatever is provided for me by Christ if I have faith enough to access such provisions. Romans 5:1-2 says, "Therefore, being justified by faith, we have peace with God through our Lord Jesus Christ by whom also we have access by faith into this grace wherein we stand, and rejoice in the hope of the glory of God."

I have learned that I must trust God, lose my controlling self-made-man mentality, lose my human fleshly self, and become childlike to God. I must not question how, but simply accept that God says it and it is so. I am in no position to bribe God or contribute to the number of rewards He will give me based on my quantifiable works, lest I should brag about how I helped God to help me; as was the case in the parable of the arrogant Pharisee and the tax collector in Luke 18:9-14. The logic, reason and predictable outcomes are of the "flesh." They exist in the natural and need no faith to get them. FEAR works in direct opposition to FAITH. Jesus the Christ spent his entire ministry trying to demonstrate the power and necessity of faith. Cancer and other conditions like this can put us in a place of helplessness. In my enfeeblement, powers of reason and logic are worthless. I can't bring them to bear on my helpless situation when I am all but dead; and let me tell you, I am at that place. I can't even reason with any clarity right now.

After the onset of this sickness, I asked God to use it and me for His good will and purpose. I know that there will be excellent outcomes. Others may even profit from the consequences of my affliction. So let it be. After all, this cancer is terminal now, but God can change that. The doctors say it is incurable. I may go into remission but will eventually relapse (so says the current evidence). So, what is the point of asking God for healing? Partly, it is self-serving, but I also asked that God make me of value to others according to His will and purpose.

I can now relate to some of the early Christians who, even in the threat against their lives, experienced such a sense of joy, excitement and peace as they advocated for Christ. For me to think that God has accepted me into His exceptional service means that I can die happy today.

For God to make me a beneficiary of miracles and favor even at this stage is something I am trying to grasp. You have witnessed with me over these months, blow by blow, as I struggled to come to terms with cancer. I posted about my confidence in healing through grace, and you have signaled that you agree with me.

Miracles and favors weren't even a significant part of my earlier writings on this Facebook board. My primary concerns were coming to terms with my physical disabilities, trying to comprehend the meaning of my mortality and how the various outcomes could impact those close to me. Now, I believe and accept that God will use me and my situation to demonstrate His benevolence. Mercies and favor are at His sole discretion, and He will do with me as He did with Job. Yes, I said it. Even as I struggle through my current situation, I am revived, hopeful, and blessed. I submit to you that God is in control of me and will show his power for you all to witness. I will be completely healed.

In the above post, I made references to miracles; the evidence of God's good work in me. I have had to use prescribed glasses for many years now and must wear them for reading. In the weeks before and at the time of this posting, I had been able to read without those glasses. I woke up one morning attempting to post a message and found I could no longer see through the prescription lenses I had been wearing the night before. I am not sure how that happened and why it has not lasted. Some said it could be due to some of the medicines I was on. The doctors did not give much credence to the possibility of me reading without glasses for any extended period.

Regardless, to me, it was an assurance that God could do great miracles in me. Maybe it was my Peter walking on water faith experience. Although I could read without glasses for weeks, by feeding into the narrative that it would not last, or that it was attributable to the medicines, I had introduced doubt and that counteracted the faith potency. Just as Peter experienced the miracle of walking on water in faith, as soon as he doubted what he was doing he started to sink. I experienced other unfathomable things during that period, not just of the transient type but such that I can prove today. Even in my suffering, God provided me reasons to be exceedingly joyful.

My wife recently reminded me of an incident she had witnessed. I cannot say when for sure, but I do believe it was after the preceding post. She told me how she had silently watched me through the slightly ajar bedroom door, dancing and singing at the top of my voice. What a sight that must have been—me, the partially crippled, emaciated, and unstable remnant of myself in an enraptured state of effervescence and merriment? I had lost so much weight by then, and my chin was immovably stuck to my chest because of the spinal collapse. Every joint in my body was painful, and my voice croaked like that of the angel of death. So, watching me then must have been a sight to behold. In a paradox of both sympathy and joy, my wife reported that she had smiled and muttered to herself with pleasure, "Look at my poor big head baby!"

Given my state, how could I have been exuberant? Things were almost certainly the worst they had ever been. But I was rejoicing in the knowledge that I was in favor with the Lord. I was filled with joy, knowing that the pleasure of the Lord was my strength. He had heard my prayers and had let me know His hand was upon me. Being joyful was a reaction to the leading of my spirit. But what would sustain this response? Choice. I came to the realization that how I react to an emotional trigger was a choice.

I turned to Habakkuk as a source from which to draw strength. He lived in an agrarian society and was a farmer. His means of survival were the produce of the fields and his animals. But there came a time when his crops stopped producing and he had no animals left. Yet he chose to rejoice in God, his Savior, his Provider, the Source of his empowerment and his joy (Habakkuk 3:17-19). I found I could also relate to the joy of the Psalmist when he declared in Psalm 30:11 (NKJV), "You have turned for me my mourning into dancing; You have put off my sackcloth and clothed me with gladness."

I derive satisfaction from the knowledge that it is not the will of God that I shall suffer (2 Peter 3:9). I had to view life from a positive perspective, notwithstanding the current reality. I could still stand and move about, which was some improvement over my recent past. Would I be able to hold fast and focus on Jesus, the source of my joy, and demonstrate it outwardly as I was doing then, regardless of whatever came? Or would I yield to the misery of the disease and Satan's deceptive subliminal lies? But even as I pondered these questions, I knew the joy of the Lord would always be there to strengthen and sustain me.

CHAPTER 21

On Faith

*Now the just shall live by faith: but if any man draw
back, my soul shall have no pleasure in him.*

—Hebrews 10:38 (KJV)

My ability to implement and sustain my faith throughout my illness, faced as I was with the myriad of issues, challenges, and setbacks that constantly arose, proved to be a colossal test. But I refused to give up. There was no other incentive for me but to stay the course. I could not shirk from my commitment and displease God. Hebrews 10:38 warned that God would take no pleasure in me if I stepped away from my resolve. Therefore, I challenged myself to endure in faith as best I could. To accomplish my healing, I needed to harness the level of faith required, believe in my ability to sustain it, and stay resolute in the face of all challenges to receive the faith product. Such was my challenge.

I have used the word *faith* a lot in this book. Unquestionably, my healing is wholly vested in faith. Without faith, I can see no way to a cure for this incurable disease. Hebrews 11:6 teaches that without faith, it is impossible to please God. Since faith is so critical, I thought it essential to give a brief overview of what faith means to me. The word *faith* is a noun. As a Christian, I perceive faith as a conduit to grace. Grace is the empowerment God grants us all to get everything we could ever need for this life. All we need to do is believe the truth that Jesus Christ is our risen Lord. Through His torture and subsequent death, He made healing possible for us all. He promised to provide for our needs, every need, even eternal life—in fact, anything we ask in His name. Grace is the repository that holds His promises, and faith is the key to unlock and access them.

In John 11:25-26 (ESV), Jesus says, "I am the resurrection and the life. Whoever believes in me, though he dies, yet shall he live, and everyone who lives and believes in me shall never die? Do you believe this?" It may seem like a redundant question to a Christian, but there is also the issue of misplaced faith. Misplaced tradition or blind faith may lead to undesirable results.

Some years ago, unsuspecting and trusting individuals were alleged to have bought what they thought was a popular brand of pain reliever. Those containers had, however, allegedly been tampered with and the contents replaced with cyanide. Regrettably, many did not survive after ingesting the poison. Although lamentable, this story illustrates that what or who we trust can result in death.

Faith cannot be intellectualized, and to try to convince non-Christians of your particular faith principles through Christ is not easy. Traditions, beliefs, and customs form the basis for many who are so rooted in their faith belief they are willing to die for it. As a Christian, I believe in John 3:16 that God so loved the world that He gave Jesus His only Son to die for me. And if Christ had not been raised from the dead, my faith would be worthless and I would still be in sin, according to 1 Corinthians 15:17. I live rooted and grounded in these core principles as an overarching credo governing how I live.

It is comforting to know that my faith is warranted on the integrity of no less a person than Jesus Christ. In John 14:13 (NIV), Jesus made the following promise about that warranty, "And I will do whatever you ask in my name, so that the Father may be glorified in the Son." So, the inexhaustible provisions of grace await the act of faith to unveil it, as Jesus emphasizes in Matthew 21:22 (ESV), "And whatever you ask in prayer, you will receive, if you have faith."

Because of the potency of faith, it helps me always to see faith as active and even relentless in its quest to achieve what it is activated to do. All that faith requires is the correlative action of belief in Jesus Christ that by His will we should receive the ideal outcome of grace. God ultimately decides our outcomes, and they could eventually fall somewhere between our lofty expectations and realistic needs. Take Paul, for example. Whatever plagued him was pressing enough for him to ask God three times to take it from him. Paul's lofty expectation was that God would in turn rid him of the issue. That would be Paul's perception of an ideal outcome, but God instead did not and declared to Paul in 2 Corinthians 12:9, "My grace is sufficient for you."

What faith produces through grace has no equivalency with magic, karma, or humanism. It did not take very long for me to acknowledge that, where my healing was concerned, faith was not like a menu with options and choices to select from. It was my only choice. There were no alternatives. I do not necessarily expect instantaneous gratification because of how desperately I summon my faith. I will have my results in God's time. Faith requires unwavering sustainability with confidence and conviction in the works of God. God rewards those who diligently seek Him. I sustain my faith by hearing the Word of God and keep listening to and reading it more and more.

Romans 10:17 tells me that faith comes by hearing, and hearing by the Word of God. I please God when I demonstrate strong faith. In Matthew 8:5-13, Jesus was so delighted by the level of faith shown by a military officer, He healed the officer's sick servant without even seeing him. The Bible cites numerous examples of Jesus providing healing based solely on the faith of individuals, or those acting in proxy for them. I am therefore assured and operate with confidence that my needs are already accounted for in the spiritual realm, even though I may not immediately experience the desired outcome in the natural world.

Faith transcends the terrestrial and accesses the celestial to produce the appropriate faith product. An outcome such as healing should eventually manifest in the natural world in God's time. Believing that, I chose to execute my faith principle. As a faith person, I had to be clear about my faith purpose and its pursuit. With my faith purpose defined, I adopted the proper faith posture. The faith process, however, is of God and beyond my capabilities. I, therefore, had to surrender the process without question to God so that in His time, He would provide my faith product. Only God knows how and when the outcome of our faith will manifest in the natural world. Instantaneous miracles present one form of faith product; however, in His omniscience, God chooses the time and method to deliver our faith outcome. I believe medical science is of God, and through His progressive revelations, science is informed.

I knew that whatever means God chose, it would deliver my specific faith product, which is my healing. By believing, accepting, and embracing the fact that things that I hoped for and that are currently intangible in the natural world will be reality in the future, I demonstrate my faith. Hebrews 11:1 (NIV) says, "Now faith is confidence in what we hope for and assurance about what we do not see." Ephesians 2:8-9 (NIV) provides a suitable summary of the relationship between God, His grace, and my faith, "For it is by grace you have been saved, through faith—and this is not from yourselves, it is the gift of God—not by works, so that no one can boast."

Our guidebook, the Bible, instructs us that the works of the flesh are enmity against the Spirit. The flesh, or carnal mind, relies on knowns such as logic and reason. Faith exists beyond the confines of things known or seen. Faith brings into our reality things that are "not," things hoped for, which to the nonbeliever may appear to be unrealistic. It permits me to expect things that are not currently in existence in the natural world to eventually be done so it can bear witness.

My faith is affirmed when with absolute certitude, I believe that the omnipotent God has already made provisions for my needs through grace, and I behave in like manner. Since it is God who has already done what I need, then God must be the object of my faith—not a thing, person, or my work efforts. Accomplishing what I hope for, in faith, rests with Jesus Christ and not with me doing what faith should. To have my work efforts contend with faith is futile; they are exclusive. However, true faith produces corresponding works. If I do any good works, they should result from the leading of my faith. Good works should not be done with self-fulfilling motives, driven by guilt, fearfulness, or some obligations or commitment, but in obedience to God. Abram's good work through faith was to leave his family and home and head to parts unknown, based solely on faith in God's instructions. That was faith producing action or work. So true faith produces good works, but works do not produce faith. As James asks, "What good is it, my brothers, if someone says he has faith but does not have works?" (James 2:14, ESV). If God has already done all the necessary work to make that which is hoped for accessible through grace, it is illogical and ineffectual to work for the same thing that is accessible through my faith in God.

Through my faith in Jesus Christ, I expect to be completely healed of the disease. Ideally, I would like it to have happened the moment I first prayed; but that was my lofty expectation and not necessarily in line with God's process. Losing faith, doubting God, and giving up because it did not happen on my schedule is unproductive; my lack of faith is not a plausible basis on which to judge God on His ability to provide my faith product, by shifting His timeline to align with my lofty expectations. The sacrificial blood of Jesus Christ is guaranteed to heal all ailments. And since I act in faith, believing in the all-powerful works of Christ and not in my own pitiful efforts, I have confidence. God has His perfect will and determines timing, progress, and final outcomes. The fact that I do not comprehend His timeline does not mean I should be any less relentless in my expression of faith. Neither should I be frustrated when my ideals do not coincide with God's perfect will. I need to be relentless in my faith pursuit, with the expectation that I will see the big picture when God's purpose becomes my reality.

Jesus Christ redeemed me to be His and gave me the investment of His Holy Spirit. My thoughts are influenced by His Spirit to be aligned with His will. If I do not allow other influences to misdirect me, I can assuredly operate with confidence that my needs for healing are already accounted for and addressed by Him.

By confidently holding in faith to the promises contained in the warranty He provides, I should cast aside all worry. He is all-knowing, so my situation is of no surprise to Him. He had already made provision for it before I experienced it. So, in faith, I am the beneficiary of His great provisions.

The workings of faith are beyond natural reasoning and human comprehension. It is contrary to logic, scientific deductions, and human instincts. The bottom line is that faith in Jesus Christ provides access to a place where all needs are met. My life's investment is in the power of faith, and my returns are the demonstrable profitable returns it provides.

CHAPTER 22

Bearing My Own Cross

Then Jesus said to His disciples, "If anyone desires to come after Me, let him deny himself, and take up his cross, and follow Me. For whoever desires to save his life will lose it, but whoever loses his life for My sake will find it. For what profit is it to a man if he gains the whole world, and loses his own soul? Or what will a man give in exchange for his soul?"

—Matthew 16:24-26 (NKJV)

*F*eebleness, *helplessness*, and even *haplessness*, are terms that would aptly describe my condition and the stage I was at when I wrote the post that follows. To complete the picture, I could also have added *mindlessness*, *mentally dysfunctional*, and *cognitively impaired*. Only through faith in Jesus Christ could one recover from all this. By His grace, notwithstanding all my ailments, I was still privileged to document and share my thoughts, but my emotions were wreaking havoc on me. Quite candidly, I seemed to have a constant urge to cry, and I had to exercise more self-restraint than ever. The strain of the illness, the isolation, and the effects of the medications on my body were significant.

As I wrote the post, I was reflecting on the embarrassment of the day before that had brought me to tears. I still clung to the belief that I could figure things out and solve problems the way I used to before my illness. I sobbed like a petulant child when it suddenly dawned on me that there were times when I was unable to understand even the simplest of instructions. My wife had bought a simple product from the hardware store that had some of the most basic instructions for installation. I read it and reread it countless times but couldn't comprehend what I was reading. It was frustrating. No matter how many times I tried, I was confounded by the instructions; nothing made sense. I was unable to focus or concentrate. Just trying to recall the previous sentence so I could string a couple of lines together was impossible for me. I was shocked, blown away, and in disbelief. "Am I losing my mind?" I wondered. I tried harder to focus and really concentrate, but the effort caused my head to hurt unbearably.

To say I was embarrassed did not begin to describe my feelings; I was beyond ashamed. Prior to my illness, I was a jack-of-all-trades. My full-time job required me to think on my feet, solve complex issues, and articulate solutions to very brilliant clients; now, it was as if I had no brain. It was distressing. Coming to terms with the fact that I was cognitively impaired was challenging and depressing. In addition to all this, I was gradually losing my ability to write legibly.

My new burden was a condition known as chemo brain, or chemo fog. The first time I'd heard of the phenomenon was a few days before when I ran into a former coworker at the infusion center. She had completed chemotherapy and shared her struggle with me. From what she said, my reaction seemed more severe. The chemo fog had rendered me stupid and dull-witted. If assessed, my IQ would have been at its lowest. Many doctors seem reluctant to acknowledge the existence of this phenomenon, or even give credence to the condition. But, for me, it was real. And although the effects diminish over time, I am not sure if it goes away completely. I could barely think or do anything that required any form of intellectual effort at the time.

"Chemo brain" is otherwise known as cancer-therapy associated cognitive change. According to the Mayo Clinic, "Chemo brain is a common term used by cancer survivors to describe thinking and memory problems that can occur after cancer treatment. Chemo brain can also be called chemo fog, chemotherapy-related cognitive impairment, or cognitive dysfunction."

The Mayo Clinic asserts that it is unlikely that chemotherapy is the sole cause. However, it notes that researchers are working to understand the memory changes in people with cancer.

The Mayo Clinic further notes that the signs and symptoms of chemo brain may include: being unusually disorganized, confusion, difficulty concentrating, difficulty finding the right word, difficulty learning new skills, difficulty multitasking, fatigue, a feeling of mental fogginess, a short attention span, short-term memory problems, taking longer than usual to complete routine tasks, trouble with verbal memory (such as remembering a conversation), and trouble with visual memory (such as recalling an image or list of words). Well, if researchers needed a perfect guinea pig or a good test case, I was he. I experienced every symptom listed above.

During those times, I did not want to speak to anyone because my voice was weak and I was unable to hold an intelligent conversation anyway. I think what came from me were more the utterances of a delusional mind that was unable to string a sentence together or hold an intelligent conversation. I avoided face-to-face discussions as I could discern people staring at me blankly or sometimes turning their heads away while I was in the middle of trying to say something. And it wasn't me being hypersensitive; body language doesn't lie. Sure, I won't deny a bit of paranoia on my part. Before posting anything on Facebook, I would review the drafts several times and, after they were published, I would still invariably find errors that I had to edit. Even after umpteenth edits, there would still be residual mistakes that made the posts almost unintelligible. Thank God for my sympathetic followers who made an effort to glean the essence of what I was trying to say rather than criticize my grammar.

There is a Jamaican idiomatic expression that aptly characterizes the confluence of issues that came with my illness. One iteration of this expression is, "What a crosses!" And what enormous *crosses* my illness brought. I can't think of a more encompassing expression. It captures the complexities, extreme troubles, tribulations, dispiritedness, and hopelessness from which only God can deliver. All I was going through fell under the umbrella of my crosses. Now, there is a clear distinction between bearing my cross and crosses—although bearing my cross at the time was my crosses.

"Bearing my cross" bears reference to our Savior Jesus Christ. The cross is symbolic of the pain and suffering Jesus bore. It meant the death of His human person. When Jesus said in Luke 9:23, "If anyone would come after me, he must deny himself and take up his cross daily and follow me," for me, it went beyond me dying to my old sinful ways and extended to my faith walk with Him. Although I had crucified my old-sin man, it did not mean that I had a life free of pain and suffering.

As overbearing as my cross was, God allowed it, and if such crosses would serve His useful purpose, then I should not complain. My commitment then was to bear my cross regardless of the pain and suffering so that God would be glorified. If my cross were "crosses," He would bring relief. He would position what or who would be impacted for His glory, and I would please God by faithfully believing He knew best and would sustain me through the journey.

Therefore, even while bearing my cross, I saw hope. My expectation was for an oasis of fruits, and what I posted on social media would be the seeds. The early harvest was borne out by steady improvement in my physical condition and the positive feedback I received from those who admitted they were inspired by what the Holy Spirit was leading me to write. The early postings, I hoped, would serve as benchmarks, reference points to be used for the time in the future when my writing would be all positive through God's grace as I reaped the harvest of progressive healing.

> I recall as a young boy in Sunday school, grieving whenever the teacher gave the crucifixion account. Naturally, I thought it was a cruel and evil treatment meted out to our "Sweet Jesus." I would wish that I could have been there. How I would boldly step to the cause and fight for Jesus, maybe take a lash or two and help bear the cross, or so I thought. Influenced by songs my grand-

mother would sing, such as, "Must Jesus bear the cross alone and all the world go free? There is a cross for everyone, and there is a cross for me," I would grieve the incident but could not imagine me having my personal cross.

Now, I can appreciate that my current condition is a cross. Although not the ultimate one, it is a cross—my present crosses. Only God knows how heavy it is for me. I embrace my cross in faith, believing that God has allowed it specifically for my betterment and His glory. Nothing happens to anyone or anything in creation without God's knowledge and approval. He knows our beginning and our end. He had our course charted from before we were even conceived and with that, begrudgingly as I may feel at times, I shall carry this cross even through the desert. What I learn in "the desert" while bearing my cross will be valuable sometime in the future. I believe they are lessons for my edification and for sharing with others who may be helped. I have learned a lot so far in this desert. Let me summarize some of these while I can.

- Pain: The rogue cancer cells, have traveled throughout my body and have nested in my bones. They are purposed to destroy my bones, and so far, they have caused my ribs and cervical spine to be eaten away and fracture. The C2-C4 vertebrae of my spinal column have virtually collapsed and, from what has been explained, they are resting on my nerve center. This is what has caused the unimaginable pain of which I speak. The cancer cells are transported by my blood and are diffused all over my body. They create holes in my skeletal structure and are clinically known as lytic lesions. Deposits of useless cancer cells nest in these holes and develop into tumors, which is how my vertebrae and ribs became fractured. When the morphine and other medications I take start to wear off, I can feel the effects of these damages by the bone pains. Trust me, pain is pain, but bone pain is the mother of all pains. It hurts excruciatingly.

- Medications: They are powerful. Some have both physical and mind-altering effects. I must take morphine as one of my pain medications even though I am aware of the dangers of this incredibly addictive, damaging, and even deadly opiate. The doctors recognize that I need the analgesic, sedative, tranquilizing, and antidepressant effects of the drug, so I need to be compliant with the doctors' order and take the prescribed medicine. I am conscious of the opioid epidemic resulting from taking medications like these, as I am aware that opioid addiction is one of the most widely discussed topics at the highest levels in the country these days.

The cocktail of medications I am prescribed seems to either complement or counteract each other, but all have significant side effects, some even compounding the side effects of others. I take one set of drugs with the hope of helping a condition and then many others to counter their side effects. Some act as prophylactics; others treat issues that are existential, while still others treat symptoms that may occur as a result of some or all the prescribed medications. Chemotherapy has further compromised my immune system, making me vulnerable to attack from external sources. I must limit my interactions and scrutinize what I eat because it appears that everything is now armed with warheads to destroy me. I take medicines to prevent severe side effects, such as shingles, nausea, diabetes, and other side effects like opioid-induced constipation (OIC). Some medicines affect my mental state, such as morphine. They keep me in an unusual state of calmness and euphoria. More than anything, I am keenly aware of those little neurotransmitters in my brain called dopamine, lest they become too opioid friendly and drive me into an addictive state.

• Physical state: Losing nearly 50 lbs of body mass makes this old man almost like a child once more. I am always fatigued, sleeping for sometimes more than 20 hours each day, most days. Each day I feel as though I had a head-to-head confrontation with a semi-truck, and guess who is the loser? I do limp around with assistance, however. Nonetheless, I fight. I do a bit of physical exercise sometimes struggling for up to an hour every other day, for now. Just imagine me in motion on an elliptical machine or trying to lift weights while being half asleep. It's paying off though; I can now see slight muscle definitions returning (I think). I am now almost 185 proud pounds of toughness aspiring for my average 215 lbs, but I feel much stronger each day. I still hate the taste of foods, although slight taste is returning. Now I am even more plagued with nausea and just looking at food makes me sick. I am quite selective about what I can stomach and how all meals are prepared. I feel the urge to vomit even just thinking about food.

- Mental state: I am aware of episodes of delusions at times; I say things I should not and react with heightened sensitivity unnecessarily. I live in a constant state of wooziness and fog, and at times, I get confused. In prior postings, I said the medicines were my friends. I have come to realize that sometimes they are not so friendly.

- The community of friends: Of all the things I have learned through this process, it is the value of friendship, and I will treasure forever the faithful support of my old and new friends. So many have rallied to my assistance. This community keeps expanding. My friends and family have been remarkable. I cannot say enough good things about how beneficial that is to me—many people just simply wanting to know how they can help. From the goodness of their hearts, they are so eager to do good for me. You express love through your comments, encouragement, cards, and other forms of expressions. I am overwhelmed with love. I am thrilled that if I don't post for a while, you hold me accountable. You, my friends, have been telling me that you've been inspired one way or other through what I write and post. There are those just wanting to be assured that I am still fighting and not yielding my faith to the alternative. I value such interactions; they are cathartic.

- God and Faith: My faith is becoming more unshakable even with the new and emerging challenges I face. Faith in God is the explicit

189

premise on which I continue to exist. There is no compromise. I am God's; I walk in faith, believing that God has purposed and destined me for His good will. Regardless of the suffering, pain, or length of time it takes for my physical healing, I stand committed to whatever God's purpose is for me. Since God is aware, then He will see me through it. I must accept my lot with pleasure. I can imagine how Jesus, faced with the ultimate destruction of the body by the horrific death by crucifixion, was agonized. He asked God the Father to let "the cup" pass from Him if it were possible. The Father, knowing His purpose and destiny for us, allowed Jesus, (God in Flesh) to die for the greater good. God allowed humans to kill His flesh. Paul is another example; he and his posse were persecutors and murderers of the followers of Christ. After Jesus called him into His service, he was the epitome of a transformed man; he suffered stoning, whipping, shipwreck, and prison. Unrelenting in his purpose for God, he brought the Gospel of salvation to all, including Gentiles like me. If those are the benchmarks by which I should compare my lot, then I am woefully below standard.

So how do I think I am doing? I am bearing my cross, noting my steps in this unfamiliar desert. I am taking this wilderness time to become even more schooled in the Word of God. That should make me better equipped for the time when I shall assume my new body from God. I will stand with confidence to impact many souls with the testimony of God's goodness and mercies to me.

I will be healed through faith. My testimony will be evidence of God's love for humanity, and my restored temple will be my proof on display. I will be the living miracle of God Almighty through Jesus Christ. God bless you all.

NB. I have now completed two of my first four cycles of chemotherapy, and it is my break week. On Friday, I resume therapy for the second half. It has been day to day for me—up today, down tomorrow. By now, I have reiterated the bad side effects from the illness and medicines several times, and they keep increasing. Added to the fatigue and cognitive issues, I now have persistent opioid-induced constipation (OIC)—a horrible thing that is obviously caused by the opioid medications. I will write more about it later.

CHAPTER 23

The Power of Knowledge

*If any of you lacks wisdom, you should ask God, who gives generously
to all without finding fault, and it will be given to you.*

—James 1:5 (NIV)

*The fear of the LORD is the beginning of knowledge:
but fools despise wisdom and instruction.*

—Proverbs 1:7 (KJV)

I was resolved that my healing would be attained from God's
grace. How and when, I did not know. It was out of my control. The fact is, grace encompassed all I needed, and for my
healing, I had it through faith in Jesus Christ. I concluded that
God Almighty had already established the duration of my condition. My cure would become evident when the Lord determined.
Psalm 27:14 (KJV) reminds us to, "Wait on the LORD: be of
good courage." I was prepared to wait, but not be deaf. But waiting to me did not mean lying in bed expecting my strength to
be miraculously renewed and my health instantaneously restored.
God provides knowledge everywhere, and I believed that in faith,
God would direct me where and how to find it. As long as I waited
and listened, I knew I could rely on the Holy Spirit to lead me

from my position of ignorance to wisdom about my illness and treatment options.

Was there a conflict in me seeking to know more about my condition when I had entrusted my healing to God's care? Shouldn't I have just sat back and waited for faith to take its course? Might not the quest for knowledge contradict the faith principle? I answered that question by asking myself, "Who leads us to discover medicines and guides the clinicians in administering the drugs that help us?" God does, through His grace. Even as I walked in faith, I had accepted that my healing might not be instantaneous, and I had to listen to how God was instructing me.

With the rapid deterioration of my health, it would have been foolhardy for me to ignore the fact that God had sufficiently trained and equipped my doctors with the necessary capabilities to play their role in my healing. Jesus was no longer on earth to touch me physically, but the doctors were here. Evidently, God could heal me through their care. Psalm 24:1 advises me that everything is at God's disposal for His good purpose. It teaches that, "The earth is the LORD's, and the fullness thereof; the world, and they that dwell therein." If God purposed to administer healing from grace through the professionals, then I must listen to His instruction through the wisdom He provides and move in faith as He directs.

God provides for not only our spiritual but also our physiological needs. He provides food for our physical needs. In response to the requirements for fuel, our bodies produce certain stimulants that motivate us to satisfy our hunger. There is a variety of plants and animals on earth, but not all are suitable for human consumption. God then gives us the wisdom to distinguish between the healthy and the harmful, and gives us the intelligence to prepare them so that they are either palatable for eating or efficacious in relieving or curing certain illnesses.

As a Christian, I know that grace abounds my healing because I use intelligence to acquire that knowledge from God's Word. God also provides me with wisdom (which is spiritual) to access the healing. It is God Who equips humans with the intellect to produce the abundance of scientific material that then guides the development of new medicines. As there is an abundance of plants and animals, so is the variety of drugs and therapies available. Some are neither safe nor effective for my condition. The clinicians use their knowledge to select and administer medication they believe will help my situation. Likewise, God equips me with intelligence to gain an understanding of some basic concepts about the disease and treatments, and provides spiritual wisdom to discern what is in His will for me. He entrusted me to the care of man, not all of whom are of the Christian persuasion or believe in God to acknowledge His divine order in everything. Therefore, I needed to be the discerning instrument of God's direction to add value to my treatment process.

To do so, I regarded it as vital to inform myself of my options as best I could. I prayed for the wisdom of my caregivers so that they would administer care according to God's direction. We all need wisdom. The great King Solomon, with all his immense wealth and distinguished status, realized he needed wisdom to be an effective king and sought it from God.

It behooves reiterating that although we are spirits, we live in the natural world. God gives us the intelligence to acquire knowledge and wisdom and to use such knowledge to empower ourselves prudently. Jesus the Great Healer gave His disciples authority and power to heal. Both Matthew's and Luke's gospels document that Jesus authorizes humanity to cure diseases and sickness (Matthew 10:1 and Luke 9:1). Jesus further extends this capability and authority to humanity in general, as shown in John 14:12, where He states, "Whoever believes in me will also do the works that I am doing. He will do even greater things than these, because I am going to the Father." In verse 13 of John 14, Jesus states, "I will do whatever you ask in My name, so that the Father may be glorified in the Son." Therefore, I embraced the privilege to ask for my healing in Jesus' name, with the confidence that through Him the "greater things" would be accomplished.

My soul was comfortable that God provides science with whatever capability it had for my benefit. Our caring Father gives to the scientists and doctors revelations and skills to heal. Scientific mysteries are continuously being revealed to them, as the omniscient God said. They, in turn, are able to do the "greater things" Jesus promised in John 14:12. I benefit because I believe in Jesus and that the practitioners are merely doing what God directs them to do in the course of my healing. So rather than seeing a conflict between science and faith, I choose to see God's awesome benevolence to mankind manifested through science and technology. That settled the science-faith conflict for me.

Does God use miracles like patient outcomes to reach caregivers and clinicians? Of course, I believe He does. God can cause miraculous healings to influence professional views about the credibility of faith in patient outcomes. So why not my outcome? The miraculous work of God in me could be their testimony to other patients. We have heard stories of doctors marveling at medical outcomes that defy science, of doctors making comments such as, "There is no longer any evidence of the tumor. We can't explain how." or "You are a miracle." These inexplicable healings are of God. I believe that, in time, I too will be the subject of inexplicable healing, the substance of my faith manifested to the glory of God. Of course, unbelievers may ascribe my healing to an aberration, a scientific anomaly, or just luck.

Regardless, the seed would have been planted to at least raise the question about the possibility of God's miracles in me to bear fruits later. It would be like productive seeds which, for all intents and purposes, appear to be dead; and we bury and nurture them, hoping for a good yield. God then mysteriously causes those apparently dead seeds to germinate and produce. The satisfied farmer testifies with joy to others of his great harvest from dead seeds. My dead myeloma cells will make room for the growth of productive antibodies and cure me of the cancer and, like the farmer, I too will be able to testify with great joy on God's behalf. Afterall, if God can mysteriously make dead seeds bring new life, why should it pose any difficulty for my loving Father to restore me to perfect health? We are sometimes allowed to be broken, but not to die, so our wall of resistance may be torn down and we can be made submissive in order to hear from God and be useful to Him. In 2 Corinthians 12:9 (KJV), He told Paul, "My strength is made perfect in weakness." There was proof that my brokenness was fertile ground for my Father to sow good seeds for witnessing or whatever was His will. I am, after all, His favored child in whom He has invested His Holy Spirit, who is no less than the same powerful Spirit that raised Jesus from the dead.

God is the head of all the sciences. He is omniscient, all-knowing (scientist in this case), and it is from Him that all knowledge and wisdom originate. Science and faith do harmoniously coexist and do so to the glory of God. Coming to terms with the harmonious faith/knowledge coexistence, I was comfortable equipping myself with knowledge while trusting in God to conclusively orchestrate my healing through His grace.

Although not every illness is preventable, there are instances when our earthly wisdom can be used to stave off attacks. It is not the will of God that we should suffer. God can prevent every illness that afflicts us, but instead He provides the route to knowledge that can help us prevent or treat our ailments. It is wrong to blame God; He gives us both academic and spiritual insight. Our bodies are temples, and it is incumbent on us to appreciate that we are wonderfully made and do everything we can to protect and preserve them. Through progressive revelations from God, we have the benefit of natural sciences to protect and keep our bodies in good order until God decides to end our life. He told us our natural earthly life would end. Until then, we have His grace.

In the post that follows, I acknowledge the difficulty in detecting multiple myeloma proactively but still believe we should seek wisdom and use knowledge to preemptively prevent unhealthiness where we can. As a beneficiary of the marvels and wonders of twenty-first-century science and technology, I have a very high regard for science, medical advancements, and the competencies of the brilliant doctors of today. Armed with knowledge, I accept that science can avail itself of tools for my physical benefit. In faith, I believe that God will orchestrate the power of science to produce my ultimate healing.

> The Bible instructs us that we perish because we lack knowledge (Hosea 4:6). We lack understanding of what God says about who we are and about any situation that we face. The joy of

living, success, and healing are always available to us. Many are ignorant of God's provisions through grace. So, what do I need? I need healing from cancer. Does God provide healing? The Bible says He does. It says by His stripes (all the scourging, beating, and punishment) all who believe that Jesus Christ is Lord and Savior can be healed from every sickness (Isaiah 53:5). If I am ignorant of that provision, or decide not to claim it in faith, then I won't benefit from it. If it sounds farfetched, let's use a simple analogy. If my wealthy uncle died and left me a fortune, and I was unaware of it, or I refuse to claim it, I would not benefit from it. My uncle's wealth could be misappropriated, and I could die in poverty.

God knows everything about me and makes provisions for my needs. He makes provisions for the birds, flowers, and all living creatures, as outlined in Matthew 6:26-29. Verse 26 (NIV) states, "Look at the birds of the air; they do not sow or reap or store away in barns, and yet your heavenly Father feeds them." God creates humans as free moral agents. He gives us wisdom and we acquire knowledge that enables us to make decisions and choices without imposing restrictions from Him. If we were perfect, our ideal actions would always align with His perfect will and would please Him. The flawed human influence on our decision-making process almost invariably contravenes God's perfect will. As our benevolent Father, He provides a way for us to be restored back in alignment with Him through our repentance. He is not quick to strip us of His grace and its provisions when we violate His will. Grace, essentially, is God's favorable predisposition toward humanity.

Our perishable human bodies will eventually fail completely. Meanwhile, everyone will experience some form of sickness in their lifetime. We are affected by everything: what we consume, the environment, and even the constant battles in our minds. Human knowledge generally provides our first line of offense. There is the inevitable cure in the bottle, and doctors who know best. Our call to God is usually the last-ditch option, either in desperation or as a hedge, seeking His blessing on our mess. We tell God what we are doing to fix our problems and ask for His acceptance. When things start to look ominous and earthly wisdom seems to be failing, we run to God who is our refuge and strength, and a very present help in trouble, according to Psalm 46. Even then, we miss the true essence of God's goodness, the giver of grace in whom we stake our claim of confidence.

Since healing is not instantaneously manifested after praying, I need to wait in faith on the process. Delay is not God's denial, but an elapse of time, so that many will know of my journey and give God glory. By restoring Lazarus to life after he had died for a while, Jesus provided indisputable evidence of His miraculous power for man to witness and God to receive glory, because they who witnessed believed. Humans had the opportunity to witness the miraculous power of God, and it glorified God.

If it is God's will that I dwell in this situation for a while, to give science and human actions the opportunity, then to His will I submit. God uses humans, their knowledge and wisdom to manifest His power. There were times when Jesus went beyond just the spoken word to heal. In one example, a sick woman only had to touch His clothes and was healed because of her great faith. We live to worship and please God. God allows situations that glorify Him.

The illness has subdued me and allowed me to be more singularly focused. With fewer distractions, I am better able to focus on God and His plans for me. I accept that the all-knowing, omniscient God, who foresees all, determines the length of my season of impairment. The progressive timestamps created by my season of illness will be indisputable evidence for my journey and the inscription for my banner of triumph.

The notion that some of my health-care providers could be convinced that God does heal those who consistently rely on their faith with conviction is not far-fetched. In my experience, many of these professionals are hard-coded to stick to evidence-based outcomes (as they should), but some are highly skeptical about the absolute role faith plays in healing. I believe that my healing, when it defies the expected scientific outcomes, could provide evidence of the power of faith in Jesus Christ. I don't anticipate any of these professionals tossing away their hard-earned diplomas and converting hospitals to churches. However, a healthy seed sown in good soil has a strong possibility of germinating. So, the possibility of miraculous intervention might just be something they are willing to consider credible and, who knows, all attributions may just go to Jesus Christ. Then all that I have been through will strengthen our faith in God, provide us with everlasting hope, and motivate us to offer Him all praises and glory of which He alone is worthy.

Most of us do annual physicals. The reports contain detailed information that can provide early warning indicators of our physical state of health. Gone are the days when basic physical parameters such as temperature, blood pressure, and weight were the only ones available to help us proactively participate in our care. These days, doctors rely on more in-depth analytics derived from complete blood count, and chemical analysis from serum, urine, and other biological substances to make specific health-care decisions. No longer are these results the exclusive purview and property of the physician. Online portals are now standard, and they provide access to our test results. These reports are archived so that we can compare how various parameters trend over time. The reports contain valuable information that both patients and physicians can use as indicators of potential or existing conditions that may have negative consequences if left untreated.

Extracting pertinent information from the data and arming ourselves with this knowledge is one way of heading off potential severe outcomes. Annual physicals are critical, but there are 364 days between when they are done, and much could change in the body during that time. When we receive the results, we should not treat them as merely another routine, with the "Oh well, another check in the box until next year" attitude. Instead, it is imperative that we use them to gain more in-depth knowledge and clarity of what changes are occurring in our bodies and use them to seek solutions to head off potential illnesses proactively. In so doing, our annuals become more purposeful, and we can engage more intelligently when it comes to our health care.

Doing so does not guarantee that we have a "catch-all" safety net; some critical diseases do not necessarily manifest in the annual lab test. Such was my case. It took an MRI to provide indications of what a disease like multiple myeloma could cause, even though it was not a diagnosis. Extensive testing, complete blood count, chemical analysis, and a biopsy had to be done before the determination could be finally made. Nonetheless, that should not be the basis for discounting the knowledge that can be gleaned from annual physicals and the reports. Multiple myeloma is one of those aberrant diseases that is hard to detect before it causes destruction. When we do our due diligence, ask doctors clarifying questions, and do our independent research, we can be our best advocates.

I was hospitalized in June 2016. The test results shown below revealed at that time how many parameters were out of range; they were prime indicators of abnormalities. Those were obtained only six months after my last physical, and the critical parameters had substantially changed. If cost was not a deterrent, I believe that after a certain age, biannual physicals would improve patient outcomes. Many potentially productive individuals become disabled as a result of late detection and treatment. Think of the pain and suffering those individuals could be spared and the economic loss that could be prevented. I don't have the actuarial training or the data to understand the economic cost to society, but in times of almost full employment as we are now experiencing, I imagine that productivity losses from preventive disabilities are significant. That is my observation and opinion based on my own experience of how this disease has debilitated me because of the late-stage detection. Below are the initial results I saw after my first hospitalization:

PARAMETERS	RESULTS	RANGE
Blood Pressure	176/93 (Very High)	80-140/89
Calcium	12.5 mg/dL (Critical Level)	8.5 mg/dL-10.1 mg/dL
Sodium	134 mmol/L (Low)	136 mmol/L-145 mmol/L
Hemoglobin	8.6 gm/dL (Low)	14.0 gm/dL-17.0 gm/dL
Creatinine	2.49 mg/dL (High)	0.70 mg/dL-1.30 mg/dL

Let's take calcium, for example. The cancer affected my bones. Calcium is a significant component of bones. The reading for calcium in my blood was at a critical level of 12.5 milligrams per deciliter (mg/dL) compared to the reference level of 8.5-10.1 mg/dL. The clinical term is hypercalcemia. Too much calcium in your blood can be an indication of bone deterioration and cause one's bone to weaken and even affect the workings of the kidneys, heart, and brain. My hemoglobin was low, which could lead to anemia. I could reasonably conclude that the bad cancer cells were destroying my precious red blood cells, and further explorations were warranted. Finally, whenever bad toxic things are in the body, your kidney is impacted. The kidneys pass waste like urine, filter blood going back to the heart, helps produce healthy red blood cells, and regulate blood pressure, among other things. One parameter that doctors look at concerning the kidneys is the creatinine levels; mine were high. I am fortunate in that my wife was able to help me make sense of these parameters. Between my primary care doctor, my wife and me, could we have seen some warning lights? Maybe, if the annual physical had shown these levels. Had that been the case, I could have adequately enhanced my knowledge and taken proactive actions to prevent the gross destruction that was done to my spine, ribs, and other skeletal structures. But if I did not go through the test, I would not have a testimony. God sets the course of our lives. For we are His workmanship, created in Christ Jesus to do good works, which God prepared in advance as our way of life (Ephesians 2:10). All things are done for God's good pleasure; ultimately to accomplish His will.

My hope, then, is that what I do is God's will and that everything that I write is led and inspired by Him. Thank God for loving me so much that He has chosen me. Please never stop praying for me, my friends; but now, having prayed for my healing and being confident in that, pray now that I will walk steadfastly in God's righteousness as I try to accomplish His perfect will.

I am not sure if the above post made it to Facebook because, now that I review it, there are so many gaps that should have been filled before posting. The idea was to convey the fact that we need to take care of our physical temples, guided by God's instructions and equipping ourselves with knowledge.

There is much that doctors can do for patients, but nothing beats educating ourselves. I have learned that I am my best advocate. But how could I advocate in ignorance? God is our ultimate source, and we should always pray for wisdom no matter how much we trust our doctors and the sciences. Although throughout my life I avoided anything to do with the sciences of the human body, such as human biology, after the onset of the disease, I craved for knowledge about my body. I finally realized how by researching and understanding the basics about the workings of the body, I could relate to the disease's progression and understand the objectives and purposes of the various therapies, which made the process more bearable for me.

I understood how doctors used specific lab results as predictive indicators to anticipate not only how my healing was progressing, but also the side effects of certain medicines, their impact on my vital organs, and whether they were causing the onset of other conditions. One example was how sugar and carbohydrates consumption could lead to diabetes. I developed the disease as a result of medications I was administered during my treatment, as noted earlier. I could not make the connection, however, as to why it was ill-advised to limit my carbohydrates when sugar was the culprit that caused diabetes. After researching the similarities between the basic building blocks of sugar and carbohydrates, I could appreciate the dietary restrictions placed on carbs. I learned that when consumed, carbohydrates are eventually broken down by the body into forms of sugar. If not constructively used, these sugars remain in the blood and are measured as an indication of diabetes. By understanding these relationships and how insulin impacts the use of sugar in my blood, I was able to reduce my diabetes levels with lifestyle changes.

God knows everything about us, and He provides resources to give us the knowledge to preserve our physical temples and act in faith to restore them when they are out of sync. He gave the ancient Jews the wisdom of natural laws concerning food, health, and other ways to live, so that the body could remain healthy. God allows us to exercise our own will, but our human imperfections mean we inevitably mess up. Whether deliberately or inadvertently, we routinely abuse our bodies, resulting in physical illnesses. Illnesses are nothing new; they have been around since man sinned. The Bible tells us that our natural life is finite. Since not all illnesses should result in the inevitable death sentence, we have a route to healing. Being impacted by cancer, I have become more aware of the power of knowledge. We need knowledge both of the natural and of the spirit in order to have a fulfilled life.

CHAPTER 24

My Last Pain— New Hope

For I consider that the sufferings of this present time are not worthy to be compared with the glory which shall be revealed in us.

—Romans 8:18 (NKJV)

There have been several times in documenting my journey when I have written about pain. Everyone has experienced some degree of pain. People have different pain thresholds, but there are some pains that can bring one to one's knees. If you have never had bone pains and the pains associated with extreme constipation, then please don't wish for such experiences. A stage 3 cancer classification meant, among other things, that cancer had spread throughout my system, grossly affecting my skeletal frame and certain organs. The fractures and lesions at various places on my skeleton were evidence of the destruction caused by the metastasis of the cancer. The torturous torrents of pains that engulfed my being were insufferable. My waking hours would be consumed with the endless sounds of my groaning and moaning.

Just raising up from a lying position, I needed assistance. My body parts were like ill-fitting appendages, with every movement providing the impetus for excruciating pains. If I sneezed, it would jerk my fractured spine; yawning had to be suppressed because it would impact my upper spine; and I had to take small bites of food when eating as opening my mouth was agonizing. It was ridiculous that flexing my toes, moving my arms, or worse, the slightest move- ment of my head, felt as though I was stabbing myself with a dull object. To turn myself from one position to another meant I had to make appointments with each of my movable body parts or I would suffer the most severe retaliation with pain, and even when approved, I had to move slowly, pausing between stages. My jaws decided to form a happy union, involuntarily trying to glue themselves together, resulting in my teeth being clenched all the time. I went through several mouthpieces in an attempt to prevent them grinding each other to dust. It was only months after my condition had improved and I went to the dentist that I realized how much damage had been done to my teeth. The dentist had to grind them down to even out the peaks and valleys of my once-beautiful ivories.

The prescribed drugs brought some pain relief, but the conse- quences were many. Sometimes I was too weak to move, so fatigued it was discouraging to get up; worse, the hallucinogenic effects of certain medications wreaked havoc on my decision-making process. There were other traumatizing side effects too, one of which I shall highlight later. Regardless of my suffering, I compelled myself to fight and push through. The few physical exercises I did supported my belief in faith that I needed to prepare my body for its healing. It was an outward demonstration that my faith would produce healing. Of course, I had also considered the consequences of staying seden- tary and knew I needed to keep moving.

The fact that God was in the process of healing me meant I had to receive it, believe it, and act in that knowledge. When Jesus healed people, they had to do something to demonstrate they were healed effectively. He would instruct those healed to perform specific actions as a demonstration of their healing. My physical exercises were testimonies to myself that the Spirit of Jesus was with me, heal- ing me just as though He was present with me, instructing me to act. I needed to demonstrably walk in my healing as though it had already been done.

I promised I would relate a painful episode I endured, which I believe was a side effect of one particular drug. I decided to do the post after a failed attempt to complete an ambitious workout that day. I was reflecting with optimism that it would be my last such painful experience.

As I sat on my workout bench rubbing my dry, ashy legs and watching the large flakes float like dry snow on a windy winter's day, I was convinced that last week I had the worst and most aggravating pain episode I could bear. I must now be in the final stages of physical healing. Just as the flakes (a direct result of this sickness) were falling away to reveal fresh, luminous skin beneath, so were the cancerous monoclonal proteins (M proteins) the root of my ailment. For clarity, M proteins are bad. They are the useless antibodies or immunoglobulins produced by the myeloma cells. These nonbeneficial cells are ultimately destructive, and they rapidly multiply and crowd out the useful cells and limit their production. Doctors rely on the breakdown of these cells into proteins that are classified in terms of light and heavy chains to give indications of the state of the multiple myeloma, as in my case. I also now have physical proof of the progress of my rebirth. However, let me tell you about what I have characterized as my last significant pain, hopefully.

For some reason, before last Sunday, I cherished the thought of going to church. I had not been to church for a while. I was ambivalent, of course, because I was not yet fully recovered. I didn't want to show up as a broken vessel, not only because of personal pride, but how would that reflect on God's good work in me? Please understand that healing had been declared on me, and I wanted to show up whole and healed as evidence of God's good work.

In one of my earlier posts, I mentioned OIC (opioid-induced constipation). I was restrained on how explicit and detailed I was with my disclosure by not providing too much information (TMI) out of sheer regard for my audiences' good taste. Well, OIC is real. It is horrible and ranks among the worst experiences I have had so far. I bear no shame in relating my personal experience. So far, I have been unfiltered, as I desire to provide a transparent, and accurate account to someone; maybe not now but someday. OIC is not directly related to cancer; it is a condition induced by the opioid medications I am prescribed for the severe pains I struggle with because of the cancer damages. This family of drugs works by attaching themselves to mu-receptors and blocking pain signals to the brain and nervous system. However, they also attach themselves to mu-receptors in the bowel, impairing orderly bowel actions.

I had not had a bowel action for many days, and it had become extremely uncomfortable. There was bloating and cramps, along with the extreme pressure of an urge I could not fulfill. I had taken every known prescription, over-the-counter and herbal medications to no avail; nothing helped. So, the pain medicine in doing its duty also effectively had shut down the receptors that make for active bowel movements. This event was pain threshold ground zero for me. It was more debilitating than anything so far; it was the pain associated with opioid-induced constipation.

When I attempted to "go," I experienced three hours of sheer agony. Excruciating pains tore at every extremity of the middle third of my body. Pain and cramps characterized my ordeal. I sweated buckets as I tried to force it; I cried like a terrified child when things would not move. I tore off my clothes, impulsively rolled on the floor, and crawled around senselessly. I prayed. I called on God. I appealed to Him in every way I ever knew of Him, as the God of Abraham, Isaac, and Jacob. The God of David, a man of God's heart, Jesus the Christ our Savior, my Lord, my source of healing.

I wish I had the healing scriptures that a dear church sister, who was also dealing with her cancer treatment, had sent me. As would be expected, even if I knew where they were, the crippling pain in my stomach would not allow me to access them. Even if I had memorized those scriptures, my brain was not cooperating adequately to recall and recite them. The only scripture I could think of was "by His stripes, I am healed," and I claimed it repeatedly.

During all this time, my wife administered all the care she was trained to; from physical comfort with soothing words to suppositories and enemas. What a horrible thing, that enema. How am I expected to hold that hot fluid in me given all the days of buildup?

I felt like I was about to explode in the wrong places. Oh! Lord bring relief please, I wailed, hollered, shouted, screamed, and prayed. Almost three hours later, after my first attempt, I decided that, at whatever cost, I was going to push with all the force I could muster—and what a cost it was. I could feel that I was being stretched in places where I shouldn't, my eyes were popping from their sockets, and my ears rang with deafening sounds. Then, there was an explosive relief and I temporarily "blacked out."

The intensity with which I expressed the substance from my gut had torn parts of my body to shreds. The thick, dark, bloody mess was splattered beyond the intended depository because large dense masses had been unleashed with such tremendous velocity. I imagined the bathroom infrastructure shook. I couldn't care less about any mess or damage at that time. Relief had come, although not without its costs. I was severely shredded, such that I am now suffering from hemorrhoids. By the time it was all over, it was much too late for church, and I was far too weak anyway, so I drifted off into my new modus operandi—sleep.

Before I went off to sleep, I pondered on what had just transpired. Had I gone to church prior to the bathroom experience, I would have had the appearance of my best self on display. My attire would be clean and well suited, and my face would bear its usual warm, polite smile to greet everyone. However, I would have been masking the physical pain within me. Pain because of the accumulation of the destructive filth that was within me. That abhorrent filth in me would have caused me to be distracted and would have prevented me from hearing the word of God. Indeed, my pristine clothes and proper deportment would portray the appearance of propriety and appropriateness, but on the inside, I would have been encumbered with the burden of the pain from the mess within me. It occurred to me that, likewise, the burden of unforgiven sins we mask inside is like mess. Such mess is not always outwardly visible, because we enrobe ourselves in self-righteousness for perfect public display.

At some point, however, Jesus calls us, and the guilt of our sins becomes weighty and over-bearing, and we need relief. Relief comes when we expel our sins, casting them on Jesus Christ for forgiveness. At that point, we must cast off our "whitewashed sepulchre" before God and reveal and confess the unsavory and unrighteous content to Him. Then, with His powerful explosive love, God brings us ultimate relief and for-giveness through His unequaled benevolence. As Isaiah said of the people of his days who were under the illusion of righteousness, their boast of righteousness was as filthy rags before God (Isaiah 64:6).

In humility, I had to acknowledge that I have no virtue on which to boast, save for the saving blood of Jesus Christ. I am always striv-ing for perfection, and I will be called to give account for my claim of righteousness. Then God will be my judge. Through the pain, I was reminded of how filthy my righteousness is before God, and that my boast can only be in Jesus Christ. Someday there will be no more pain. That said, I have declared that incident to be my last significant pain.

On a more uplifting note, having completed half of my planned chemotherapy, I met with the oncologist last week. To all who have believed I will be healed, the results were quite favorable. Now, I don't expect anyone who is reading this to be an expert on all the indicators the doctors use to determine my progress. However, two of the critical gauges are "free kappa" and "free lambda," a subset of the M proteins I mentioned earlier. The reference levels for them are 3.3-19.4 and 5.7-26.3 mg/L respectively—those are the normal ranges, not my result. Mine were nowhere near those numbers; however, in a relative sense, you can see from the numbers below that they are trending in the right direction and that the treatment has been hugely effective. My free kappa at the start of the illness was 133,518 mg/L. At the half-way mark, it stands at only 1,827.0 mg/L. That is progress, although far away from 3.3 mg/L.

How am I feeling? Happy, of course! I have boldly all but weaned myself off the opioid. So, I am in pain. The pains in my bones and neck are quite severe, but I am feeling almost great. My head is clearer; I am stronger and working out like crazy (I would like to think). I still get exhausted and fatigued every day, but otherwise, just as the flakes float away from my dry skin to reveal new shiny growth beneath, so is cancer. It will be drifting away, and I declare this in Jesus' name. My fractured bones and damaged structure are getting ready for new super-growth that you will bear witness to someday. Will you give God thanks on my behalf, please?

CHAPTER 25

The Body of Christ

*Just as a body, though one, has many parts, but all its many parts
form one body, so it is with Christ. For we were all baptized by
one Spirit so as to form one body—whether Jews or Gentiles,
slave or free—and we were all given the one Spirit to drink.
Even so the body is not made up of one part but of many.*

—1 Corinthians 12:12-14 (NIV)

I wrote the post that follows out of sincere gratitude to my church
and to those who donated blood on my behalf and, most importantly, to our bishop's wife, Denise. There were three instances that
I had blood transfusions, twice while hospitalized and on my first
day of chemotherapy. Somehow my church was made aware of it,
and without a formal memorandum of understanding, or an elaborate affirmative response, Denise had organized a successful blood
drive on my behalf. In a matter of days, my wife brought home a
Certificate of Appreciation, indicating that a significant amount of
blood had been donated to the Red Cross in my name. Imagine, I
did not have to move a muscle to have this done. A body of Holy
Spirit-inspired members had joined with unity of purpose and effectively executed a plan to accomplish a feat that, in the world outside
the church, would require extensive planning, maneuvering, and
promotional activities to get done.

The action of my church positively demonstrated the power of love from a unified body and epitomized the virtues of the "body of Christ." The body of Christ should not be construed as referring to the physical body of Jesus Christ. At the Last Supper, Jesus blessed and broke the bread and gave it to his disciples, symbolically referring to it as His body in Mark 14:22. He instructed them to remember Him every time they gathered as they did then.

As Christians, we immortalize the memory of Jesus' death and resurrection for our salvation by partaking in the Communion celebration. The body of Christ represents Christians who, by accepting Jesus Christ as Lord and Savior, individually share the common pursuit of doing His will, thus, in unison, striving to please God. It is individuals, joined by the Holy Spirit, who create the body of Christ, as we see in 1 Corinthians 12:12-14 (NIV), "Just as a body, though one, has many parts, but all its many parts form one body, so it is with Christ. For we were all baptized by one Spirit so as to form one body—whether Jews or Gentiles, slave or free—and we were all given the one Spirit to drink. Even so, the body is not made up of one part but of many." Although I was physically sick and unable to be at church, I was still a member of the body of Christ.

Paul illustrates that each member of the body has a role to play. The members of our church remained convinced I still had a role to play regardless of my temporary inactivity and that my well-being was vital to a fully functional body. Paul further details the various roles individual members of the body can play. In 1 Corinthians 12:27-28 (ESV), he says, "Now you are the body of Christ and individually members of it. And God has appointed in the church first apostles, second prophets, third teachers, then miracles, then gifts of healing, helping, administrating, and various kinds of tongues." The will of God is fulfilled when each member accepts her/his role as an imperative to ensure the wholesomeness of each other.

Although I have many friends, who would give a lot to see me get well, they were not as organized or as unified as was the body of Christ represented by our church. Unselfishly, members were undaunted by the fact that I was unlikely to receive a single unit from that blood drive. They understood the depth of Leviticus 17:11 (KJV), "For the life of the flesh is in the blood." There were other lives that needed to be saved. In turn, those benefiting from their sacrifice could one day be witnesses to the most critical blood sacrifice of all—that of Jesus Christ. And by their sacrifice in faith, my recovery would be substantiated. At the time of writing the post that follows, I was very encouraged. The beautiful acts of generosity uplifted my spirit, and I looked forward to the day I would be healed and regain my place as a functioning member of the body of Christ in the church.

These days, many of us have become obsessed with our physical bodies. We are overly conscientious about what we intake to ensure perfect health and longevity. When we are in physically good health, we concern ourselves about our appearance. So perfect is the human body that many machines and devices we use try to mimic features and functions of the human body that God has "fearfully and wonderfully made."

The individual body can accomplish greatness when all its members work in harmony, each part doing the specific function for which it was designed. When all members of the human body do not work in harmony, illnesses and dysfunctionalities are among the consequences. We become miserable, chaos ensues, and outcomes are unpredictable. Because of cancer, there are many things I cannot do at this time that were generally routine for me. What about Christians as a segment of society? How do I relate "body" to this group of people?

Paul, the Apostle to the Gentiles, coined or popularized the concept of "the body of Christ," to which he made several references, such as in Romans 12:5, 1 Corinthians 12:12-27, Ephesians 3:6 and 5:23, and Colossians 1:18 and 1:24. Our Lord Jesus the Christ is the overall head of the church. Members who accept Him as Lord and Savior are referred to as the body of Christ. Each member serves as a functional element of the body. Although we are from diverse backgrounds with various skills, personalities, and talents, we are unified in Christ to form that whole, competent body. Paul illustrates that "the body" has not one but many parts, each uniquely performing functions complementing each other. I am a proud member of the body of Christ. I am a Christian individual and a member of my local assembly known as the East-West Church in Marietta, Georgia, which collectively functions as a body and a part of the body of Christ.

Our church demonstrated how the unified body of Christ can accomplish God's purpose. Through my regular postings on Facebook about my illness, the bishop's wife, Denise, became aware that the hospital administered blood to me as a part of my treatment. She contacted me advising that she could arrange for a blood drive to be made on my behalf. I gave very slight acknowledgment to the proposal as I was groggy and drained and hardly grasped the importance of her generosity at the time. And, after all, why should anyone devote such yeoman efforts on my behalf? Think of all the coordination, logistics, and getting willing volunteers to donate blood.

I had not been back to church since my illness, but that did not stop this great "body" unifying in purpose, without any effort on my part, to organize a blood drive. Before the deadline, the drive was 100% subscribed. That "Body of Love" to which I belong rose up with full motivation and donated 34 units of blood in my name. If my calculations are correct, it means that the contributions could impact the lives of 102 individuals—a phenomenal accomplishment. Note that I made no contribution or effort to this cause; all this came through LOVE from the incredible BODY OF CHRIST. It is highly unlikely I will receive any of this blood. However, I pray that anyone who benefits from this blood donation is made whole and gets a great revelation from the Divine God Almighty and goes on to develop a great appreciation for the unselfish love of the body of Christ.

Historically, and even more so today, the Church, Christians, and their leaders have been the subject of wide-ranging criticisms. Admittedly, some have merit. However, concrete examples like this illustrates why the name of Christ Jesus has to be continuously elevated above the distractions of critics. If the body of Christ is unified in purpose with "love," there is nothing it cannot do through Christ. The feeling of belonging gives hope and inspiration; my church and the loving members reinforce my conviction of God's love.

My healing is guaranteed and has been reinforced by the results from my third of four cycles. Last Friday, I got my third cycle results. It is now 500 "bad stuff." In context, my first readings were 133,518 mg/L, then just over 1,800, and now 500. Why would you not rejoice on my behalf and praise God for the body of Christ? You have been my persistent witnesses and supporters to date and bear witness to the hand of God on my life in various ways, not least of which is this unselfish act of generosity by my church. Through faith in Jesus Christ, I am a new creature; you will be my witnesses.

TO ALL WHO UNSELFISHLY DONATED
BLOOD ON MY BEHALF, PLEASE ACCEPT THE
DEEPEST AND MOST SINCERE GRATITUDE
AND AFFECTION BOTH FROM ME AND
ON BEHALF OF EACH RECIPIENT OF YOUR
PRECIOUS BLOOD. I PRAY THAT GOD WILL
GUIDE YOU INTO SOLUTIONS FOR YOUR
MOST PRESSING NEED.

I am not sure how easy it is for anyone else to appreciate what that act of unity and generosity meant to me, unless they were in my position. There I was, barely able to think or move; my only hope of staying alive was through faith. And here was a body of people expressing their confidence not just in me and my ability to fight the good fight of faith, but in the promise of Jesus Christ for my healing. That gave me even more courage to fight through all that confronted me. Their action encouraged and strengthened me. I was motivated to fight through the adversities and believe that God could move armies to my rescue if He needed to.

With great hope, I looked forward to the beautiful life I could expect after recovery, especially knowing there were good, caring people in the world who loved me. Their act of kindness has been indelibly etched in my mind. I keep reflecting on how beautiful this world would be if we all lived lives of selflessness. The concept of the body of Christ is foundational in most churches. Imagine a world where actions like these move beyond the boundaries of our churches and become standard behavior among people in general.

CHAPTER 26

My Next Stage

Let us hold fast the profession of our faith without
wavering; for he is faithful that promised.

—Hebrews 10:23 (KJV)

My postings were becoming less frequent because I did not believe I had anything new and exciting to communicate, and I was getting tired of whining about my aching body and pathetic state. Self-indulgence, solitary reflections, reading the gospels, and listening to selective teachings then meditating on them became the order of my days. Whatever would distract me from the pain demons that plagued me became my preoccupation. At times I felt like I was in monastic training. Oh yes, it was lonely—self-imposed loneliness mostly. However, from time to time, people would inquire why they no longer saw my posts. Some stated how much they missed the inspiration contained in the posts. It was reassuring to know these posts were considered significant in their own right and were not just about me. That was moving and gave me renewed inspiration to keep my followers up to date and informed. I still needed prayers of thanksgiving and words of encouragement, and it was hugely in my interest not to extinguish the beneficial flame I'd lit at the commencement of my illness. Maintaining my lifeline of encouragement would become even more important as I transitioned to other forms of treatment.

At each doctor's visit, I was overwhelmed with excitement to see my latest test results. I was anticipating improvements and better overall outcomes through faith, believing that the Lord's will for my healing would be progressively better and manifested to strengthen my faith. But, as I kept learning through this process, God never promised a smooth, progressive trend. The school of faith was in session, and I would be faced with new and varying challenges that I would need to appreciate as necessary incidentals to demonstrate my progress. In so doing, I was empowered to marshal the courage and strength needed to maintain faith in the process and not to yield to them in defeat. The more I bragged about the strength of my faith, the greater the challenges that arose. The resiliency and long-term endurance of my faith depended on the strength of the foundation on which it was established. For me to profess faith with any level of conviction after this, I had to appreciate that endurance was a part of my faith walk, and that God was honorable to His Word of providing healing through grace. If I was to fight the disease successfully, I needed to effectively use the sharp sword of the Spirit, weaponized with the Word of God.

Following my latest doctor's visit, I posted that my results showed a significant reversal in trend; it was in the wrong direction. What's worse, it was at the critical juncture where the course of chemotherapy was expected to end. The next stage was supposed to be the autologous stem cell transplant, and lower levels of "bad stuff" would be ideal. I was subjected to a barrage of tests, including scans, extensive blood evaluation, and the dreaded bone marrow biopsy. I recall how weak and exhausted I was in those days, when my lungs could not sustain me walking more than a few yards before I had to sit. I was always disoriented and confused. Sometimes it felt as if I was getting worse, not better. My physical reality was challenging my faith, even as I was being encouraged to stay strong, fight, and exercise my faith. I held on to the hope that God would not relinquish His hold on me and that His will was for me to be healed and reconstructed.

When the ominous dark clouds of the devil were poised to overwhelm me and envelop my faith, I would reach for reinforcement in trusted sources, such as my wife whom I regularly asked to relay excerpts from our bishop's message of the day, after she'd attended church. One particular Sunday, she related a point the bishop made about how easy it was for people to tell others how to have faith, regardless of what they were enduring, but how difficult it was to exercise that faith when faced with their own predicament. It was such a timely word in season for me as I was acutely able to relate to that truth then. I resolved not to lose my grip on the slippery slopes. Even if I slipped occasionally, as long as I did not completely let go, or allow myself to fall, I could keep climbing in faith. If I fell, there was still hope for me. All that was required was that I get back up with renewed faith in my pursuit and climb with even more vigor, confidence, and purpose. That injection of hope reinvigorated me to press on even stronger in faith. Jesus Christ knew the faith walk would be challenging, but He also knew how much I was able to bear.

Things were not as rosy as was expected. The next treatment protocol promised to be challenging. I did not know, for example, what the bone marrow transplant (BMT) process entailed; all I knew was that it was risky, and the most recent results did not help. I could not afford to loosen my grip on my faith in Jesus Christ. I had to accept that my expectations and times would not necessarily align with God's.

When I wrote the post that follows, I had psychologically prepared myself for the transplant, hoping that my healing was on the immediate horizon.

Time has flown by so speedily. I realize it has been more than a month since I last posted an update on my progress and treatment. Hopefully, by now, you have a sense of where I have been, and now you will have a perspective of what is planned for my near-term future. There should be no doubt that I have embraced God's healing for me and have a healthy appreciation and respect of "process." All processes of God are executed in His orderly manner to achieve His will and purpose. Humans introduced time as we know it so that they can frame and plan within a time domain and predict outcomes within that domain. As an example, God creates constancy and regularity in His creation, such as sunrise and sunset, and the seasons. They follow the orderly and timely operation of God. Humans then wrap time around it in hours, months, and years, to be able to plan, organize and understand things based on discrete time periods.

Just over three weeks now, I completed the final round of chemotherapy based on a scheduled four cycles. At the halfway mark, I reported that the bad stuff, as analyzed, had fallen from the initial 133,518 mg/L to 1,827.0 mg/L. Since then, I have had readings in the 500 and sub 300 mg/L levels. The last reading, however, indicated a reversal in that downward trend, showing an upward trajectory to more than 1,000 mg/L of bad stuff. Should I be concerned with the numbers? Well, it is not the best sign, but what does God say? In Judges 7, God demonstrated the inconsequence of numbers when he had determined a path to victory. With 300 men, Gideon was able to confuse and defeat the Midianites, Amalekites, and the sons of the east who were as numerous as locusts. So, whatever the number of bad stuff, and regardless of how they are trending, God can make large numbers into nothingness, and in my case, affect my healing as His process determines.

According to the oncologist, the outcome of my bone marrow biopsy will significantly influence further actions. Speaking of bone marrow biopsy, if you ever need to have one done (I pray you never will), don't pretend to be tough and opt for local anesthesia, as I did. Go for general. I was shocked when I realized last week that the gentle, unassuming physician's assistant (PA) would be using a drill to penetrate my flesh and drill through to my bone. When that drill hit my pelvic bone, I screamed like a teenager at a rock concert. Just imagine me biting into the pillow and begging her to stop. Extracting the bone marrow sample was not much fun either. It felt as though every substance in my body was being pulled out. It was a very exhausting day anyway, considering that only a few minutes before the biopsy I had had countless tubes of blood withdrawn and, just before that, a full body imaging.

I think I have completed the required chemotherapy protocol for this stage, so, I guess the next step is to go to the bone barrow transplant (BMT) team. I have been transferred from the oncology team to the bone marrow transplant unit. I have been subjected to a series of tests and prep work, all leading to hospitalization for the transplant. For that process, I will be induced with certain drugs for a period to liberate stem cells from my bone marrow into my bloodstream. My stem cells will be harvested and frozen to be transplanted in me later. I was advised that later this week an access port will be implanted in my chest, through which my blood will be extracted, the stem cells siphoned and frozen, then the remaining blood will be restored to my body. Depending on the desired amount of stem cells required by the transplant team, the harvesting could span several 6-8 hour days.

After successful harvesting, by the end of October, I will be admitted to the hospital for a few weeks. During this time, I will be treated with an extra-strong dose of chemotherapy, the aim of which is to wipe out all remaining cancer cells. This process, however, is destructive. In addition to attacking the bad stuff, it will deplete my bone marrow, leaving my body completely defenseless and vulnerable to almost everything. Also, many of my useful cells could be destroyed, and this poison could damage several of my organs. It is anticipated that my body could be grossly compromised, which is why they must administer RESCUE therapy by infusing the previously removed stem cells into my body. As you can imagine, interactions with people will have to be restricted after this procedure. My body will be defenseless, so there will be even tighter restrictions on my activities.

I believe my healing is guaranteed through Jesus the Christ. I also accept the universal laws of nature. If I expose myself to anything that may cause me harm, it could be devastating as my body is defenseless. The same God who empowered a defenseless boy named David to slay a fully armored giant will protect me and give me victory over this illness. The will and purpose of the Lord God the Almighty will be done.

I am further comforted by your fervent and unceasing prayers. As in James 5:16, I believe you will continue to pray that I am healed because the effectual fervent prayers of you, my devoted well-wishers, avail much through Jesus the Christ.

CHAPTER 27

Bah, Humbug

The righteous cry out, and the LORD hears them; he delivers
them from all their troubles. The LORD is close to the
brokenhearted and saves those who are crushed in spirit.
The righteous person may have many troubles, but the LORD
delivers him from them all; he protects all his bones.

—Psalm 34:17-20 (NIV)

After being transferred to the bone marrow transplant (BMT) unit, I had longer commutes, my times at the clinic were more frequent, with more extended hours, and I was subjected to much more testing. I became easily disoriented and found it difficult to follow directions or navigate the hospital complex, no matter how many times I went there. Had my wife not been with me, I would have been hopelessly lost. It was an astonishingly sad state. What was worse, I couldn't keep pace with her, even at her slowest. As we walked from one department to the next, she had to stop and wait for me every few steps. I would be quickly out of breath and lethargic. It was unbelievable how incapacitated I was. The chemo brain and the side effects of the medicines were wreaking havoc on my physical and mental well-being.

I was at the pretransplant stage, being evaluated and treated to undergo autologous stem cell transplant. According to the oncology team, I had failed the first line of treatment and as a next step needed to have the transplant. As a point of information, there are two types of stem cell transplant. The Dana-Farber Cancer Institute differentiates them as follows:

An autologous transplant uses a person's own stem cells. In this procedure, stem cells are collected from the patient and frozen in liquid nitrogen before transplant conditioning. Stem cells are intrinsically healthy, and they are collected to allow blood cell recovery after the administration of high-dose therapy that would otherwise irreversibly damage them. Following conditioning treatment, the patient's stem cells are returned to the body to help it produce healthy red and white blood cells and platelets.

An allogeneic transplant, on the other hand, uses stem cells from a donor whose human leukocyte antigens (HLA) are acceptable matches to the patient's. The stem cell donor may be related to the patient or may be an unrelated volunteer found through a donor registry, such as the National Marrow Donor Program.

After reading both official literature and reviews from others who had undergone the procedure, I was not totally optimistic about it. I had a childlike curiosity about the process, and that was it. I hoped the doctors knew best and had the professional expertise and competencies to administer the treatment. But I trusted that having surrendered my course to God and functioning exclusively under His guidance, He would direct it all for my best outcome. I was so thrilled they had secured the correct quantity of the required blood product in one procedure, I could not resist posting the following somewhat whimsical account on Facebook.

> The truth is, the past couple of weeks have NOT been fun. You'd think that after chemo I would be home free. What's the big deal with stem cell transplant anyway?
>
> Check this out. I have to rise before the first rooster's crow, then fight traffic for almost 30 miles to the hospital, where I am practically ripped to shreds before I leave. Yes! I have been prodded

(EKG and Echo), probed (colonoscopy), drained (blood work), drilled (bone marrow biopsy), lit up (more than enough X-rays, CT scans, and MRIs to make me glow in the dark) and, as if that isn't enough, been injected with so many different drugs, I would fail every drug test. So, you think I am whining? Try being pierced up to six different times each day to deliver a myriad of drugs, all in the name of getting me prepared to harvest and transplant stem cells.

Still want more? Check this out: last Friday I had my first surgery to implant some fancy device known as a tri-fusion catheter; Sunday, my day of rest and worship, I had to show up to have seemingly gallons of blood drawn and then be injected with some weird drug cocktail. Finally, today I spent almost six hours on a fancy device. I think they call it a hemapheresis machine. Don't be too impressed; it's just a little thingamajig used to extract blood, separate and collect stem cells, and return the remaining blood to my body.

Now if you promise to keep this between us, I am sharing a picture of this machine (Appendix II). If you look at it closely, you may see a fine specimen of a man hooked up to it today (Yeah right, a specimen is all that I am right now) but check out that fancy gown I am modeling. I want one for Christmas. The color is spot on, goes well with my blue bunny slippers. Oh yeah, have you noticed that I have regained most of the weight I lost earlier this year?

So, this hemapheresis procedure was scheduled for up to four days to collect eight million stem cells. Guess who your perfunctory overachiever was? Not to brag, but I produced thirteen million of those fertile stem cells in one day!

Please! Hold the applause and awards. So, tell me, who has God blessed and favored in every possible way? Meanwhile, I need to get rid of this excruciating headache. Let me go and meditate on the words my wife comforted me with last night before today's procedure.

CHAPTER 28

Setbacks or Opportunities

Consider it pure joy, my brothers and sisters, whenever you face trials of many kinds, because you know that the testing of your faith produces perseverance. Let perseverance finish its work so that you may be mature and complete, not lacking anything.

—James 1:2-4 (NIV)

Even though I faithfully believed God's will was being accomplished for my good with setbacks and delays, I was disappointed. I was tired of chemotherapy, the biweekly trips to the infusion center and, most of all, the side effects of the medications. I longed to taste food again and to be rid of nausea. I wanted to be removed from under the fog of cognitive disablement and be able to walk again without pain and dyspnea (breathlessness). The results of the test, however, apparently did not meet specifications. I had relapsed even before I went into remission. Since the chemotherapy cocktail had not achieved the expected goals, I would be administered a new line of therapy, meaning a different set of chemotherapy medications. To undergo chemotherapy again was absolute misery.

That setback was not just about the delay in my healing process, but also about how aggressive the cancer was. A few weeks without medication, and the remnant rogue cells were at their prolific best, multiplying so rapidly as to cause a drastic reversal in my readings. As

I would later learn from the BMT doctor, mine was a very aggressive form of the disease. As I understood it then, over time, these rogue cells develop a defense mechanism to the cancer treatment, rendering the current therapy ineffective. With a new set of chemotherapy drugs, I hoped God would be merciful to me and I would get to the stage where my test results would satisfy the requirements for autologous stem cell transplant.

A colleague told me his wife had recently been through the transplant procedure and was doing quite well. That made me so very optimistic that soon, I too, would have excellent outcomes. I prayed the new line of chemotherapy drugs would be effective so that I could get through to the transplant phase. Who could blame me if I chose to lament over the disappointing news? However, Nehemiah 8:10 assures me that the joy of the Lord is my strength. So, I accepted that joy was from God planted in my spirit, but my reaction was the emotional response of the flesh, over which I had control. My fleshly mind evoked negative emotions, but I chose not to accept them.

"The mind governed by the flesh is death, but the mind governed by the Spirit is life and peace. The mind governed by the flesh is hostile to God; it does not submit to God's law, nor can it do so," according to Romans 8:6-7 (NIV). So even as negative emotions were rising within me, I chose to be positive. My confidence was that God foreknew and had predestined me for healing and that all things were working together for good because I was called to His purpose, according to Romans 8:28-29. I had no doubt I was still in God's favor and that, with enduring faith, God's will would be accomplished. It was with this assurance and optimism that I shared my next post.

> Based on my recent posts, you should have expected that I would be hospitalized this week for stem cell transplant, as was prescribed by my doctors. Well, that won't be the case. Recent results indicate that my bad numbers have reversed, meaning that the trend of bad stuff is

increasing. The trend reversal is not new news. I had personally noticed it and highlighted it in a previous post titled "Next Stage of Treatment." Even though I raised it as a concern to the oncologist at that time, he had not seen it as the ultimate determinant to influence any change in my course of treatment. Oh well, doctor knows best!

Chemo again! Yes! I will have to be subjected to that horrible chemotherapy once more, maybe up to three more months. I am NOT excited about that. I was starting to feel like a living human again, with the restoration of physical and cognitive/mental capabilities.

So that is the report of "man." I wonder what God says? You, Team Facebook, and I have been united in our approach as instructed by Psalm 18:6. We agreed that in my distress I should call to the LORD for help, and you have assured me continuously I am in your prayers. We know that God has heard our prayers; our prayers came before Him, into His ears. That being the case, through faith I believe, as Philippians 4:6-7 advises, that I should not worry about anything; instead, I should pray about everything, tell God what I need and thank Him for all He has done. In fact, I have moved beyond mere hope to earnest expectation for my healing.

Rather than viewing this recent news as a setback, I believe it is an opportunity for God's work. First, consider my long-term recovery. I would not be happy if I had gone through the transplant only to later realize that I had an aggressive form of cancer that would return after the transplant. Therefore, our omniscient God, knowing all things, allows this opportunity for everything to be revealed upfront and be dealt with once and for all. I will not sit around worrying. God is love, and He knows what sways my emotional impulse in the wrong direction. It is not His will that I should suffer.

Jeremiah 29:11 declares that He knows the plans He has for me, plans to prosper me and not to harm me, and plans to give me hope and a great future. What then should be my stance, all things considered? I will let 2 Corinthians 1:3-6 advise me, "Praise be to the God and Father of our Lord Jesus Christ, the Father of compassion and the God of all comfort, who comforts us in all our troubles, so that we can comfort those in any trouble with the comfort we ourselves receive from God. For just as we share abundantly in the sufferings of Christ, so also our comfort abounds through Christ. If we are distressed, it is for your comfort and salvation; if we are comforted, it is for your comfort, which produces in you patient endurance of the same sufferings we suffer."

"What, me worry?" No, I walk boldly in faith, fully trusting that my future is secured in Christ. Matthew 6 advises me not to worry about life because God in heaven knows my needs and will provide. What sweet hope. So, OK then! Bring on chemo again. If that is God's prescription, let's do it. Then, stay tuned and see the results and God's report.

CHAPTER 29

Introspection in the Desert Place

Yea, though I walk through the valley of the shadow of death,
I will fear no evil: for thou art with me; thy
rod and thy staff they comfort me.

—Psalm 23:4 (KJV)

The medical reports had started to inform my state of mind. The cumulative negative news, setbacks and disappointments over time would periodically leave me dispirited and questioning the strength of my faith. The frequently bad news fed my natural tendency to rationalize and speculate on logical outcomes that were not in line with what I believed. I was at times tempted to ask whether I was denying my reality. I was clinging to the mystifying concept called faith, expecting its power to produce some phenomenal solution that would confront and mitigate the source of disappointing news before it impacted me. Wasn't the testing of my faith supposed to produce perseverance, according to the Bible? After so much progress walking diligently, I was allowing my human, fleshly reasoning ability to distract me from my purpose and destiny. During these challenging periods, I had to summon the power of my soul and spirit into willful action to mitigate the overpowering negative influences that were challenging my faith.

My journey had been extended, and I longed for a sense of wellness. I had to keep reminding myself I was no longer in control or on my designated timeline, that I had committed it all to Jesus. The knowledge that He understands human frailty and knows that fear and panic would always be trying to overwhelm me throughout this lengthy process was reassuring. I took comfort in Psalm 103:14 (NASB), "For He Himself knows our frame; He is mindful that we are but dust."

Understandably, those days of sickness were like walking in an endless desert with mirages of hope that vanished when I reached for them. My natural impulse was to crave more tangible evidence of my assured healing. Of course, I was mindful that 2 Peter 3:9 says God is not slow in fulfilling His promises; but like David in Psalm 13:1, who asked of the Lord, "How long, O Lord? Will you forget me forever?" I grew weary and felt deserted and would contemplate what I could do to help myself. Such is humankind. Back in Biblical antiquity, Abraham and his wife felt the wait for the promised child was too long and they intervened. It resulted in major family conflicts and abandonment. God did not need their help in executing His plan then, and He certainly did not need mine now.

It was always so helpful, however, when the Holy Spirit within me spoke. He is my timely Helper. In a still, small voice, I would be reminded of how far I had come in faith on this journey. It was not the time to try to wrest control from God. I needed to wait on the Lord because He would renew my strength, so that I would be able to run and not be weary and walk without fainting, as Isaiah 40:31 tells us. This process was not by my design and not within the purview or control of Mr. Fix It. Rather than trying to strong-arm the process, which would return me to my peevish, irritable state, I needed to persevere in faith because, as Matthew 24:13 teaches, "The one who endures to the end will be saved." To be saved from the destruction of my affliction, I needed to reflect on the goodness of God to me and the hope I had in His promises. Each setback was an opportunity for God to clear the way for my progress. Every time I stumbled, He picked me up. I was assured that I could depend on Him, validating His Word in Isaiah 41:13 (NIV), "For I am the LORD your God who takes hold of your right hand and says to you, Do not fear; I will help you."

It is incredible then how when I meditated under the guidance of the Holy Spirit, I could see more victories than defeat. My desert experience then was a place of learning. The footprints of God were everywhere, and His right hand was always outstretched to guide me; even more, He was leading me each step of the way. My reflections below represented an outpouring of my heart, guided by the Spirit, as I looked back at the milestones God had led me past. I was telling my story, which made it so easy for me to write. The metaphorical desert represents my struggles through this illness and draws from my whole life experience. It was my heartfelt prayer reminding God about me, His suffering child; offering thanksgiving for how He had taken care of me in the past; and appealing to Him for His compassion. It was also a reminder to me that if He did then, I could believe in faith that He would be there to deliver me from that place of sickness desert.

Introspection in the Desert Place

As I walk through this desert, its parts are unknown;
Lord, help me to share the lessons I now know.
From fear into faith, Your way now is clear.
This desert is barren, O God, help me carry on
The scars on my feet are of burns from the heat,
The taste of my sweat, living waters refresh.
When things get so horrid with me, please do tarry
With a cloud by my tent, no evil shall harry.
I win, and I lose, I pass, and I fail
You save me from perish, that life I may relish.
When the journey is tiresome, then, God, You are awesome
Your angels You send, to them I can vent.
With the terror of death no longer a threat
When death was at my door, then Christ I implored
The splendor of life has an enduring allure
But Jesus, my Lord, of You I want more.
Those onions and leeks, I no longer seek

Past deeds that were sweet, I lay at Your feet.
When I spoke profane, I felt all insane
I sought much to gain, but my life was in vain
The times spent in sin, You were nowhere within
For these I repent, my soul please defend.
Hope is eternal through mercies and grace
Lord, let me not waste, so I'll see Your great face.
I've grasped for illusions where there was profusion
This desert's a fusion, of all things confusion.
With struggles persistent, You, God, are consistent
On You I'm insistent, and not on my sixth sense
Secure me, O Lord, and please be my guard
I seek no award but Your richest reward.
Lord lead me by faith as humbly I quake
With pure childlike innocence, I offer my penitence.
Your words have new meanings; with joy, I absorb them
I ask not for pride, my thoughts You please guide.
Time has no essence; Your good work is the key
Like purifying of silver, keep working in me
Lord, make me so shiny, Your image to show
In deserts and mountains, I'll effervescently glow.

Reviewing the preceding poem took me back to that place of cognitive dysfunctionality. I was weak and submissive. The chemo fog was weighing heavily on my brain, and the side effects of the medicines were wreaking all kinds of havoc on me. I did not need the added disappointment that I had relapsed to the extent that I would have to go back to chemotherapy before I could have the transplant. I needed reassurance from God that my healing was still on track. It was time for me to pour my heart out to God, reminding Him of all the times I had wandered away to the attractions of the world and how He chose to draw me back to Him. I felt the need to remind God that I was still His child, waiting in suffering. If I expressed to Him how grateful I was for all those times He had rescued me when I called upon Him previously, He would hear me and be gracious and merciful to me again in my time of need. I needed Him to remember me. If by any stretch of imagination or in reality I had heard His promises for my healing, then I wanted to remind Him as Isaiah 43:26 (ESV) guides, "Put me in remembrance; let us argue together; set forth your case, that you may be proved right."

God knows my tomorrows and what challenges will confront me. His grace will allow me to survive the barren desert and be stronger and better for the experience, and for that, I prayed.

CHAPTER 30

Giving Thanks

In everything give thanks: for this is the will of
God in Christ Jesus concerning you.

—1 Thessalonians 5:18 (KJV)

It was Thanksgiving Day, so I was moved by a sense of personal gratitude to God, my friends, and followers. I felt compelled to let it be known. I was tolerating the new chemotherapy medications much better and the side effects were more bearable. I was thinking more clearly and was less fatigued and sleepy. The pains too were subsiding, so I had every reason to be thankful. Even moving around had become less challenging. Of course, I was still impaired and in pain, but I was much better. Having had such a prolonged experience of awfulness, I was appreciative of the slightest feeling of improvement. Relative to how I was during the past months, I felt ecstatic. I was happy and thankful. My spirits were high, and I was greatly encouraged. Finally, I could share joy, not just the anguish, hurt, and threat of impending disaster I had feared over the past months. How could I not share this with those who were the pillars of encouragement for me?

If there is anyone who has every reason to give thanks today, it is I. God has guided me through unfamiliar circumstances and situations. He stabilized me when I was debilitated physically and mentally and protected me in my vulnerable and defenseless state. Suffering and helplessness made me surrender in humility. I had to let go and let God. He took control and is taking me through a process of transformation. Today, I am here at peace, and I am grateful. I am doing better by the hour, and I am thankful to God that He chose me for something special that is yet to be completely understood. What I know is that all this experience is for something good. God is good.

Today I thank God for allowing me to have this experience that I am still being schooled in, and for the things I have learned through the process. I have been changed by them, and I look forward in faith to a new life ahead. I thank God for you. I have chosen to reflect on the positive benefits of going through this sickness. Otherwise, I may miss so much good, such as the beautiful side of people shown through love. Each of you, my friends, has been contributing to the process of my healing in your individual, unique and remarkable way. And I relish the fruit of your spirits as therapy.

In my state of helplessness, you adopted me with love. You expressed your love and faith through constant prayers, cards, positive feedback to my postings, and support of every kind. You gave me hope and encouragement. You promised to pray for me continuously. With that, you strengthened my faith and encouraged me beyond my natural capability. I told you that God's will would be manifested through me as a witness of His goodness. I can tell that I am getting much better. I THANK YOU ALL.

Your treasures are in God's keeping, and you can unlock the treasure chest with your faith. Here, I offer my note of sincere gratitude and thanksgiving for all your tireless support of me and my family. For every prayer you have prayed for me, I pray that God will count it toward your worthiness, because each is an act of faith.

As far as updates are concerned, I was able to attend Wednesday and Sunday services a few weeks ago, as I was between chemotherapy treatment and I had faith that my weakened immune system would tolerate the exposure. Thank God I went because I was very blessed. Taking Communion, receiving prayers from the bishop, and the warmth extended to me by everyone was not just spiritually refreshing but physically healing. My cognitive competencies have improved. My clarity of thought and my faith are stronger, and I am proving God's love more each day. Today, we celebrate Thanksgiving; I thank God for everything. I thank you for your compassion for me.

It is interesting how the little things we take for granted can become enormous treasures when we no longer have them. I could list the host of things I was grateful for when I wrote the preceding Thanksgiving post. Simple clarity of thought and the ability to walk, eat, and move about with less pain were miracles for me. The awakened discernment to recognize and appreciate common human virtues I once took for granted, I accepted as enlightenment from God. Most of all, the fact that our loving Father had brought together a devoted, diverse group of friends to cheer me on through my challenges, was heartening. Very basic things I had generally taken for granted, having lost them for a while and now seeing evidence of their return, were incremental highpoints I appreciated immensely. This was my first significant illness, and I had never ever lost so much before. I could appreciate the significance of being a fully functional human being, as well as the positive contributions of support and encouragement. The significance of a sustainable faith walk with God and His desire that I should not perish, which are vital imperatives found in the Word of Jesus Christ, had helped me to appreciate a purpose-focused life.

CHAPTER 31

Merry Christmas and Year-End Update

He came to that which was his own, but his own did not receive him. Yet to all who did receive him, to those who believed in his name, he gave the right to become children of God.

—John 1:11-12 (NIV)

Being Christmas, when most Christians celebrate the birth of Christ, I chose to reflect on how Jesus Christ came to us and was rejected. How apropos that our landscaping team would present me with such an analogy to demonstrate Jesus the Christ coming to earth, being rejected by His chosen people, but gladly embraced by others.

My first cycle of the new chemotherapy drug was complete, and the BMT team advised me that I had to have an autologous stem cell transplant posthaste. According to the BMT doctor, I had an aggressive form of cancer. That was not very encouraging. However, confident the God I served had an aggressive kind of cure, I refused to make discouragement linger or daunt the prospects of my healing or ruin my Christmas. Just for once, I would give anything for a comment of hope. People with other forms of cancer would be told that after a certain course of treatments they would likely go into remission, but not me. To be reassured that after the stem cell transplant there would be a guarantee of remission would have been helpful. Regardless, I was scheduled to undergo the risky and rigorous procedure in the New Year. But I accepted that the procedure would be good for me and clung to the belief that I would come through it successfully, led by the hand of my Lord God. Not a bad way to end the year. The New Year would mean new birth for me, and so I posted this Christmas update.

> With not too many exciting changes happening, I thought I should be quiet for a while. Before I give my update, I will share a personal anecdote about a different take on Christmas as I experienced it this morning.
>
> Since becoming ill, I have not been able to manicure my lawn as I was accustomed to. So I hired a professional, and he showed up with an assistant this morning to do the job. While they were working, I thought of how I could make his Christmas special. I descended into the storehouse and retrieved one of my exceptional vintages, bagged it in one of those lovely wine bags with frills and Christmas decoration. With great excitement, I presented the gentleman with this beautiful gift, with high expectations of an Oscar-like acceptance speech. Much to my dismay, he exclaimed, "I don't drink, but maybe my assistant could use it." Before I could object (if I wanted to) his assistant, who was a few feet away, had gleefully grabbed that bottle with such speed I did not have time to raise a protest.
>
> What does your wine story have to do with Christmas? you may ask. You see, my bottle of vintage was special to me. By giving this gentleman this special gift, I thought it would likewise be valuable to him and he would appreciate it. Likewise, God thought of His special peo-

ple. Jesus the Christ was His special gift. Jesus the Christ, Emmanuel, Messiah, a part of the incomprehensible triune, manifested Himself in mortality so that He could live with humans for a time. Did His chosen people wholeheartedly accept Him? No! He came to His own, and His own received Him not. Some Jews did. We, as non-Jewish people, are fortunate to be offered the opportunity for salvation and heirship of God by accepting the "rejected Christ." Some Christians choose to celebrate this time of year as his birth or manifestation here on earth. Just as the lawn care assistant enthusiastically claimed the wine and will hopefully enjoy and cherish every drop, we who claim Christ and Christmas should cherish and enjoy every day with gratitude to God.

Update: In previous updates, I informed you that I had begun a new regime of chemotherapy using different drugs and protocols. Part of the game plan was for me to participate in a clinical trial for new (experimental) medications. That will not be happening at this time. The decision has been made for me to be hospitalized in January for stem cell transplant. The bad news: they anticipate that after this process, I will need chemo indefinitely.

As I stated in earlier postings, I feel better by the day. Most of my pains and issues are centered in the area of my neck/spine. I am comfortable with the decisions made by the doctors; after all, with all the earnest prayers from you, I am assured that I should only expect positive outcomes from God the Father as a result of this process. I will reiterate, Jeremiah 29:11 declares that He knows the plans He has for me, plans to prosper me and not to harm me, and plans to give me hope and a great future.

This year for me has been transformational and humbling; certain realities confronted me that I could never have otherwise fathomed. I have experienced things that were incredible, painful, and uniquely spiritual. The sudden onset of the disease forced me into making changes I hadn't planned on or could have foreseen, yet there have been so many positive aspects. I have a better appreciation of love. Through this journey, God has allowed me to understand the value of the simplest of things and to appreciate His awesomeness.

I wish I could thank everyone individually, but as best as you can, please accept a simple THANK YOU. Just doing what you did made the pains more bearable, helped with my sanity, and developed my faith. Since everything is created for God's pleasure, then as evil as cancer is, by afflicting me, I have been able to see God's goodness in humanity and creation.

My prayers are that you and your families will enjoy the best Christmas ever, appreciating Jesus, and that God will make your New Year the best that you have had so far.

CHAPTER 32

Finished Work

Until now you have asked nothing in my name. Ask,
and you will receive, that your joy may be full.

—John 16:24 (ESV)

Precisely what made me use the analogy of painting and display a picture of one in the post that follows, I really cannot recall. Maybe I needed assurance, or recognition, or perhaps I genuinely wanted to cement in my mind the concept of the "finished work" through this process. What I knew for sure was that my hospitalization would be the next day, and it was another step in the realm of mysteries. I was hoping the operation would commence the finished work of God healing me. I prayed that I would come through it successfully. My paintings, when finished, could accrue financial gains to me. Jesus the Christ, through His finished work, provided for my healing and other blessings.

The next few weeks for me represented the juncture at which significant changes could happen. The objective was to be rid of the bad myeloma cells by removing my old bone marrow and implanting functional stems cells to make good plasma cells. My miseries would be over, and this disease would retreat into remission precursory to my eventual complete healing—what better way could there be to start the year? I would have a great testimony, and the witnesses to my suffering would have every reason to proclaim the goodness of God through faith. The professionals performing the upcoming operation would validate the effectiveness of current science. While waiting, I posted the following prehospitalization update.

> Some of you know that one of my favorite hobbies is oil painting. I paint various subjects, from portraits to landscapes to abstracts. I am not sure what type of painter I am by classical definitions, but I love to paint.
>
> Tucked away in our basement where I paint are several unfinished paintings. At some point in time, I would love to transform them into "finished works." Some of them may have potential financial value. But without finishing these paintings, I may not derive any financial reward for my efforts. Knowing this, I need to act to complete them so that they become marketable. So, from my finished works, I may earn money that will empower me to acquire other things of value that satisfy our wants and needs.
>
> One of the biggest challenges I have as a non-professional artist is determining when a painting becomes a finished work. I have never reached the point where I am completely satisfied that my work is finished. I am always very critical of every painting I do and can always find something else to modify and make better (and in some cases worse). So, I am thinking why not get help? I am inviting *you* to be the judge of one of these paintings so that I can have a finished work by consensus. Tell me what you think. Vote "yes" to let me know if you think it is a finished work, otherwise vote "no".
>
> There is a more significant and universal "finished work" that was not done by consen-

sus and it avails much to us all; in fact, it avails all we need. For many Christians like me, we believe this was accomplished by Christ Jesus through blood sacrifice. Jesus the Christ gave up his human life (Luke 23:46). He confidently declared that His work on earth for that time was thoroughly done when He said in John 19:30, "It is finished." Later, He spiritually resurrected himself to human form before returning to His place in glory. That act represents the "finished work." This "finished work" empowers believers through faith to obtain all good things for our human and spiritual needs by Christ. Things like healing, peace, prosperity, and all the abundance of God. To benefit, one must first recognize this "finished work" of God and accept it. As for me, by faith, I rest in the confidence that I will have my needs met through the "finished work." Tomorrow, I will be hospitalized for a few weeks.

As I have previously detailed, my treatment will involve a high dosage of strong chemotherapy followed by stem cell transplant. So far, we have prayed for my healing. God's agents at the hospital will align their human works with His directives and treat me by His perfect will. We are agreed that it is God's will for me to be healed. I will walk out of that institution a new birth. Through faith, I will reap of the finished work of Christ Jesus. You will be my witnesses and brag with me about my complete healing in time. Please never cease praying for me, as I do for you, so that we will continually benefit from the finished work of Jesus the Christ.

From what I had read, autologous stem cell transplant was not a typical, run-of-the-mill procedure. It involved killing all my bone marrow, effectively reducing my blood supply and depleting the antibodies that protect me from diseases. But despite it being a risky procedure, I was not scared. I welcomed the prospects of the outcome. To be cleansed of the source of cancer and be infused with the seeds for new, perfect stem cells to produce healthy, cancer-free blood cells was worth any risk. My mind was more focused on the end of cancer. The finished work would be the successful outcome of this high-risk procedure.

So, upon reflection, I guess I wanted to complete a painting before I went through the operation as a sign of hope. It would remind me of Jesus ending His sojourn on earth and bringing future hope for humanity. Maybe I also wanted a confidence booster before the operation. I wanted to emerge from the procedure as an example of God's finished work through my healing. The positive responses I had to this post were extremely encouraging. I went into the hospital with the firm belief that, after the transplant, I would manifest the finished work of God. God was the Master Painter, and I trusted He would apply the final brushstrokes to obliterate cancer so that His artistry in me would be exemplary of His finished work.

CHAPTER 33

Through the Valley of Dry Bones

*The hand of the LORD was on me, and he brought me out by
the Spirit of the LORD and set me in the middle of a valley; it
was full of bones. He led me back and forth among them, and I
saw a great many bones on the floor of the valley, bones that were
very dry. He asked me, "Son of man, can these bones live?"*

—Ezekiel 37:1-3 (NIV)

I n this next post, I was hoping to provide an objective review of my
stem cell transplant. I didn't think it necessary to lay out the gory
details. Everyone apparently has different challenges and outcomes,
so my experience could very well differ from the general population
of transplant patients. The few people I knew who went through the
process had had excellent results, and in fact, some went into remission not long after. I did not relish a single moment of the procedure,
neither would I care to relive any part of it. I was still seething from
the experience when I wrote the post and indicated that I did not
enjoy talking about it.

The best analogy I can provide is as follows: Imagine a graph
shaped like a bathtub, downward sloping, then flattening out for
some time, then gradually rising to form the upward side of the tub.
Such was my life cycle for the period during the transplant process. A
summary of my transplant experience follows. Very high-dosage che-

motherapy was administered to me on my first night of admission; melphalan was the chemotherapy drug used. Then I was transfused with my previously extracted stem cells. Chewing on ice for hours is not the tastiest fare; however, it was recommended, and I did so while being administered the chemotherapy to help prevent mouth and throat soreness.

As the days progressed, the effects of chemotherapy started to impact my whole being. Just as the graph slopes downward, so were both good and bad cells dying, and my body began to feel as if I was creeping toward a slow death. The strong dosage of chemotherapy was purposed to attack and destroy all fast-multiplying cells, like those in the linings of the mouth (causing mouth sores), in the stomach, and other areas where there are rapidly multiplying cells.

With the progression of time, my health degraded. Referencing the bathtub graph again, this stage of the process would be beyond the downward sloping side of the bathtub toward the flattened stage, referred to by some as the bottoming-out stage. That was the danger zone, when most of my bone marrow and other cells were destroyed. I ached so much and was so fatigued, I found it a challenge to stay awake. But my body told me in no uncertain terms where I was on the graph. I call it the near-death stage, and it was here that I had what I called the "dry bone" experience. Note: this is my term for it. I felt as though I was being battered and pounded from both inside and out; I was totally wiped out. At regular intervals throughout this process, my blood samples were taken and analyzed. The analysis indicated the rate of cell destruction.

After the bottoming-out stage, the results became even more critical. They were keenly observed for indications as to whether the infused stem cells had been successfully grafted and the rate of new cell production. The infusion of stem cells was a rescue procedure because the chemotherapy had destroyed the existing cells in my bones, which could mean death. Without the protection of my antibodies, I was vulnerable to attacks from basically everything. Visitors were only allowed in my hospital room under rigorous protocols.

The side effects were real. Every inch of my body hurt, and nausea and diarrhea ruled, so eating was almost impossible. To top it all off, I was expected to exercise every day; now, that was painful! I wondered how Joe, a very pleasant and courteous fellow patient, was able to take all that misery in his stride as though he were comfortably piloting his plane. Maybe it was a reflection of his resilient faith, which he and his wife were never shy to speak about.

A successful transplant is supposed to mimic the upward slope of the graph. As soon as specific parameters from the test results indicated that the new blood cells had grafted and were growing satisfactorily, I was discharged. Regular outpatient follow-up was mandated. From that point forward, I was sent into isolation at home because, with my immune system so severely compromised, I was vulnerable to be hurt by almost every living organism on earth. I was too weak and listless to want to leave my bed anyway.

Nonetheless, I was able to pen my first post-transplant update after leaving the hospital. Speaking of pen, post-transplant, I had completely lost my ability to write. For months, I could not correctly form the letters of the alphabet. My penmanship was completely gone for the first time in my life. I wanted to send thank-you responses to the people who had sent me get-well cards and ended up laughing stupidly when I realized it was just not happening. It took me quite some time before I could personally chicken-scratch a response to those who had diligently sent me cards throughout my illness. Thanks to touch screen technology, I was able to post the following:

> I felt as though my bones were made dry during my recent high-dose stem cell transplant. The unwanted cancerous cells and, to a large extent, my bone marrow, were destroyed, and my dry bones were infused with life-giving stem cells. As a reminder, blood and platelets are products of the bone marrow. The objective of my treatment was to remove the bad cells and their sources and empower my bones with fresh capabilities to make functional cells
>
> How great is our God that even though He does not walk among us healing the sick, He

equips us with the knowledge to assist in healing? Imagine being able to completely remove the defense mechanism that you need to live, and then using these multipurpose stem cells to reproduce the cells that were destroyed. Stem cells are characterized by their potency, or their potential to differentiate into different cell types; specifically, they can create oxygen-carrying red blood cells, infection-fighting white blood cells, and clot-forming platelets. In my case, all my cells were impacted. At the bottoming-out stage, my white blood cells became almost undetectable (destroyed by the high-dosage chemo medicine).

I am now home, after 15 days in the hospital and almost a full day in the outpatients' department. I feel as though a tornado has devastated my body. Would I like to discuss all I experienced during this process here? No! Maybe one-on-one to someone either scheduled to go through the procedure or someone who has already been through it. I shall no longer characterize my stay at this hospital as going to enjoy "the resort experience." Sigh! Suffice it to say, the caregivers were terrific, and I did meet a wonderful Christian couple, and we shared our faith conviction about the power of healing through faith.

A good outcome of this recent experience is that, by the hour, I already feel marked improvements. Sometimes I believed I could get up and run for a while. But I am still very vulnerable, and the doctors' restrictions are firm and many. That means I must love from afar, for now, so you can see me later healthier, vibrant and handsomer (if that were possible).

Your prayers avail much. Your support and encouragement have given me strength. I am your witness of the healing powers of God the Almighty. Thank you, thank you, and thank you. Next step: I will be tested through various means—blood work, radiography, and biopsy—so that I can be restaged from stage 3 cancer to cancer free (which I claim). Praise God the Almighty to whom only, I offer all worship.

CHAPTER 34

Recovering from Transplant

The LORD is thy keeper: the LORD is thy shade upon thy right hand.
The sun shall not smite thee by day, nor the moon by night.
The LORD shall preserve thee from all evil: he shall preserve thy soul.

—Psalm 121: 5-7 (KJV)

There were some post-transplant challenges, but I was prepared to ride through them. I was still in pain, but it was
surprisingly less intense than before the transplant. The aches
and incomprehensible instability and impulses generated in my
body compelled me to clench my fists and teeth continuously. I
would unconsciously lock my jaws and grind my teeth uncontrollably, and I could feel the unevenness caused by such actions.
The destructive high-dose chemotherapy administered during the
transplant did not help my brain post-transplant. It made things
worse. I was disoriented, forgetful, and still challenged figuring
out basic instructions.

The hemorrhoids had worsened while I was hospitalized and
had become bothersome. So as not to aggravate the myriad of pain
points throughout my body, I had to move cautiously. When I tried
to rise from the lying position, I first had to sit up for a while before
my feet made contact with the floor; otherwise, I would pay the
pain price. It was as though my brain had to be told what my next

action would be, and it would commandeer blood flow and energy to awaken my feet before they could be functional.

In time, though, I began to experience the benefits of the transplant and started to feel the best I had in months. Although the doctor cautioned me that it would not last as I had an aggressive form of the disease, I would not allow him to steal my newly found joy. Since I was no longer being administered regularly scheduled chemotherapy, the mental fog was lifting more frequently, lasted longer, and started diminishing with time. I was not as fatigued, requiring sleep maybe twice each day. One of the most favorable outcomes was my ability to move about on my own. I could now walk for some distance unaided. Shortness of breath, however, remained a challenge. When I walked, I had to take frequent breaks, and my lungs would burn so viciously, I would try not to inhale too deeply; it was another side effect of my medication. Because of my vulnerability, I had to wear a mask and dress appropriately in cold weather. But the desire to be outdoors again and free from my cage was just too liberating, and whatever the cost in pain and discomfort, I was prepared to pay.

At first, I could only walk a few yards before stopping, but I would push the envelope, doing more than was safe or comfortable. I ignored every warning not to overdo it in my determination to seize what I saw then as life anew. Faith becoming substance manifested in my physical healing was my goal. Going beyond whatever was defined as safe limits was my attempt to walk in faith, stripping myself of the encumbrances attributable to fear. I suppose this is a natural reaction to being so near the point of death so often, then being given the opportunity to return; you embrace life with passion. Every inch of progress I made was a huge milestone. Whatever I did was in recognition of faith in action, tangibly bringing my healing into reality, and I would not allow anyone or anything to limit or steal my joy.

Of course, there were negative consequences associated with my defiance. I attempted exercises involving twisting and bending, but had to beat a hasty retreat to the confines of my bed for days afterwards so that I could recover. One day, I went to pick up the mail and stubbed my toe. It caused my spine to hurt for days.

There were also external drivers that kept emerging to distract me. The news of influential people dying from cancer seemed to have been more widely proliferated through the media. Was it the season? Or was I becoming more sensitized to the apparent number of casualties from cancer, and to my own mortality? The emaciated image of a famous Georgia pastor suffering from cancer being repeatedly displayed on TV and his subsequent death haunted me for a long time. The smiling face of the brilliant television anchor suddenly erased from this life left me wondering who would be next. These folks were like extended families, still in their prime, with so much potential, all gone too soon. Did I have more faith than they did? Was I more in favor with God than they were? Did they not have access to the best care science and medicine could provide? What right then did I have to live?

I had to assure myself that who I was could only be defined by God alone. My purpose was exclusive of anyone else, regardless of how much we esteemed them. Only God sees the heart of individuals, and as Peter says in Acts 10:34-35 (NIV), "I now realize how true it is that God does not show favoritism but accepts from every nation the one who fears him and does what is right." My relationship with God is on an individual basis. I ought not to, therefore, sacrifice God's favor on me based on whose robe my eyes perceived as whiter than my own. God loves me as His child and created me for His specific purpose. I had a right to be healed, as God, and only He, determined.

Shame on me if I surrendered my rights of sonship by trading them in fear of the prevailing winds of doom. My duty in faith was to gird my loins with the truth of God, stand on the promises it contained, and claim and assert my rights to all benefits and privileges provided, among which was my restoration to perfect health through faith. My "greater things" were yet to be realized, and I needed to accept that in faith. Healing was merely precursory to God's plan for the rest of my life. So then, I did not need to yield to the distractions presented by my environment, nor my apparent compromised capabilities. My focus should be on my personal relationship with God. His perfect promise further assured me of my inheritance, among which is healing and a fruitful life with Him. Here then is one of the more positive posts I wrote in a more personal, whimsical, and entertaining way, to share my joys of the progress I anticipated ahead.

It has been a wonderful experience for me to give voice to my progress through this medium since I became sick. At times they were rather self-deprecating and inglorious, as I was trying to be transparent and relate my condition in real time. I believe that God is greater than whatever I was or am experiencing at any time. Through faith, I rely on God for deliverance, and I am confident that He will ultimately take me through all my afflictions completely. Sharing with you has become a part of my cherished experiences, and you will eventually share in my healing reality. My testimony is also yours. Our testimonies are foundational for our faith. We share them to reinforce each other's faith and strengthen our relationship with God. Through it all, God is honored and glorified.

So, how is the Old Guy doing? It has been just over a month since I received my stem cell transplant, and I am happy to let you know that I am doing exceptionally well. I try to walk, sometimes for nearly two miles continuously, although I become winded. I have to wear a mask when I venture outdoors. I grunt like a fat hog trotting uphill, huffing and puffing like the big bad wolf but lacking the strength to blow the little pigs' house in. Imagine what my poor neighbors are subjected to when I go for walks. I can do minimal, very basic exercises, if they don't involve my neck or back. If I keep on pace, I should soon be able to qualify for some seasoned citizens exercise group. My taste buds are reblooming like the profusion of Georgia flowers at this time of year. It is allergy season, which is very bad for me; I suffer severely from seasonal allergies. My appetite is returning, and regular food is once again becoming palatable. I no longer require as much sleep, and my baby blanket is relieved. Speaking of which, do you realize that I will have to be revaccinated as though I am a young child?

My neck still refuses to cooperate with the rest of my body to carry my head; I have a disproportionately large head. If you did not laugh at that, I will be forced to show you some pictures in this post (Appendix II). My neck's familiar method of protestation is to bring on the hurt. It has imposed certain restrictions on me, such as no yawning, head shaking, or looking side to side unless the rest of my body is consulted and agrees to full body rotation. Vertical head movements are explicit exclusions; any violations are paid for dearly. My old lytic bones have thrown their support behind the recovery process, and although they no longer rattle and squeak, I get subtle reminders via my sensory system that they will not be pushed beyond certain limits. I still avoid crowds, have not had visitors for a while now, and await doctors' orders to emancipate myself from my confinement. In a few weeks, I will be restaged.

I love, trust, and worship God the Almighty and, in faith, believe that all things are possible and that my healing will soon be completed. I am blessed to have you as my friends, supporters, and advocates.

Now how about them pictures? I told you I had hair many decades ago. I am not Ole Baldy, just Follicly Challenged. You know what? Not sure that I will be too bothered if hair does not return (Appendix II).

God bless you, my friends. See you all one day soon.

CHAPTER 35

After the Storm

*And I will restore to you the years that the locust hath
eaten, the cankerworm, and the caterpillar, and the
palmerworm, my great army which I sent among you.*

—Joel 2:25 (KJV)

I had very high expectations that the autologous stem cell transplant procedure I had undergone would have completely rid my
body of the nasty cancer, as it had done for others, but the results said
otherwise. I would have to reserve the glowing tributes of a cure for
another day. All was not lost, however—there were glimmers of hope
and some positive outcomes. The disease was apparently no longer
metastasizing as it previously was and, in fact, its footprint in my
body had been reduced. I was experiencing less pain and felt stronger,
so any discouragement I felt was short-lived. What was disheartening
was that I had to restart chemotherapy. I was, however, ambivalent
about the next step in the process—the allogeneic transplant. That
process would not be using my stem cells but those of a matching
donor. If it were standard protocol and the will of God, then I would
have to comply. I remember my immediate concern at that time was
how much the previous operation had changed my appearance.

Funny how easy it is to characterize others as vain. Yet, in all
of us, there are streaks of vanity. Maybe it could be said that I was

even more vain after my transplant. I was quite unhappy with the image staring back at me from the mirror. That reflection was ugly. All my hair was gone, I was scrawny, and my once deep-set eyes now seemed droopy. My skin was tar black as though it had been mummified or severely burnt. I am of African extract, so I am naturally on the darker end of the pigmentation spectrum. However, I had slid several shades down into the darker area of the color scale (hyperpigmentation). My nail beds, fingers, and toes were equally discolored. I felt the need to creep up to the mirror so as not to cause a scare, then quietly reintroduce myself to the reflection that stared back at me. In all honesty, several times I looked at myself and thought not even a mother could love someone that looked like me. I became so sensitive about my appearance, I kept expecting my wife to be startled each time she saw me. Thank God, she looked passed the old scary flesh man, allowing her to admire the handsomer imperishable spirit man.

Dwelling on unmet expectations was futile. When the impulse to revert to self-pity arose, or counterfactual thoughts like "I would be much better off without the transplant" presented themselves, I would consciously switch my thinking, focusing instead on how fortunate I was as a favored child of God. I had survived the most advanced stage of multiple myeloma (stage 3) and was making progress toward complete restoration.

With this mindset, I could engross myself in admiration and praises to an awesome God who, even though preoccupied with the care of the tremendous infinite universe, found time to reassure me that I was still actively in His thoughts. Regardless of whether I saw myself as a nondescript, all-but-dead remnant of humankind, God saw me as relevant and essential. As is the will of God, nothing bad can last forever in this fearfully and wonderfully made creation of His. As time passed, I enjoyed the familiar image of me returning, with lush hair growth, even thicker than before, newer skin with an added glow, and nail beds restored to their former healthy appearance.

God heard my prayers and those of the people who prayed on my behalf and demonstrated His benevolence to me by orchestrating my recovery. Through the evidence of His work in me, I could appreciate the awesomeness of His sovereignty and allay all fear and doubts. The basis of my faith, as contained in His Word, was being realized. Who then could fault me for documenting a reiteration of my faith? I wanted to have my statement of faith memorialized for future reference. Even though my expectations weren't being fulfilled in my timeline, I still firmly believed that I would be healed and, further, that I would be cured of the disease entirely and not just go into temporary remission. My fractured skeleton would be made whole again, and my old lytic, fractured, and worn-out bones would be replaced with newly generated ones. Anything in me that was destructive would be completely eradicated. Remarkably, my faith was finding bedrock on the progress I was experiencing, and I was daring to test its ability to reach into the depths of the storehouse of grace for even more substance. My progress was now becoming evident, and I had an urge to declare it publicly and acknowledge God with unrelenting praises, as I tried to do in the post below.

> I often contemplated how I would survive the prevailing storm if I did not have absolute faith in God the Almighty. On what or whom would I base my belief for a successful outcome? I had been diagnosed with an incurable disease. Without God, I don't know on what I would dare base my claim for healing. Medicine and the competencies of man are not failure-proof. What other higher power is there? To claim that I will have a complete cure requires me to speak of a failproof source, a deliverer or some infallible being, and to only God do I know to ascribe such authority. The overarching question is: Where would I be without Jesus the Christ? I am proud to declare that I have a foundation for my faith. My faith is biblically based and centers on the promises of the Triune God Almighty.
>
> To walk in faith, I make a conscious effort to believe that the endgame will be what I hope

for, as expressed in my prayers. Walking in faith requires that I let go of comfortable and familiar deterministic concepts such as time, place, and forced actions. I cannot harbor fear, facilitate anxiety, or wane in confidence even as my humanity (flesh) urges me to.

The fundamental tenet of my faith, found in Hebrews 11:1, stresses the need to have confidence in what I hope for (through prayers) and to be assured that even though I am not yet experiencing what I pray for, it will eventually happen in reality. I conclude that, if I can rely on a man-made aircraft to safely auto-pilot me to the other side of the globe, I can have faith that the omnipotent God Almighty will heal me from this incurable cancer in His time. I don't know when my healing will be manifested, but I am confident that one day, I will write a final update on this board declaring my healing. My journey has not been the most straightforward battle; it has been my biggest singular life challenge. But through it all, I feel the empowerment of God, and on this basis I keep making these bold, very public declarations of faith. God will NOT allow my affliction to be more than I can bear. From 1 Corinthians 10:13, I learn that God will not let us be tried beyond what we can handle. In fact, the very trial I am experiencing now keeps providing ways for me to endure it. What exceptional comfort!

Two days ago, I went for the long-awaited results of the post-stem cell transplant. Although the results were not the spectacular outcomes we anticipated, I am encouraged. The "bad stuff" (the free light chains) did not show any meaningful reduction, but neither did they show any increase. The bone marrow biopsy revealed less than 5% cancer in my bones, and PET-CT imaging did not show a widespread distribution of the bad indicators. The bad news is that as long as there is a remnant of the bad stuff, they can potentially multiply rapidly. Another bit of good news is, I feel physically great. The BMT doctor advises me that my feeling good is the short-term effect of the stem cell transplant. Nonetheless, I am enjoying this feeling of well-being. So much so, I even allowed myself to be dragged out (kicking and screaming) to an amazing "surprise" birthday party, the only real escape from my imprisonment for a long time.

The immediate future looks like this: I will be repeating the dreaded chemotherapy, which is projected for another six months. After that, I will be hospitalized for another three weeks for a miserable bone marrow transplant if they can find me a match. I am not enthusiastic about it, but it is a part of the process, and as long as it is God-approved, then I am all signed up.

I will survive this storm and emerge stronger and better. While being tossed in it, I will try to learn from the experiences God allows. I believe God will teach and equip me for the work of my future. I appreciate your continuing prayers. Please stay encouraged because my successful outcome will strengthen your faith in God. He is kind and merciful. God bless you all.

Sometime after writing the previous post, the feeling of rejuvenation, strength of faith, and just hearing from the Holy Spirit compelled me to share the following affirmation:

One day I will write on this board: "From Stage Three to Cancer Free." Foremost among my reasons for believing this are:

1. I dare to believe that I have the authority to claim through faith in Jesus Christ my complete healing by His grace. I have done so and continue to stand on that premise.

2. I believe the Holy Spirit of God has revealed my impending healing to me. Since this comes from God, I will be able to confirm that His Word never returns void without accomplishing its purpose.

3. I have declared that you will be the witnesses of my healing. Then, I hope that you will give God glory for His miraculous works in me. With that, God will be well pleased. AMEN.

CHAPTER 36

A Praise Offering

You intended to harm me, but God intended it for good to accomplish what is now being done, the saving of many lives.

—Genesis 50:20 (NIV)

As I started feeling more energetic and healthier, I became more cavalier. I was venturing into areas that I should not, exposing myself to things that were unhealthy for me. I threw caution to the wind, interacting with the things that were prohibited. I was keenly aware that I was operating outside of the doctors' guidelines and venturing into forbidden grounds. The impelling force of confidence, bravado, and just the sheer excitement of feeling well again presented the illusion that I could, once again, easily handle "manly" duties. I was a fool lost in my own conceit and arrogance. Twice in a matter of a few months, I became ill. In both cases, I had severe bronchial infections and had to be treated with antibiotics. My haste to demonstrate God's good work in me could only be matched by my enthusiasm to help God do His job. I was forcing myself to get fit again by attempting forbidden, extraneous physical activities, which I could easily justify, if questioned, as being a demonstration of my healing through faith.

But God doesn't need my help in setting His timeline, I came to appreciate. For every cautionary advice I defied with vigorous exercises, physical work, or venturing beyond safe domains, I would suffer corresponding ailments. There would be pains lasting weeks, infections requiring serious treatment, and frustration with my arrogant actions. These were my efforts to force and control my healing, but they were producing outcomes that were to my disadvantage. The consequences of my impatience, breaching natural laws, were definite no-no's, but they were parts of my new training regimen. That aside, I was obviously on the mend. My mind and body had been laying waste for too long and needed action.

With the fantastic overall improvements I was experiencing, I became convinced my faith was now manifesting substance through my progressive healing. I was elevated to new heights of happiness and enthusiasm. My heart was abuzz with praises. God is good, and if I did not know it all the time, I knew it then. Praises to God were always on my heart, and I spoke them with my mouth continuously; I had to share even if it took me several attempts. Each time I attempted to write my praise offering, something would come up to cause its loss or destruction. Many other negative influences tried to emerge to mute my exaltation.

My goal was to overcome all obstacles, whether they were negative spirits masquerading as innocuous support or physical impediments emerging to block my praise. I needed everyone to know I was on the mend, even if it was during my infusion with chemotherapy. Had I not feared it would cause too much excitement, the post that follows would have been written in CAPS, colored in red, and underlined. It would be punctuated with scriptural praise quotes throughout, such as, "You are the God who sees me" (Genesis 16:13); "Great is the LORD and most worthy of praise; his greatness no one can fathom" (Psalm 145:3); "There is none like You, O LORD; You are great, and great is Your name in might" (Jeremiah 10:6); "For the Mighty One has done great things for me; And holy is His name" (Luke 1:49). And I could keep going with praise to our great, wonderful God Almighty, but I had to control my enthusiasm and posted a shortened version of my praise offering.

Have you ever felt like the forces of darkness are
unleashed with a specific assignment to muzzle

269

you? Well, before this, I was not exactly the type disposed to place much stake in anything to do with the concept of a triumphant evil spirit over me, a child of God. I always felt that evil spirits would somehow pass me by, being clothed in the armor of God. I now realize that I am such an ever-learning child. Up to recently, if you had attempted any discussion on the ability of evil spirits and their power over me, I would be dismissive. I would acknowledge the existence and power of evil spirits, but I would discount any potential impact on me. Maybe I attempted to cover my head like a child believing that not seeing the boogie man meant he was not there, even though he was.

Biblical evidence to support the existence of evil spirits and their power over humans are easy to find. The Bible does provide ample evidence of the power of evil. Its influence was unleashed on Job. Jesus cast out evil spirits but, even more significantly, Jesus the Christ was tempted several times by the Evil One. There are many examples of the activities of evil spirits cited in the Bible. The attacks are relentless when the Evil One perceives that we are favored by God, and I think that I am in God's favor, enough to be visited and harried by the Evil One.

Since Sunday, I have been motivated to document some recent experiences that give me cause to demonstrate how the Evil One takes God's truth, repackages it in a beautiful lie that looks credible, convincing enough to be believed, even though it's a big lie, not unlike what he did with Eve.

Below is my third attempt to write my praise story of the day. I started it at the outpatient's earlier today, and I lost the data for different reasons each time before I could post it. I refused to give up, I had to stick it to the Evil One. So here I go.

As I comfortably reclined at the infusion center, while being administered my customary chemotherapy, I took time to reflect on the beautiful day it was. On my way for treatment, I found myself just totally engaged in constant prayers of thanksgiving to God the Father. Boy, it felt good to thank God, because of His goodness and mercies to me. I had this fantastic feeling of positivity, the past notwithstanding, which, in fact, may have been in large part because of my recent history.

The last couple of weeks were not too good for me. Aside from "the bug," I had other issues. I'll spare you the details, having evoked more than enough sympathy from you by posting about my bleak disposition so pitifully. But remember, it was my commitment to use these posts explicitly for such a purpose.

Today, however, I feel like I am on cloud nine. I feel great, really great! I have no pains from the cancer; in fact, no pains at all, and I have voluntarily discontinued all pain medications for some time now. My mind is clear, I am physically strong, and I can turn my previously fractured neck very slightly with little pain. I have relatively improved stamina. I can walk and even jog a little, and if you rain enough dead presidents on me, I may do a little jig for you if you play my favorite country music. (Please feel free to laugh at the thought of this belt-buckle holding, boot-kicking, square-dancing Jamaican. Yah man!! Hee haw!!).

So, they tell me I have cancer, that I will need indefinite chemotherapy, and that I may even need the dreaded bone marrow transplant. OK! Fine, if that is what God says, so be it. The outcome will favor me if it is, "thus saith the Lord." Let me tell you what I heard from the Holy Spirit. I will not just be healed, I will be reconstructed. Not only will the ailment disappear, but I will also be in much better shape than I was before this trial. There is God's process to all this, and to Him I yield. It has all been an experience from which I have benefited, and I pray that God's purpose is being accomplished. God is merciful; I am unique to Him. I am Spirit. It is not just my beautiful body that is fearfully and wonderfully made, my soul and spirit are too. My body may have been ravaged, but my spirit and soul are still in great shape. As long as they are intact, then it is well. It is the exercise of my faith through the spirit that touches God the Father, who is SPIRIT.

As you read this, please believe as I have that I have triumphed over the forces of evil that have attempted to prevent me from sharing my praise account. Again, thank you, my friends, prayer warriors, well-wishers, and sympathizers. I can only hope that at the time when I declare the final word of God, confirmed by the medical practitioners, you will still be here. I believe that your faith will be further strengthened and that God will be glorified. I love God the benevolent, merciful Father, I praise and worship Him in spirit and truth, and I trust Him unreservedly. He has taken me through and is leading me where He desires. Lord, please let your will be my duty always, in the name of Jesus the Christ. Thank you.

CHAPTER 37

Hold That Allogeneic
Transplant for Now

*Call unto me, and I will answer thee, and show thee
great and mighty things, which thou knowest not.*

—Jeremiah 33:3 (KJV)

At what point do your caregivers regard your action as pompous and overbearing, rather than you just being your best advocate as a patient? Well, I did not precisely allow my doctors to make that distinction when I told them I wanted to postpone the planned allogeneic transplant. I am not sure that sat well with the BMT team. The BMT doctor was a fantastic, personable, and brilliant individual, who took time to explain every procedure I would undergo so that I would be comfortable. Under his supervision, I went through the previous transplant with much confidence. According to the plan of care discussed with the doctors earlier, I was fully aware that the allogeneic procedure would be the next step in my care.

The BMT team had done its due diligence and had located a good match for me. All the necessary approvals had been received, and I was scheduled for the routine prep work before undergoing the transplant. It must have been a shock and disappointment to the members of the team when I showed up for my pretransplant meeting and told them I was not comfortable doing the procedure. I advised them that I wanted to allow myself time to explore other options, specifically the CAR-T (chimeric antigen receptor T-cell) method that was in Phase 1 trials at the time. I intended to seek enrollment in one of the ongoing or upcoming trials. Maybe they thought I was out of my mind then; however, I really was not comfortable with the allogeneic transplant. It was, in my opinion, the nuclear option. My spirit was guiding me against it, and the risks were a bit weighty for me at the time.

I chose to be obedient to the voice of my spirit. I believed that God would see me through my healing without the challenges posed by the allogeneic procedure, so I was comfortable declaring my intentions to the doctors. That choice meant the end of my relationship with the BMT department. I was referred back to oncology, where I told my oncologist about my desire to be part of the CAR-T trial. He gave me his support and started me on a previously administered cocktail of chemotherapy drugs. This set of chemotherapy drugs is given to multiple myeloma patients who have relapsed. So, here I was, defying the wisdom of science and going against the advice of the very distinguished professionals. Under whose authority was I doing so? Under the power of the Holy Spirit, and I had faith enough to be convinced that I was indeed hearing from God. Considering my state of health, I hardly had legs to stand on, so I was publicly putting my faith to the test, believing that God would support me, with demonstrable evidence of progress, without the allogeneic transplant. So, I laid it all on the line and posted the following with confidence.

> Just over a year ago, I was diagnosed with a blood cancer known as multiple myeloma. After my stem cell transplant, the medical teams advised me that I would be kept on chemotherapy indefinitely. I would then be moved to a bone marrow (allogeneic) transplant (using a matching donor's bone marrow). This is a rigorous process. The prospect of doing this more aggressive transplant, with unpredictable outcomes and

risks, lengthy miserable hospitalization, and the tedious post-op care, is daunting to me. I am not motivated physically or spiritually. I still believe that through faith, my healing will come. I am just not motivated by the allogeneic route at this time. My constant and persistent FAITH still holds, and I am stating it as a modified version of Paul's Hebrews 11: 1. Now FAITH is: Substance—the curing of the cancer that science has deemed incurable, but through the grace of Jesus Christ, will be cured, without the recommended transplant. My Hope—is based on the confidence that my will lines up with God's will.

The challenges presented by the enemy, however, are significant. They are even borne out by the reports of the professionals. The disease has affected my chromosomes, the BMT doctor tells me. The reports are what they are; we live in the natural world where we should not ignore natural laws and substantiated realities. Such reports, however, are powerless when God's plan is to deliver me from what prevails.

My most recent results indicate that the cancer is now stable; please note that I am not yet in remission. Being stable is encouraging news and supports my faith belief of an eventual complete cure and reconstruction. My current challenges are the necessary isolation and restrictions imposed by my condition. My immunoglobulin levels are very low, which means I still have to avoid large crowds and limit my exposure to many things. Most days, I feel quite well, but I must avoid any jarring motions as my bones will ache severely. The chemotherapy, as expected, wears me down tremendously, and I suffer from fatigue. The side effects of the various medications I take are more pronounced than those of the disease itself.

I chose not to be subjected to a procedure that I believed God had revealed I should avoid. With no disrespect meant to the well-learned professionals, I had to test my faith to confidently declare its effectiveness. God works in mysterious ways. Consider this: I have been dabbling in stock trading for years. A few months ago, while researching pharmaceutical stocks to invest in, I stumbled on specific companies that are doing novel and cutting-edge research in gene therapy, to treat cancer. How amazing it was for me to find out multiple myeloma was now being investigated through Phase 1 clinical trials. Yes, I was excited.

When I first mentioned to my BMT doctor that I was postponing the bone marrow transplant, I could tell he was stunned and maybe amazed at my apparent defiance. Revealing to him that I was opting instead to be enrolled in one of the trials, precisely the CAR-T method, might have had him thinking that I was a little green man with my spaceship docked outside. But through my research, I had discovered not only stocks, but companies that were actively engaged in the exploration of using the CAR-T method for the treatment of multiple myeloma. It was difficult for me not to spiritualize the CAR-T acronym. For my purpose, I translated the CAR-T acronym as "C"—Christ, "A"—Almighty, "R"—Revealed, "T"—The Omniscient, Omnipotent, and Omnipresent. However, the scientific translation for CAR-T is chimeric antigen receptor, with the "T" being T cells. T cells detect and fight invading bad stuff, from flu to cancers.

With the CAR-T method, the patient's cells are extracted and sent to specifically designated labs, where the T cells are genetically modified by adding receptors to recognize and fight off toxins and other foreign substances—in this case cancer cells. The modified cells are then reinjected into the body. Just imagine, as I have, God using the most unlikely source to reveal my potential cure. I live by faith believing.

Will I be eligible for a clinical trial? Maybe not anytime soon. There are stringent criteria, limited studies, and at my disease stage, I am not deemed critical enough. There will be later stage studies that will be opened to a broader population with less stringent prerequisites. Hopefully, the FDA (Food and Drug Administration) will provide expedited approval of this groundbreaking method of treatment as standard protocol sometime soon. At this developmental stage, however, there are still several known and unknown side effects to be ironed out. The results of these studies are so far stunningly positive. Is my deliverance coming through this therapy? Against the persistent reports of the enemy, God keeps revealing His power to me, an insignificant creature such as I. In one of my recent postings, I opined that with all the current treatment I could be made into a bionic man; well, let's modify that. If I eventually receive the therapy, please don't hesitate to label me as GMO positive. Hold to God's unchanging hands all, keep the faith, and let's continue to thank God for how He loves us.

I did not consult with anyone about my decision to opt out of having the allogeneic transplant; I am not sure if I even told my wife before meeting with the BMT team. It took faith for me to believe I was hearing from God, yes, even the unction of the Holy Spirit, to act with such authority that could negatively impact the predicted progress of using the established medical protocol of care. On the other hand, I had to test my faith, believing God was guiding me.

It would be disingenuous and maybe even dishonest of me to say I did not also consider the risks, adverse side effects, and consequences of going through with this bone marrow transplant. One of the most severe risk factors I deliberated was a condition known as graft-versus-host disease (GVHD). GVHD occurs when the donated bone marrow or stem cells view the recipient's body (the host) as foreign and attack it. No two human cells have the same genetic markers. Much like fingerprints are unique, cell types are genetically differentiated by what is called human leukocyte antigens (HLA). T cells know the cells that are like themselves and can distinguish them from others with dissimilar genetic markers. Acute GVHD usually manifests within 100 days after transplantation, while chronic GVHD generally manifests later (after 100 days). Either way, the condition can cause organ damage and could eventually lead to death.

So now I was considered a relapsed case and would be reverted to chemotherapy treatment. The Multiple Myeloma Research Foundation distinguishes between relapsed and refractory disease as follows: "Relapsed (or "recurrent") multiple myeloma is the term for when cancer returns after treatment or after a period of remission. Since multiple myeloma does not have a cure, most patients will relapse at some point. Refractory multiple myeloma refers to when the cancer does not respond to therapy. In some patients, the cancer may respond to initial treatment, but not to treatment following a relapse."

For the new round of chemotherapy, I was prescribed Kyprolis (carfilzomib) via infusion, and Pomalyst and dexamethasone orally (please see the brief descriptions and side effects of these drugs in Appendix I). So even as I was considered a relapsed patient, in faith, I believed that God was still in charge. Whichever chemotherapy protocol was prescribed in the interim, it would have to work, or at least sustain me until such miracle or new medication God prescribed became available; otherwise, I did not hear from God. Notwithstanding the current evidence, I posted the preceding account with confidence in my healing through faith.

CHAPTER 38

In Control

*Humble yourselves, therefore, under the mighty hand of
God so that at the proper time he may exalt you, casting
all your anxieties on him, because he cares for you.*

—1 Peter 5:6-7 (ESV)

Some years ago, when my children were younger, they bought me
a T-shirt for Father's Day. It had a picture of tools and the inscription "Mr. Fix It." It evoked a feeling of invincible, superhero dad,
with power over his perceived domain. In the eyes of my children
(who did not know better then), I was "in control" at home. Of
course, my wife knew better.

Not too many things evoke a sense of empowerment as being
in control. Whether delegated, elected, or assumed, being in control
meant I had authority over things or people. I was able to make
things happen through others. Being in control allowed me to motivate people and manipulate things to satisfy my ego or meet some
expected deliverables for myself or whomever I was accountable to
then. We all encounter occasions, however, when we feel less than
capable of handling things in our span of control. Such things could
be related to the job, personal issues, financial challenges, illnesses,
family or relationship situations—you name it.

When external situations challenge or undermine our authority to exercise control, we may experience a loss of standing, become unconfident, and feel destabilized. These often lead to stressors, which not only bring into doubt our capabilities but also question the very source from which we derive our power and authority to exercise control. Losing control gives way to insecurity and negative, self-defeating manifestations. I could not bring to bear the power and authority of Mr. Fix It to hasten my healing. God was in control. Yet, when gripped by impatience, I would spend hours thinking of ways I could leverage my wisdom to fix my brokenness. It was about time I was healed. I felt my waiting period had been extended and now exceeded reasonable expectation. There had to be something Mr. Fix It could do. There had to have been a word from God with instructions requiring my input to speed up the healing process and I had carelessly missed it.

I was unaware that I was subconsciously scheming about how to wrest control from God, which is precursory to rebelliousness. Obviously, even at my holiest, my efforts toward full surrender in faith remained vulnerable to infiltration by my sin nature. My imperfect human side was still nurturing pride and controlling impulses so deep, they would spontaneously sprout doubt and unbelief from the depths of my subconscious.

But God despises a proud heart. Proverbs 16 tells us that God detests the proud of heart, that continuing to be that way will lead to punishment, and that pride goes before destruction. However, the good news is that I needn't struggle with things that are beyond my control. My efforts to change my situation would be woefully inadequate. And why should I contemplate self-help anyway when Psalm 46:1-2 provides me the comfort that God is my refuge and strength, an ever-present help in times of trouble? Those were the days when Psalm 27:14 had so much relevance, I needed to recite it frequently. "Wait for the LORD; be strong and take heart and wait for the LORD."

God the Father creates us with the innate ability to exercise our "own free will." All-knowing, He understands that power-craving humans are more likely to wantonly vacate His perfect will and instead do rebellious deeds. Such actions tend to spring from man's controlling nature, where he selfishly amasses power and uses it for devious schemes. It was not lost upon God that with too much power man can be horrendously destructive. In Genesis 6:5, it says that every intent and thought of man were evil continually. Being love, God never removes His protective guardrails, otherwise we would have self-annihilated eons ago. When we use the brute force of our will to take and maintain control, adverse outcomes often result. Throwing our hands up in frustration for fear of defeat or failure and not seeking God's will is, likewise, unproductive and possibly just as destructive. In either case, the devil wins.

Remember, our adversary the devil walks about like a roaring lion seeking whom he may devour, according to 1 Peter 5:8. He seizes opportunities of rebelliousness, fear, and weakness to manipulate our thoughts. We become weakened without God because our humanity is exposed; we are unprotected and vulnerable to the wiles of the devil. In Ephesians 6:10-12, we see that if we are not covered with God's armor (the precepts of God), we are subjected to the schemes and deceit of the devil. Our devilish spirit of self-sufficiency convinces us that we are in control of our destiny, leading us to our eventual demise. In all things, it is better to let go of our controlling spirit and let God guide us. Psalm 55:22 says we should cast our burden on the Lord, and He will sustain us.

If only we could honestly believe and accept that all things are attainable from God through His grace by our faith, as stated in Mark 11:23-24. Imagine the power of faith to trust in our hearts without any doubt that what we speak with our mouths, believing in faith, will be accomplished through our God the Omnipotent. So, being genuinely in control is, in effect, being empowered by God the Almighty.

In the past year, I have had the most humbling experiences of relinquishing control and allowing God. Mr. Fix It was unable and disabled. Things I thought were in my domain of control, and the innate power I believed I possessed, were the delusions of someone being controlled by the devil. So now, even as I acknowledge that I possess a little wisdom, a bit of learning, a clutch of talents, and some functional physical abilities, I am mindful that I am "powered by God Almighty," who has ultimate control and without whom I am worthless.

It is clear to me the fruits of complete self-reliance and control are arrogance, selfishness, pride, and the feeling of self-aggrandizement; they are precursory to all the things the Bible says God hates in Proverbs 6:16-19 (NIV). These are: "Haughty eyes, a lying tongue, hands that shed innocent blood, a heart that devises wicked schemes, feet that are quick to rush into evil, a false witness who pours out lies, and a person who stirs up conflict in the community." We see evidence of these many times in our lives and in the actions of power-grabbers, whose motives are to seize power and control and hold on to them at all costs. Maybe I was guilty of some of these ills or was being driven in that direction.

God sees ahead. He chastens those He loves so that they may avoid self-destruction and ultimately incur His wrath. Happily, though, He gave me a period of time-out and reflection. My life is a work in progress, in which I learn humility and respect for boundaries. In doing so, I relinquish control of things and situations over which I have no authority and should never have sought to control in the first place. In humility, I yield my life to God for His absolute, permanent, and total control. With this, the Holy Spirit will counsel me and delegate to me whatever He entrusts to me as my responsibilities. By embracing these guiding principles, my will should highly likely be aligned with that of God the Father, in whose domain ultimate control dwells.

These days, I try to live one day at a time, acknowledging the weaknesses I formerly perceived as strengths and seeking all I need through God's grace. The gift of life itself is a reason to rejoice. The ability to do simple tasks I could not do last year is a reason to praise God. I take nothing for granted anymore. I crave to stay in the presence of God and seek his guidance so that I know what to do. God has blessed me with much; He brings the most delightful people into my life. Many of these people are parts of "the body of Christ," and since each element is dependent on the other to properly function, I have a greater appreciation of each member.

I consider myself duty-bound to share my humbling experiences so that others may benefit from them. There can be no greater privilege than to be the evidence of God's mighty, marvelous, and miraculous works. If there is anyone who wants to question or judge the awesomeness of God, please, look at me first. Just by being alive with my physical and mental capabilities restored, I am evidence of His awesome mercies and grace. Even my eventual death will not erase what has been His good work in me. I give glory, honor, worship, and highest praises to God our Father Almighty, and may I never be derelict in my duty to His service.

CHAPTER 39

The Substance of Faith

In trouble, deep trouble, I prayed to GOD. He answered me… I was as far down as a body can go, and the gates were slamming shut behind me forever—yet you pulled me up from that grave alive, O GOD, my God! When my life was slipping away, I remembered GOD, and my prayer got through to you, made it all the way to your Holy Temple. Those who worship hollow gods, god-frauds, walk away from their only true love. But I'm worshiping you, GOD, calling out in thanksgiving! And I'll do what I promised I'd do! Salvation belongs to God!

—Jonah 2 (MSG)

After I had sunk to the lowest levels of human frailty and fallen into the bottomless pit, who pulled me up? When my bones were inexplicably broken and wouldn't mend, who would be my healer? When all the resources of my brain had been overwhelmed by pain, so much so that I lost the power of comprehension and reason, and I felt as though I was losing my mind, to whom were my thoughts directed? When my body had been subjected to years of dangerous drugs that were designated to cure me but instead threatened to damage my vital organs and kill me, didn't faith become my panacea? When the myriad of treatments, therapies, and procedures failed to meet their targeted objectives, wasn't there a place for hope I sought after? After hearing the sincerest platitudes in love and having sufficiently whined, complained, screamed, moaned, and cried floods of tears, there was now a sweet, soft voice that I could hear.

I had rationalized, analyzed, reasoned and bargained, and the medical professionals had told me they couldn't help because my condition was so grave. Then, with sincere repentance, I cried out to the Lord in faith, believing He always hears, never fails, and would send me a rescue plan. Having lived through this for such a long time now, what should my attitude and reaction be when the evidence, which is the substance of my faith in God, starts to become real? With my healing now becoming manifest, how do I suppress the spirit of rejoicing that floods my soul? The proof of my healing was now compelling, as shown in my test results. Now, even that experienced and well-learned professional, my trusted oncologist, was convinced enough to characterize me as a "miracle." The prospect of my complete healing was now beginning to show tangible proofs.

Here it was, finally. The process of faith was transforming my hope into real-world tangible substance, producing visible evidence, not just for me to feel, but for all to see. If never before, the time had come to worship and esteem the Lord God Almighty. All my prayers in prostration became shouts of praise, supplications became rhapsodies of joyful exaltation, and invocations were transformed to heartfelt gratitude and thanksgiving. God is magnified and manifested through His work in me. The evidence of things not seen, but which were hoped for, through faith, was becoming substance.

The doctor's endorsement of what I already knew through faith provided the ammunition to slay any doubter, even the devil; here was proof that validated God's promise. Up to that point, saying I was feeling much better without the doctor's endorsement of my healing progression was little more than a hope and a prayer for those who required proof. For my oncologist to attribute my progress to a "miracle" was more than a good thing. That good thing had now leapfrogged into the realm of a God thing. The word *miracle* perfectly described the resonance achieved by my faith product to the healing outcome. Faith and substance were coming to a place of harmony, with evidence. With whom do I first share my joy? Those who had endured with me in my struggles: my friends and faithful supporters.

So, again, I took to Facebook. In this post, I tried to recall as best I could the words that transpired between me and my oncologist.

> If you were a fly on the wall, privy to the following conversation yesterday, what would your reaction be?
>
> Speaker #1, "You are a MIRACLE, you know."
>
> Speaker #2, "I am a CHRISTIAN, you know."
>
> Speaker #1, "I know that."
>
> Speaker #1's claim to fame—Director of Hematology and Medical Oncology, Director of Community Oncology, Medical Director, Infusion Services, and Assistant Professor in the Department of Hematology and Medical Oncology at one of the foremost teaching medical centers in the world.
>
> Speaker #2's claim—A simple, flawed Child of God, living by FAITH in the Risen CHRIST JESUS, through whose GRACE he is currently experiencing an unmerited privilege of being selected to go through a unique experience to discover the awesomeness of GOD the ALMIGHTY.
>
> All Praise to God the Almighty, in the name of Jesus the Risen Christ.

CHAPTER 40

Their Science, My Faith

*Then your light shall break forth like the morning, your healing
shall spring forth speedily, and your righteousness shall go before
you; the glory of the LORD shall be your rear guard.*

—Isaiah 58:8 (NKJV)

There are specific vital themes that may appear to have become repetitive throughout my postings, and you may well ask yourself the question, "Haven't I read this before in an earlier post?" The answer is clearly yes. Not that I had planned for this to happen, as I never foresaw this as a book with a logical flow with the need to avoid redundancies. Each post represented my evolving truth, and since I never reread any of my previous postings until recently, I had no gauge on what to avoid in future posts. If the Lord desired that some revelations were repeated so that they could be more effective, then I am privileged to have been given authorship to write the words as He guided me. As I said earlier, faith comes from what we hear, and what we hear should come through the Word of God (Romans 10:17). Do we hear the Word of God one time and it adequately sustains our faith eternally, or is it not essential for us to hear and hear and hear the Word continuously so that our faith can be established and continue to develop and be reinforced? So, as the Holy Spirit leads me, faith and healing are the revolving themes, and their repetition is consequential.

I possess neither the intellectual nor theological competence to settle any argument suggesting conflicts between science and faith. What I have are my guiding principles, which are the truths that sustain my beliefs. Science and faith do not have to be conflicted; they have happily coexisted forever. If we acknowledge that the common source of all creation is God, then all conflicts disappear. Every element, every nanoparticle that science discovers has an origin—I believe they are from God. The theory that presupposes the origin of the universe was sourced from elements of unknown origins validates the alpha attributes ascribed to the Almighty God. He is the Beginning, before anything else, hence the source of everything. God created natural laws for the order and stability of all things. There are infinite capabilities and potentials yet to be harnessed by humankind; today much remains to be discovered about the mysteries of the omniscient God.

Common cures for past deadly plagues were once mysteries. As God reveals cures for disastrous terminal illnesses, the quality of life of His human creation improves. We bask in the knowledge that historical epidemic diseases, such as bubonic plague, cholera, polio, and smallpox, are a rarity these days as a result of progressive scientific enlightenment. However, new scientific discoveries are really orderly releases from God. With progressive revelations to science, one day current cancer survivors like me will be elevated above the tenuous categorizations of "in remission," to the distinct designation of "God completely cured him."

The solution to the cancer problem remains today's mystery. In His time, God will unveil the cure to man. What I write about today as transcendental healing will be the routine treatment of tomorrow through science as God progressively reveals cures to man. Because of our limitations, it is impossible to understand God's grand universal purpose. If during our times of tribulation we could get just a glimpse of God's greater purpose, we would, perhaps, be better able to appreciate our individual inconveniences. We would patiently endure our sufferings and possibly come to see them as privileged service to our Creator. How many parents have abandoned their children for whatever reason, only in later years to see how positively they have impacted the circumstances of others? If they had had foresight, wouldn't they have sacrificed to whatever extent necessary to keep and care for those children? Would I regard as joy every pain, agony, and displacement while I was experiencing them if I could clearly see God's purpose? I pray that the will of God is accomplished through my sufferings.

"You are doing so well, Mr. Mullings. You know, I think you're going to be cured of this disease." This was my oncologist speaking to me last week. Did flesh and blood reveal this to him? Remember, multiple myeloma is an incurable disease. Isn't such a statement then in conflict with the current scientific facts?

Through faith in Jesus Christ, I have persistently reiterated my truth, that you and many others will have proof of my healing. To be cured goes against the grain of established scientific facts, which are objective and backed by evidence and measurable outcomes. This form of cancer is incurable (today); however, I am a Christian believing in Jesus the Christ, whose words bear the ultimate, irrevocable truth. Faith in Jesus Christ governs my beliefs. When God promises anything, rest assured we can rely on that as an unalterable truth.

Unlike science, faith is not based on any established, predictable formula or empirical data. It is subjective, non-scientific, and specific to individuals. For Christians, faith is foundational. At its core is the acceptance of Jesus Christ as Lord God. Through Jesus the Christ, there is access to grace. Grace is the provision by the merciful God that makes all things possible by the exercise of one's faith. Therein lies the basis for the declaration of my healing and the persistent reiteration of this belief throughout this narrative. Being dismissive of the evidence and value of science is foolhardy. The facts are I am taking medicines for the disease, and I am seeing positive outcomes; that is indisputable. God gives us human beings knowledge and wisdom to advance science for our good. I am not conflicted. Whereas the facts are quantifiable, provable, and evidentiary, they may change with time; eternal truth from God is, however, everlasting. The fact is, stage 3 cancer ravaged my physical body, with years of terrifying pains and physical destruction, residual evidence of which still linger and impact me. I know that the eternal truth of my complete physical healing is in sight through faith in Jesus Christ.

If you accept my premise so far, you should reasonably conclude that faith is of the "spirit man," based on the truth that the omnipotent God is capable, and He will do things that defy logic. Science is of the "flesh man" based on facts derived from logic, evidence, and predictable outcomes. I am still undergoing chemotherapy, albeit at reduced levels. My oncologist has placed me in what he calls observation mode. I expect that I should be in the remission state next. Then finally, as the doctor now affirms, a cure for the incurable will be mine. Malachi 3:10 recommends that we should "prove God." I comply. Thanks for your prayers. Thank you for being my witnesses. You are witnessing the "hope" of Hebrews 11:1, becoming the "substance" of "faith." You are witnesses of God's love, as He heals me through grace by faith.

As you bear witness to my healing, your faith is being strengthened; Christ is being glorified, and my truth is becoming a demonstrable fact with conclusive and supportable evidence—the impossible made possible only by the grace of God the Almighty Father.

CHAPTER 41

I Stubbed My Toe

For all have sinned, and come short of the glory of God.

—Romans 3:23 (KJV)

Just look at him now! Who died and bequeathed him the supreme authority of knowledge and wisdom, that he is now king of his destiny? That's what I thought about myself after realizing my errant action. My arrogance haunted me for a while after a discussion with a brother in Christ. I knew what I had done wrong the minute he said, "My brother," in his calm, deep baritone. How could I have been such an ingrate? A few months ago, I would have given the world to have the numbers in the recent test results attributed to me. That day they were actually my results, results that were the best. Now, here I was, forgetting all the faith I had employed to get me to this point.

My feet had regained enough strength so that I could stand aloof with prideful smugness. No longer plagued with intense pain, fatigue, and exhaustion, I was regressing to the old pre-cancer, opinionated, assertive flesh man. My brain was no longer as clouded by the fog of chemotherapy. I had now regained some level of cognitive competence, and I could once again read above the first-grade level. My tongue was back freewheeling, such that I could maintain a dialogue. There I was, analyzing my test results, as though I was a trained professional. I was nitpicking about what could have been better and forecasting doomsday scenarios based on my logical projections. I had usurped the role of doctor, caregiver, and was even preempting God's will and timing. It was a blatant contradiction of the faith walk I had so ardently professed over the past months when I was in despair.

Such was my audacity and unfaithfulness. But God is so wonderful that He strategically placed His messenger of correction in the position of my sounding board, the listener of my conflicted utterance. Wasn't I the one who, when disability and incompetence were the order of my life, stoutly advanced the platform of faith triumphing over logic to achieve God's divine healing for me? I allowed the leaven of logic to permeate my human mind. Is it any wonder the omniscient God keeps giving me more developmental time? Obviously, I have not yet completed my forty years of desert journey needed to kill the old man of logic and reason so that the faith man can strive and prosper.

The wonders and mysteries of God continue to amaze me. We sometimes lose faith or seek to take control before the purpose of God is accomplished. As we experience perceived delays, our logical assumption is that our prayers in faith are not being answered. When we perceive that things are not working out at points in time as we expect, why are we tempted to force our will and forfeit the greater good that is God's plan? God knows how much time is needed for His works to be perfected in us. Clearly, I was not fully ready for service. I stubbed my toe while attempting to walk by sight and not by faith. I was back to being the old flesh man, reasoning and grasping for control. I was jeopardizing the final stages of my palpable faith healing by injecting the leaven of logic into my faith.

But God was merciful to me and spared me from the stronger discipline I so richly deserved. As Hebrews 12:6 (NIV) teaches, "The Lord disciplines the one he loves, and he chastens everyone he accepts as his son." Fortunately for me, I considered myself favored by God because of what Psalm 37:23 (KJV) tells me, "The steps of a good man are ordered by the LORD: and he delighteth in his way." So, I confessed to my friends on Facebook in the post that follows. Honestly, I had stubbed my toe, and it was good so that I could be corrected.

> Interesting how easy it is for us to slip away from the foundation of what brought us "THROUGH." As soon as the things we HOPED for prayerfully in FAITH start to manifest, we forget how desperately we clutched to the belief that only God through faith could help us. We suddenly slip back into human reasoning of how much outcomes could be improved with our intervention. We become masters of our destiny rather than, in faith, allowing God's will to accomplish what we earnestly prayed for in faith. Who among us is guilty? In humility, I plead guilty. Over the last many months, when I could hardly hobble around, when every millimeter of my natural fabric was in pain, I was grateful for even the slightest positive outcome. I would rejoice and proclaim with gratitude every micron of improvement in both my physical abilities and test results that demonstrated how the mysteries of faith were producing miracles for me.
>
> I have been contrasting the differences between faith and fleshly actions throughout my posts. Fleshly thinking, I stated, was based on logic, predictable outcomes, and previously proven facts. In contrast, I used the familiar scriptural reference of Hebrews 11:1 to show how what we hope for in faith (not knowing what exact formulas God uses) would become substance and be manifested clearly to bear witness and serve as testimony. How soon I forgot.
>
> God never forgets. He is so merciful that even when our foolish thinking and expressions go against his perfect will for us, He does not

instantaneously move in anger to punishment mode. Instead, as our merciful Father, He provides us with options for our correction. It is then incumbent on us to be attentive to his leading and take corrective actions. I believe that God sometimes communicates to us through individuals. I have never personally seen a biblical angel; therefore, God's messengers can be people like us. Weren't the prophets humans? Yesterday my messenger was one of my kindest, most genteel friends, a person of whom I think the world. He never misses an opportunity to applaud my faith and speaks of my professed walk as a Christian with admiration. This time he was the one who stood me up and straightened me out.

My friend had also boldly traveled the unpaved desert road that cancer presented him, but is now delivered by God through faith. I was reviewing with him the vast improvements shown in every area of my last test results except for one parameter. To the devil's pleasure and delight, it was the one that I saw as the barometer of my progress, even though the doctor only uses it to factor into a resulting ratio that he uses to show my progress. So here emerged my all-powerful FLESH dynamic. Although most of the other markers were now within suitable ranges, showing how God's good work was being accomplished in me, human reasoning dominated my evaluation of the results. Logically, if that one parameter continued to trend, as it seemed to be doing currently, basic math told me that the ratio would be off and that would be bad news; that's fact.

At the urging of my flesh, I mounted a stellar case about my concerns. My friend, in his clear, calm voice, subtly but profoundly remarked,

"Brother Courtney, at the urging of the Spirit, I have to tell you that you are focusing on that which is not in line with your faith." Before he had even completed his thought, I became acutely aware of the power of my tongue and the fleshly content of my heart. I could only imagine how Peter felt when he heard the rooster crow the third time. Proverbs 18:21 tells us, "The tongue has the power of life and death." And Luke 6:45 notes, "For out of the abundance of the heart the mouth speaks."

Could I have been more ungrateful and acted more contrary to my faith belief? I was like one of the nine ungrateful lepers cleansed, according to Luke 17:17-18. After Jesus had cleansed ten lepers, only one returned to give God glory. Rather than extolling God's goodness and expressing my gratitude to Him for all He had taken me through, there I was, all pompous and too smart for my own good. I was speaking to the logic of what I could calculate rather than, in faith, patiently resting in the continuing revelation of God's mysteries in my life that I could not yet see.

Thank you, my fearless brother, for with boldness you declared what God had placed on your heart for my correction. As Paul states in Acts 20:27, "For I did not shrink from declaring to you the whole counsel of God." Through this, I am reminded that a message from God may come from anyone He singles out, even the good gentleman, whom I least expected to stand to my face in such a casual conversation. Proverbs 27:6 makes it clear that "the slap of a friend can be trusted to help you, but the kisses of an enemy are nothing but lies." Remember who the enemy of your soul is. He will bring you into the field of the flesh where logic and reasoning breed fear and doubt, which will ultimately defeat the power of your faith and limit your access to the abundance of grace.

So why am I posting my failings today? Shouldn't this be my shame? Am I not a "loser" here? Much to the contrary, I see this whole episode as me winning; and maybe just like me, someone reading this may have slipped a bit in exercising their faith and is miserable because of it. I am not sure that I have read any biblical account of any perfect earthly human that God has ever called to greatness. No, not even Job; read Job 38, and you will see. All have sinned not only before they received Christ as Savior and Lord, but even after. Our merciful Father, however, provides the route for the forgiveness of sins. It is not about how many times we fall, but how often we get up and the strength we gain from getting up. It is so comforting that Jesus said in Luke 5:32 (KJV), "I came not to call the righteous, but sinners to repentance." Most importantly, I post this because, in doing so, I am doing the exact opposite of what the devil would want me to do. I believe his intentions were for me to focus on something that seems logical, even factual, something easily measurable, so that I would be distracted from the real working of my faith. By posting this account, I am saying, "I caught you in the act old feller, I won't remain in condemnation for my error."

My friends, don't stay distracted or dwell upon what you can see, compute, or deduce after you have deposited your concerns in faith as I did. Remember why we choose the faith approach.

The lure of believing in what is logical and predictable does not require faith; it is the easy out-route and the path taken by most. By doing so, you are allowing a little leaven into your truth. In Galatians 5:9, Paul says a little leaven leavens the whole dough. In Matthew 16:6, Jesus cautions against allowing in the leaven of nonbelievers. Let's give God thanks for ALL He provides, including the people He places in our lives and the provisions of His grace that we can access by exercising our faith. Meanwhile, watch out for the workings of the flesh; it is the gateway for a little leaven at a time, used by the devil. Finally, as James 4:7 advises, "Resist the devil, and he will flee from you." I love you all.

CHAPTER 42

Those Were the Days

Blessed be the God and Father of our Lord Jesus Christ! According to his great mercy, he has caused us to be born again to a living hope through the resurrection of Jesus Christ from the dead, to an inheritance that is imperishable, undefiled, and unfading, kept in heaven for you, who by God's power are being guarded through faith for a salvation ready to be revealed in the last time. In this you rejoice, though now for a little while, if necessary, you have been grieved by various trials.

—1 Peter 1:3-6 (ESV)

Let me reiterate: according to science, my affliction is an incurable disease; that is a scientific fact. I could interpret that as a warning to start the countdown for my end of days on earth and prepare to die in short order. It may appear silly to have nurtured a belief that was contrary to the facts; however, as a Christian, believing that God's truth could overrule earthly realities, I looked forward with hope that I could have life, and more abundantly, as promised in John 10:10. The secrets to the cure for multiple myeloma are contained in the mysteries that God will eventually reveal to the domain of science.

Having presented my request through prayers to God, I needed to wait and not be anxious about anything, as instructed in Philippians 4:6. The fulfillment of my desire to be healed was beyond my control and would be done according to God's timeline and plan. Science would eventually catch up with God's preexisting revelations. My level of spiritual maturity became such that I felt no compulsion to find an excuse as to why the substance of my faith was not evident when I summoned it. As I have confessed throughout this book, I felt the walls of my faith shaken several times, especially when the journey seemed endless and I kept failing various lines of therapy, particularly the failure of the autologous stem cell transplant. I would speculate that maybe my request of God was overly ambitious. Then I would take hold of myself.

It was evident I could not pay, bribe, or bargain my way through the process. The fact is, it was not so much about what I could do in a transactional manner with God, but what He had already done in His grand plan, and I was favored to be a part of it. My willpower and all I could mobilize trying to wrest control from Him were futile. I was powerless and incapable of accelerating God's process. Therefore, I concluded that it was never about me, my will, or my willpower; the fact is, the ultimate will of God must prevail. I behave with the confidence that, being redeemed by Him, my petitions for healing line up with His perfect will and that He will never cease to be merciful to me because God is mercy, not an act of mercy that changes. Lamentations 3:22-24 (KJV) teaches me, "It is of the LORD's mercies that we are not consumed, because His compassions fail not. They are new every morning: great is thy faithfulness. The LORD is my portion, saith my soul; therefore, will I hope in him."

Why did I have to go through all I did anyway? A friend raised this point in response to one of my posts. His concern resulted from the age-old paradox of why a loving, merciful God would allow His redeemed children to suffer. That is beyond me, and any response I offer will fall way short of what is the mind of God. It remains a pertinent question for Christians and nonbelievers. But another way to phrase the same question would be: Why was the devil allowed to unleash such a juggernaut as cancer on me?

Is God powerless over the devil's actions? We read in Job that the devil had to request God's help to remove the protection God had on Job before he could execute his evil work. God is aware of everything even before it happens. He didn't have to wait for the cancer to afflict me to deal with it. He foresaw it and planned for my healing. As sovereign LORD, He has power over everything. Indeed, He could have prevented what had befallen me, but He never promised I would be free from trials. It was not the worst thing that could have happened to me; I still had life. I will never know how many worse situations God aborted or diverted so that they didn't impact me. My illness then must have been a part of His greater divine plan, not so much for me to suffer, but that I be reshaped for His divine purpose, through which there would be suffering. God did not spare Jesus Christ our Lord, His only begotten Son, from the crucible of pain. This was a part of God's grand plan to mercifully redeem mankind back to Him. Because of His suffering, death, and subsequent resurrection, I claimed the privilege of unparalleled access and opportunities for deliverance from my ailment.

What then were the positive outcomes of my journey? First, I was convinced that my illness was not reprobation from God; in fact, it was a process of helping me to develop the right relationship with Him. I receive of Him not just the things that satisfy my wants, but also the spiritual bread for my soul. I have the confidence that as long as I am cloaked in the righteousness of Jesus Christ, my works are aligned with His will, which in turn glorifies God the Father. Through the process, I heard from God in many ways, and He taught me a great deal.

I grew spiritually through the experience. Although I would not dare to suggest I have the answer to that age-old question, what I can conclude is that God desired me to have an improved relationship with Him. In my suffering, I completely surrendered my will and was dependent on Him. I desired and craved His presence. My ear and brain were tuned to His voice so keenly, I would not lose that coveted spiritual connection. In my weakness, I found strength in God, and I was revived to gradually appreciate each step in the continuing healing process. Since I had no control over the pace of my recovery, I was made to appreciate the virtue of patience. It is impossible to fathom the infinite mind of God and His ways to unduly try to influence actions contrary to His will, so submission was another lesson I had to learn.

God knew I would derive a renewed sense of loyalty and dedication serving Him. He foreknew I would be sharing my story about His marvelous work in me as a testament of persistent and sustained faith in Him. I can reasonably conclude that the sovereign God foreknew my diagnosis. He allowed me to go through the crucible, provided the means for my healing, and trusted me to develop a stronger relationship with Him. He could then give me the benefits of a spiritual makeover and, out of it all, I could become a good steward with all He has entrusted me. And after all that is said, why did God allow me to go through the suffering? As His masterful handiwork, He knows what's best for me.

More than thirty years ago, I gave my sister what I believe is one of the best paintings I had ever done in my youth. After years of neglect and mishandling, it had fallen into severe disrepair and no longer showed very well. She treasured the piece and placed great value in it. The canvas was shredding, the paint was crumbling and falling off, and even though it lacked its previous luster and appeal, she treasured it. The task to remount and restretch the aged canvas was extraordinarily intricate and needed a high level of care. It was so brittle, I had to handle it delicately. I still have not completed the task of retouching the painted areas, and I expect it will be a long, tedious process to restore it completely. I think, however, that it will be well worth it and I hope it will continue to delight her once the process is completed. Just like that painting, in which we take tremendous delight, is my great work, so too am I God's great work. If He in His infinite wisdom needs to stretch my very fibers and retouch my fading colors so that others can appreciate His great work in me, and I can continue to bring Him delight, then I can only thank Him for the process, regardless of the suffering.

Now that I can reflect on the dreary days of my illness, I appreciate the journey. I feel a great sense of gratitude to God and thank Him for the caring earth angels He sent to bear me on their wings with the tenderest of love and attentive care. Aside from my chief caregiver (my wife), the clinicians who administered my care are unsung heroes. I now recall how every change impacted on me. I would stress over my days of therapy. The drive to the infusion center would be agonizing. Every bump and turn would cause pain to my fractured spine, and then there were the seemingly endless hours at the treatment center and the longing to return home to the comfort of my bed. It was during those troubled times at the treatment center that God allowed me to appreciate the frailty and vagaries of our humanity. Just seeing people in their suffering gave me a fresh perspective on life.

The waiting area at the infusion center provided me some of my most interesting lessons. Not unlike the world outside, whatever conclusions I came to about my fellow patients were erroneous. I could not establish a reasonable opinion of who was who by their material presentation. One's attire was mostly for comfort rather than for show, so what people wore did not define them. Decoding the vacuous stares on most of the faces belied their life's history and accomplishments. Smiles were rare but sighs were plentiful. Pride was put on hold and status in life was unimportant. Regardless of classification—ethnicity, social standing, or financial status—there was a sense of commonality among us. In silence, we knew we were all bonded by a common dilemma, the consequences of cancer. As I frequently surveyed the room and glanced at other patients, I would find myself musing about each person's particular story and how different they would be from my own. The dejected blank stares and polite smiles we occasionally exchanged masked the truths of our souls.

In surveying the waiting room, there were times I would conjure up countless metaphors I associated with life. In the short span of a lifetime, an individual can gain much fame and accomplishment, but life itself is tenuous. Just trying to guess how much unrealized potential was in the waiting area was stunning. The marauding parasite that is cancer was purposed to wreak havoc on us. Indiscriminately, it could suck away the hope that sustained us and could, in short order, put out the light of talented lives. Based on the sheer number of patients in this single-treatment center, I could imagine how many families were being impacted by the horrific scourge that is cancer.

We were not just victims controlled by a doomsday prognosis; we were unrelenting fighters hoping to become overcomers.

We showed up for treatment because we dared to believe that as brave warriors still nurturing ambitious dreams of future outrageous accomplishments, cancer was a temporary impediment that we would endure without sacrificing our unyielding expectations for even greater futures. Behind the veiled faces and fragile bodies were lives of remarkable successes and profiles of courage. Prior to our current state, we were initiators of joy, the lives of parties, pillars of strength, and influencers of world changes. On any given day, I could be sitting next to someone of worldly accomplishment or a pauper. The irrationality that the guy next to me was a doctor and current cancer patient was a cursory enigma. As an accomplished physician, he had successfully resolved many patients' issues and provided them hope. Now he, too, was just another cancer patient in the waiting area dependent on someone else to prescribe and administer treatment for his cancer, just like me.

Looking past the shell-shocked masks of endured pains and mental and physical disabilities, it was evident that many were eager to reassert their prideful independence, silently hoping to recover respect and not be pitied; to be shown understanding, not condescension; and to hear words of hope and positive affirmations, not be reminded of the ominous consequences and potentials the horrifying disease bore, regardless of their factuality.

I often pondered what provided a basis for hope for those who did not believe in a higher power beyond the doctors and their therapies, as the death prognosis progressively stole the oxygen from their life-sustaining flames. Do those of wealth and earthly prosperity consider the folly of what they have sacrificed in pursuit of material gains and the futility of not being able to enlist their wealth to their cure? And how about those of little means? Do their hopes hang on the fickleness of the day's political ideology that determines how their health-care bills will be paid? As for those of us of a faith persuasion, when failures and disappointments are persistent outcomes, does faith provide the motivation to keep holding on and sustain the resolve to not let go? Medications may temporarily delude us from reality. However, like the fleeting winds, their effectiveness eventually diminishes. Only the intangible hope through Jesus Christ is all-sustaining. It can last for as long as you compel your faith to believe that Jesus "is" and "will," as you believe through Him. On that foundation is hope eternal built.

With the correct mindset, it is remarkable how the tedious biweekly rendezvous with the dreaded infusion center became a pleasant routine for me. Just breaking from the boredom and solitary confinement of my bedroom was a welcome change. Over time, I even started looking forward to chemotherapy, although I can imagine the poor care team could have used a break from me at times. You see, as a pitiful, caged bird, I spent my days longing for normalcy, more human interaction, and just simply to share in some meaningful conversation.

So the excellent clinicians and caregivers became my victims. I would engage them on any subject that came to mind. To capture and hold their attention, I became an expert on every topic (or so I thought). I pretended to be smart, venturing into discussions on subjects I could only fake my way through. It was my way of engaging real people in intelligent conversation, since the walls in my bedroom refused to talk to me. God bless those busy professionals for humoring me with any form of acknowledgment. I desperately wanted to prove I was still capable of engaging in intelligent conversations.

Even my oncologist, although seemingly in the highest demand among his peers, could not help but accommodate me in my mania. As busy as he was, he was not beyond being one of my captive victims (if only for a minute or two). While executing his core professional tasks, he would be compelled to politely facilitate the myriad of wild topics I would contrive to throw at him during our brief sessions.

He was quite humorous, but never allowed himself to laugh at his own jokes. He reminded me of a certain silver screen character. But best of all, he was a most positive advocate and made my visits very interesting. He would make time to address my concerns, and we would engage in discussions that were just short of fixing world hunger. The range of topics would change with such rapidity, and were so varied, I had no time to contemplate or fake intelligent responses. I thoroughly enjoyed my visits with him. Now that I think of it, was he really interested in the substance of my responses, or was this just part of his therapy to keep me distracted from my dreaded ailment? Or maybe he was evaluating my cognitive capabilities? If only he knew how much restraint I showed in not turning the tables on him with a few wisecracks of my own, as is my normal disposition. But I feared he would take me seriously and prescribe me some appropriate looney medications. He's my doctor, remember! And no matter how nice a guy he appears to be, he has a little pad and paper, writes ugly in illegible codes, and knows my pharmacy. Nonetheless, I felt empowered, as he would always find ways to debunk my fears, treat me as a capable and intelligent human being, and provide me with encouragement and inspiration, which made me look forward to my next visit with him.

I was blessed too to have brilliant, sensitive nurses and technicians administering care to me. By politely engaging me, even in my absurdities, these blessed, long-suffering professionals were my incidental therapists. Unwittingly, they provided me more than just medications; their warm, caring smiles and words of encouragement were therapy for my soul. I am sure I would be embarrassed to hear a replay of some of the irrational nonsense they were forced to listen to during my treatment.

As I would discover later, my attitude gained me much love and respect from them; maybe the charm offensive was my best asset in those days. As my mind cleared in the latter stages of my treatment, I had a sense that I was a favored patient; at least it helped my ego to think so. Most of my caregivers knew me by name, and thus, when I made an entrance into the infusion center, I would receive a rousing reception, with pleasantries and genuine interest in my well-being. I could tell they were duly pleased by the positive, progressive outcomes to which they had contributed. God had allowed them to witness the various stages of my journey, from my worst of times, when I was hobbling in pain and confusion, to the point where I had become a healthy, functional human again.

It just shows how, as the Spirit of God produced the right attitude in me, it evoked the most positive responses. Busy professionals, who might have otherwise regarded me as just another forgettable patient as they went about their very demanding jobs, instead recognized me as an individual with potential and worthy of their care. I wish I could mention them all by name and relate the unique and positive experiences I enjoyed with each of them individually, but they know who they are and I thank them.

CHAPTER 43

My Caregiver

A good woman is hard to find, and worth far more than diamonds.
Her husband trusts her without reserve, and never has reason to
regret it. Never spiteful, she treats him generously all her life long.

—Proverbs 31:10-12 (MSG)

Caregivers are among the least heralded and underrecognized players in the healing and recovery process. It is they who assume the awesome responsibility of guardianship, protection, and administering to most of the emotional and physical needs of the sick entrusted in their care. I refer specifically to family members who voluntarily commit themselves to the 24/7 role of attending to the infirmed. They selflessly accept an indeterminable assignment to be on the front line of care. There they are inevitably saddled with both the physical and mentally taxing job of ensuring the comprehensive needs of the demanding patient are met promptly.

My wife, as caregiver, is the focus of the next few lines. This is not to diminish the role of the other professional care providers, who are loyal to their codes of ethics and sacrifice so much for their professions. I noted earlier how the medical professionals, including doctors, nurses, and technicians, displayed the highest levels of sensitivity and professionalism as they cared for me. It is not until we step back from our suffering and put into context what it takes for these professionals to show up to care for each patient that we are sensitized to them as individuals with needs of their own. They have to deal with the unique personalities, moods, and behaviors of a diverse set of patients, while suppressing their personal biases, struggles, and demons to smile and encourage the patients as they diligently deliver care ethically and professionally.

My spouse is a nurse and my chief caregiver. Contrary to what would be assumed to be a seamless operation, various complexities can arise. I was not just the testy patient of my wife; we were conjoined spirits. Whereas in her professional practice she has the option to greet, treat, and move on to the next patient, she was stuck with me (I hoped). The umbilical linkage of our souls through holy matrimony meant I was not just an abstract individual but a part of her, lying in suffering. She was constrained to stay near me, where she was subjected to hearing my woeful moans and groans and panicked expressions while trying to anticipate my next unpredictable action. She was not only burdened with my physical care, she was also forced to carry her grief in silence to accommodate mine. She wore a mask of bravery for me, but I could sense that inside she was continuously grieving, filled with foreboding that the worst could happen to me.

Sadly, there was nothing I could do to assuage her fears. I lacked the credibility to speak on the disease's progression and did not have the intuition to try. Not only did I lack the physical strength to extend her a comforting hand, but I also did not have the mental competence to compose a soothing word that might comfort her. My mind was always consumed with my dilemma; I needed her strength even as I was oblivious of her needs. God bless her for the indomitable courage she showed in coping with my constant demands on her while remaining stable.

I became aware that she had established a diligent and steadfast routine of praying and fasting. I could sense the purity of her intentions. My sudden disablement had had an impact of seismic proportion on her, but she remained resolute in her faith that God would provide the most favorable outcome. I was both her spiritual and physical partner, a source of strength she had grown accustomed to relying on over the years. Before this, she allowed me to play a lead role in many of the affairs of our lives, and now there I was, a use-less, incapacitated remnant. Undoubtedly, she must have wondered several times what the future would be like without me. The pathetic mass lying helplessly on the bed might not be around for much lon-ger. Having to assume responsibility for all the affairs of our lives would definitely place unbudgeted demands on her.

The essential task of caring for the health, safety, and general well-being of the patient is paramount. However, the assumption of a range of new and continuously emerging personal responsibil-ities—including resource and logistics management, financial man-agement, and the management of external relationships—without the luxury of getting up to speed in time to cope with these demands can lead to disaster. She now had to take full charge of our combined responsibilities and to account to the myriad of stakeholders, a task that would normally fall to me.

A person's normal lifestyle can become totally reordered to that of a caregiver overnight. One does not necessarily sign up for the indefinite time required to serve in this role. There is generally no specific, predictable agenda outlining a schedule; neither is there any preparatory training available to adequately equip the individual to become a caregiver. The role requires on-the-job training with zero allocated resources and no supervision to provide guidance and over-sight. The challenge imposed by the possibility of losing a loved one in your care is enough to cause anxiety and stress, without the emo-tional entanglement of watching that person suffer.

As if she was not bursting at the seams with enough new responsibilities, as my immune system progressively weakened, it became imperative for me to spend months in isolation. My wife had to valiantly stand guard against all potentially dangerous, infec-tious invaders as my life could be jeopardized. With my phone dis-abled, she became the default point of contact, fielding the endless stream of inquiries about my status. Then there was the challenge of meticulously managing the delicate balance between facilitating the desires of friends and family to physically interact with me and the need to protect me without appearing to spurn their genuine attempt to reach out in love. The confluence of these demands took a toll on her. There were noticeable changes in her bearing. The physical and emotional tortures were sucking the flesh from her bones. In no time she had lost quite a bit of weight, the wear and drag on her face belying her age. Challenged as I was, I could tell her movements lacked cadence and coordination, as though she was simply floating mindlessly.

The strength of a godly woman is immeasurable, and her ability to always mobilize inner resources to maintain her sanity while reinforcing my hope and conviction for recovery was testimony to her deeply rooted faith. To augment her spiritual courage, she found inspiration through the church collectively, our bishop and the pastoral team, the family, and a cadre of reliable and devoted friends, whose unrelenting support and solidarity were unbreachable. Church attendance was an imperative for her. On Sundays and Wednesdays, I would expectantly await the nuggets of spiritual wisdom she had gleaned and would relay to me for encouragement and the strengthening of my faith. She celebrated the slightest evidence of my progress and provided me with positive anecdotes to counter any negativity that came from me.

To reinforce my positive development through God's favor, she would task me to do things so I could prove it myself. In one instance, she reminded me of how, even as I was drowsy, weary, and unable to move without discomfort, she came to me in pain. A fragment of broken glassware had become so deeply embedded in her foot, it was impossible for her to remove. She reminded me of how I confidently asked her if she believed that I could pray and have God remove it, to which she responded affirmatively. Her testimony is that after my prayer, the embedded material miraculously disappeared. Such was her confidence that, even in my weakened state, she believed God could empower me to perform miracles.

I can only imagine that the manifestation of God's divine power served to reinforce her faith and renew her strength. Even in my physically and mentally weakened state, God provided me with strength and power I had never before realized. What she had witnessed also encouraged her that God the Father had secured my healing. My recovery got to the stage where I recognized I had significant memory gaps, but my caregiver wife was a reliable truth teller. She would validate and inform me of things that still mystified me or that I had no knowledge about.

When the caregiver is rooted in the faith that God will provide the ultimate care, the need for worry is lessened. That answers the question of who cares for the caregiver. There are emotional taxes, unreasonable demands of patients, and unpredictable external stimuli always clamoring for attention. There are also the stresses imposed on the caregiver to assume the roles formerly handled by the patient. The demands on time and attending to necessary dependencies are unquantifiable, such that even sleep becomes a when-possible event.

Caregivers deserve the highest level of respect, forbearance, and understanding. They need every kind of assistance and support. Their responsibilities are unquantifiable, yet their time and resource budget do not increase to facilitate the added responsibilities. For a spouse or close family member to assume that role, there is the emotional drain that plagues them. They sacrifice so much as providing care moves beyond the scope of mere duty to the incredible demand placed on the soul to not just preserve life but to be a confidant, a spiritual adviser, and a source of hope in many ways.

I realize this episode has changed my wife by how sensitive she is to my well-being. I am convinced that it is impossible for anyone thrust in that role to ever regain a sense of normalcy. It should be easy to understand that the caregiver may become indelibly scarred for life by their experience. My takeaway from this time of illness is that God anoints special people with the mental fortitude to be caregivers. In addition to all the other personal attributes that qualified my wife as the consummate caregiver, she was rooted in her faith in God and trusted in His goodness and mercy for my healing. It is not a stretch for me to believe that she is an angel from God.

REFLECTIONS

The Voices

Holding fast the faithful word as he hath been taught,
that he may be able by sound doctrine both to
exhort and to convince the gainsayers.

—Titus 1:9 (KJV)

Therefore, dear friends, since you have been forewarned,
be on your guard so that you may not be carried away by the error of
the lawless and fall from your secure position.
But grow in the grace and knowledge of our Lord and Savior
Jesus Christ. To him be glory both now and forever! Amen.

—2 Peter 3:17-18 (NIV)

There were times when it was difficult for me to process the streams of advice flowing toward me from various directions, including my brain. Much of it was just babble and, given my weakened state, confusion abounded. So many conflicting theories and beliefs were being thrown at me, I had to implement various forms of filtering. Oftentimes a polite "no" became grounds for personal condemnation and extended arguments. To defuse tensions, I had to become a master pacifist. I quickly learned that, given my distressed state, my interest would be best served by not even uttering a polite disagreement when confronted with much of the dogma. It was ridiculous how many people would claim to be the authority on cures, diet, theology, and prophecies. In many cases, their sources were unverifiable; at best, some were roadkill retrieved from the information superhighway (the Internet), where everyone can be adviser in chief. Had I taken a fraction of the strongly recommended sure fixes and panaceas, who knows where I would be now? Of course, I tried a few, but concluded they would be ineffective for the type of cancer I had.

Not to be outdone, I had my share of freshly minted theologians, who evidently found my hapless state fertile ground for their versions of what was righteousness for me. Merely saying I had cancer was enough for some to say I had effectively named and claimed it upon myself, as though the existential disease was some abstraction "out there" and would materialize by me mentioning it. Wasn't the insurgent pestilence already within me ravaging my entire body? I would ponder such spurious speculations that presumed I was vested with inherent powers to inflict myself with what had already afflicted me. This was in direct opposition to my belief that my prayers, in faith, would eradicate the affliction. While I was languishing in misery and torment, the last thing I needed was the confusion of the next version of some catchy-sounding doctrine. I purposed not to compromise my core understandings of God's Word to accommodate the many iterations of other people's theology.

Regardless of the compelling urgency I felt to be rid of the torment, I challenged myself to be anchored on the sound doctrines that governed faith, and not be "tossed to and fro, and carried about with every wind of doctrine," Ephesians 4:14 (KJV). I was in no position to pass judgment and condemnation. I understood that even well-intentioned individuals could be used by the devil. Unsuspectingly, they could be innocent pawns who had given heed to seducing spirits and doctrines of devils, as Paul characterized it in 1 Timothy 4:1. I stood firm in the knowledge that faith in God would produce my healing, regardless of the disease's origins, or any words or characterization I could call into reality. With all confidence, therefore, I boldly enunciated to God my Father that I was suffering from a form of cancer called multiple myeloma and prayed in faith that I would physically experience my hope of healing.

I did not doubt that God already knew about it. I felt the need, however, to voice it so that my ear would hear it, and my soul would be entrenched with my appeal to God. Continuously doing this would also be a reminder that I should be relentless in my faith pursuit to achieve the faith objective I had been praying for. In Luke 18-1:8, Jesus related the parable of the widow and the unjust judge. Her persistent appeal to the judge eventually earned her the justice she relentlessly sought. This taught me that my prayer in faith for what I needed should be specific, persistent, and consistent, with the hope that the promises in the Word of God would produce the conclusive justice I sought, which was my total cure from the disease. God would eventually produce a cure as the fair judge whose words are unfailing. If I failed to tell the world I had cancer, then what would I say I was delivered from in my future testimony? My apparent depressed state must have signaled to some that I was not in right standing with God and had committed some doctrinal breach. Isn't this so much like the experience of poor old Job? When he was destitute, his friends found it the most convenient time to judge and convict him on the merits with which God was pleased.

Being a Christian, I stood firm on my core beliefs, trusting that the Holy Spirit would guide me in all truths. Again, I do not doubt that those who sought to guide me were well-intentioned, but I had to make the distinction between what was right-sounding and what was righteous. In aspiring for spiritual guidance, it was necessary for me to filter out those voices that were not divinely inspired. I could then carefully allow in the things that God had declared for me. God gave authority to those who were chosen to make prophetic revelations that would instruct and guide me. I am duty-bound to acknowledge and take heed of their words from God. In so doing, God would allow me to discern what was of Him. It was easier to distinguish between His words, the traditions of men, and dogmas founded upon someone's ideas that had morphed into doctrine. To refuse correction from those God had directed to me would be arrogance and disobedience, for which there would be consequences.

God desires obedience, as He instructs in Hebrews 3:7-8 (NIV), "Today, if you hear his voice, do not harden your hearts." When voices declared terrible news to me, and I could count them as joy, I knew they were under the guidance and direction of the Holy Spirit.

We live in a time when there are many sources influencing what we hear. The proliferation of falsity, conspiracy, and subliminal messages of ill intent makes truth questionable. The inerrant Word of God has been subjected to so many interpretations, it has become difficult to distinguish between what the intellectually astute ascribe as their faithful interpretation of the Word and what has been spiritualized by others. Science also provides us with treatment that may enhance the quality of our lives and it is foolhardy not to heed such wisdom. Today's clinicians are well equipped with knowledge from God for the benefit of His creation, and they need to be respected. Nonetheless, it is advisable to be aware that there may be other influences that can affect the soundness and wisdom of their decisions. These well-intended practitioners are also fallible humans trying to follow the protocols and ethics governing their professions.

But there should be no mistake; the wisdom of God supersedes everything. There is His inerrant Word in the Bible, and He gives us the Holy Spirit to teach us all truths. He is not boisterous and imposing, but respectful and gentle, and guides us appropriately. In times of decision-making, we are often aware of His leading, but our human fleshly self hears the voice of the Spirit as an irrational annoyance and creates opposition to Him, supplanting His directives with the comfortable rational alternatives of the day.

I was mostly compliant with the recommendations of the clinicians throughout my illness. However, at the urging of the Holy Spirit, I also opted out of certain medications and treatment. So far, the outcomes have been to my benefit and I truly believe that I heard God's instructions and that my actions honored Him. I am aware that my eventual cure may not be from some miracle but could come from God's revelation through science administered by the hands of man, and I look forward to how God will order it.

God is in the business of restoring and extending life. In 2 Kings 20:1-6, it is written that God pronounced death on King Hezekiah.

After he prayed to God, with humility and much emotion, reminding God of how he had been loyal to Him, God, in response, added fifteen years to his life. God can do that and more for me. In faith, I keep praying, reminding the LORD of my status, never losing hope that what I pray for will eventually be manifested. Having been near death and experienced cognitive and physical disability, to be where I am now at my current state of recovery, I am overwhelmingly optimistic that I shall bear witness of what I have been acting on in faith for the past three-plus years. I have seen some of my worst disappointments and trials transformed into my best opportunities. There were times in the past when I prayed that God would change some specific trouble so that I would no longer be plagued by it. However, God, in His holistic wisdom, would instead change other conditions around me, usually with me as the beneficiary of those changes. How magnificent it is that the all-knowing God did not fulfill my selfish, shortsighted prayers but, in His wisdom, addressed the issues in my environment for my betterment. Sometimes apparent unanswered prayers produce the best outcomes.

Christians are not immune to challenges and sufferings. I find comfort by not dwelling on the disease these days. God has helped me to appreciate that nearly all of us are living with some type of disease or medical condition. Mine is cancer, and cancer is just another disease. Multiple myeloma remains a deadly disease only because the scientific community has not yet received the revelation from God about how to cure it. At this point, I have bettered the odds. I have exceeded the twenty-nine month survival rate for stage 3 multiple myeloma.

It may sound irrational for me to say that my affliction has brought me some good, but I would not be the first to say this. In Psalm 119:71 (KJV), David reflected, "It is good for me that I have been afflicted; that I might learn thy statutes." I have devoted hours thinking about how much good my affliction has produced. The mere fact that I came back from near death, to where I am currently, is a miracle in itself. What I gained through suffering is unparalleled. My current existence is God-approved for now, and I will seek to maximize the best of it as long as God continues to favor me. There is so much yet for me to do and accomplish, why would I not seek to prolong my life?

There is a saying, "In the midst of life there is death." Of course, I will die one day, as will most of us. I am prepared to die. The Bible tells me it is inevitable. Potentially, it could even be from something unrelated to the current disease. But, in faith, I believe that before I die I will be cured of this deadly plague. Someday I will lose this body of imperfection but retain my imperishable spirit. Later, when my body is transformed into its glorified state, cancer-free and God perfected, I shall again be clothed in perfection as God desires it. There is a better life after this, but I want to make the most of this life that God has approved exclusively for me.

Writing this book would never have happened had I not gone through this experience, so there is some blessing to be had from my misery. The journey has reshaped me. I am wiser, transformed, and have a greater appreciation of the fruit of the Spirit. The term *value* is more extensive to me, with all of God's creation now part of my value system. How can I not conclude that God has been good to me when I have heard Him and experienced His goodness and mercies in so many ways?

*"You will seek the LORD your God, and you will find **Him** if you seek Him with all your heart and with all your soul. When you are in distress, and all these things come upon you in the latter days, when you turn to the LORD your God and obey His voice (for the LORD your God **is** a merciful God), He will not forsake you nor destroy you."*

—Deuteronomy 4:29-31 (NKJV)

LESSONS LEARNED

I will praise You, O LORD, with my whole heart;
I will tell of all Your marvelous works.

—Psalm 9:1 (NKJV)

Maybe it is a paradox for me to say that I am thankful for the terrible sufferings I have had to endure. In this book, I have used many words to express the range of horrifying experiences I suffered. How, for example, many of my dreams and aspirations have been altered or aborted; how I have been scarred physically and mentally; the negative impacts wrought on my family and friends. My perspective on life will be viewed through a different prism hereafter as my life has been completely repurposed. What good, then, could result from such a tragedy? Pains and setbacks do not invoke positive thoughts.

As God would have me realize, the pains were not just reminders of my human vulnerabilities and mortality, but a dashboard with a light warning me of the need for a comprehensive spiritual checkup and repair. The diminished cognitive experience brought me to a place of humility, where my inability to function as an intelligent adult reminded me of Jesus' instruction that we have to be like children to inherit the kingdom of God. The physical disablement and debilitation meant I had little use for my accumulated material possessions. How apropos is it that I should reflect on 1 John 2:15 (NIV), which states, "Do not love the world or anything in the world. If anyone loves the world, love for the Father is not in them." This is so because we can become double-minded, shifting our priorities to vain earthly things in deference to what our Father desires of us.

To become conscious, as it were, of my nakedness before God, as Adam and Eve did, was spiritually humbling. Pride was not a quality God wanted in me. As my fecklessness and inadequacies became evident, I was awakened to my dependence on the leading of the Spirit. It was all that remained intact as my mind and body declined. Life took on new meaning when I fully realized that, regardless of how well I took care of myself, I had no control over the length of my days. My time on earth was beyond my control and was within the domain of a higher power—God Almighty, my Father and LORD.

Fear and anguish tested the foundation of my faith as to whether it was built on rock or sand. Illusions from the dark presented me with a quick escape from my misery rather than a plan for endurance through devotion to God and His promises. When the frailty of my physical being was exposed and my mind was tossed into a whirlwind of confusion, I discovered peace and hope in the promises of God, as in Isaiah 66:2 (NKJV) he assures me with the words, "But on this one will I look: On him who is poor and of a contrite spirit, And who trembles at My word." In destitution, I found sufficiency in His grace to provide for and sustain me.

My bout with cancer was something I would rather not have had. I knew I was dangerously close to death at various stages. In fear, my initial focus was on what I could do to earn God's favor. I reflected on Job and others whom I saw as righteous, but was riddled with guilt when I tried to measure myself by their standard of righteousness. God corrected and comforted me, in that even if I tried, my efforts through good works to prove my righteousness were unnecessary. Continuing to do so would be a demonstration of my unbelief in the "works of the cross" previously done by Jesus Christ. He had already done all the works necessary for my righteousness. Besides, it was not by my works that I should be made righteous because, according to 2 Corinthians 5:21 (NIV), "God made Him who had no sin to be sin for us, so that in Him we might become the righteousness of God." Jesus was already standing in the gap for me, having done what was necessary for my righteousness through Him. All I had to do was believe, accept, and faithfully live by it. Jesus Christ offered me the gift of grace, and through faith in Him was salvation, redemption, atonement, and healing from cancer specifically. I accepted that the will of God was for me to be healed, live, and prosper, but I needed to completely remove my fleshly impediments to reveal the image of God as He had created me, so that His attributes would have dominance and govern the spirit that I am. Only then could the transcendental faith be effective and heal my physical being.

I am now better able to appreciate the mysteries and awesomeness of our magnanimous God. He mobilized other humans in the form of doctors, friends, and families to sustain me throughout His process. Through Facebook, I could count on encouraging words of love and prayers. The body of Christ, as I highlighted earlier, played an instrumental role in my recovery. My inspiration came from many sources but, nonetheless, I developed an even stronger awareness of the necessity to guard my heart. I believe in the concept of "trust but verify" where humans are concerned, based on my pessimistic view that we are inherently flawed by virtue of our fallen state. It means that, by default, we are more inclined to do evil and have to make more of an effort to do good. Genesis 6:5 (NIV) supports this position, as it records, "The LORD saw how great the wickedness of the human race had become on the earth, and that every inclination of the thoughts of the human heart was only evil all the time."

Satan infiltrates people and uses them for evil, inadvertently making them delivery mechanisms of ungodly motives working in opposition to what God designates as good. This is verifiable throughout the Bible. In Matthew 12:22, people brought a demon-possessed man to Jesus and He healed him. These spirits will even speak at times. In Mark 5:7 (NIV), the evil spirit dwelling in a human actually pleaded with Jesus, saying, "What do you want with me, Jesus, Son of the Most High God? In God's name don't torture me!" It was not unusual for the unusual well-wisher to be less than positive at times, and I had to implement filters as directed by the Holy Spirit. That meant I had to be conscious of God's voice and be obedient to the guidance of the Holy Spirit for directions as to whose messages I should allow to direct my behavior.

On the question of messages, I cannot resist the urge to make a humorous commentary on the differences in the way the genders communicated with me. *Men Are from Mars, Women Are from Venus,* the title of John Gray's book, has become something of a popular idiomatic expression. It implies that men and women behave differently. The stark contrast between how my male and female friends reacted to me during my illness reinforced the theory that the way men think and act are extremely different from women. Of course, those of us who consider ourselves "smart men," eventually fall in line, not just for peace sake but for our own good. Despite the dissimilarities in approach, I am grateful for both. My female friends were generally warm and nurturing and explicitly voiced their compassion with much affection. My male friends, on the other hand, were mostly measured and reserved in their delivery. When I occasionally heard from the guys, their reactions were brief and studiously delivered. The stark contrast in how the sexes showed concern reinforced the idea that men and women are from extremely different planets.

When I was well enough to ask my male friends about their reaction, or lack of it, while I was unwell, the typical response would be something like, "What could I say to you man?" It wasn't that they cared any less or wanted to neglect me and see me suffer, but us guys are awkward in our approach to caring for a member of the herd. It's a "man thing," I guess. Of course, there are exceptions. There are a few who were magnanimous in their outpouring, both physically and spiritually. Poor us guys. When we can't fix it with hammers and nails, duct tape, or WD-40, we are basically helpless. So, I am thankful to everyone, both male and female. Overtly or covertly, I knew love had helped sustain me, and I am grateful to God for having furnished me with love and support from so many.

I once heard that, while going through a desert, one should also grow through it. My growth and maturity during this journey were extensive. I experienced God in amazing new ways. My spirit became more finely tuned to the Lord's voice and I heard Him more clearly. I realized I could have an even deeper relationship with Him, so I developed a more solid expectation that my faithfulness would bear evidence of my obedience. When I prayed, it was the opportune time to reveal my heart, so that where corrections were needed, God would provide them to me. Because of God's demonstrable love, my appreciation for love and the need to show love increased; my desire to help others was also more pressing. Many people spoke words that helped me with the burden of my cross. As a result of that, I am more keenly aware of how the appropriate words spoken at the right time can accomplish dramatic results. When they are inspired by God, they can sustain life itself. Because of my experiences, my time on earth has new values. Now, my desire is to use whatever time God extends to me for His glory.

My confidence in God's promises has grown magnificently, and I am thankful. I am a testimony of God's mercies and goodness to a believer. He honors the faith of us His children. He chose me as one among the billions of His, to assure you that, even as He is the highest exalted, the God above all, He desires a relationship with us mere mortals. As our Father and LORD, He knew our beginnings before we were conceived, and He knows and controls our eternity. He, who created every nanoparticle of our physical being, has the final call on our eternity. He understands cancer and other so-called critical diseases. He was never unaware of anything I went through or will go through in the future.

NEXT CHAPTER

And all these blessings shall come upon you and overtake you, because you obey the voice of the LORD your God: "Blessed shall you be in the city, and blessed shall you be in the country. Blessed shall be the fruit of your body, the produce of your ground and the increase of your herds, the increase of your cattle and the offspring of your flocks. Blessed shall be your basket and your kneading bowl. Blessed shall you be when you come in, and blessed shall you be when you go out."

—Deuteronomy 28:2-6 (NKJV)

There is yet another chapter to be written. It will be the chapter of hope fulfilled, of faith producing tangible evidence for the world of sight and reasoning to witness. That will be of my total and complete healing. Since I have not yet declared my complete physical healing, what is the point of this book? The doctors have deemed multiple myeloma an incurable form of cancer. The lab tests further continue to support this fact. Even now, after each doctor's visit, I have ample proof of remnants of the disease still in me, and I have to continue taking medications to control its spread. Should I have waited for complete healing to write this book, so that I could provide a fairy-tale, happily ever after story? Only after I had completed most of the manuscript did that thought occur. That then must have been a distraction to prevent the publication of a book God has authorized. But God always provides clarity whenever there is confusion and doubt.

It was such a revelation of peace and comfort when the Holy Spirit reminded me that most people over 50 have some form of chronic illness. Hypertension and diabetes are rampant among this age group. Notwithstanding, many of those afflicted live and function as productive members of society. My classification currently is a recovering cancer patient who is being progressively healed. That realization has changed my thinking about the cancer. Reflecting on the apostle Paul, he did not allow his affliction to hinder or deter him from the extraordinary accomplishments of spreading the Gospel for our benefit. He did not pout, become despondent and disobey God for not relieving him of "the thorn in his flesh." Paul chose not to dwell on his selfish desire, but instead, took pleasure in doing the greater good that God had appointed him to do. Looking beyond his affliction, he believed, in faith, that God's grace was enough to empower him. In so doing, he had God's blessing and the privilege to be arguably the greatest voice of God to humanity. What esteemed and distinct blessing from God!

As my benevolent, merciful Father, God provides me knowledge to appreciate His process and avoid anxiety. Recently, I had an epiphany; it was a guideline for clarity about the purposefulness of God's timely process. Just the power of what it meant to clearly hear and appreciate the meaning of purpose to God's process was powerful. Because of His omniscience, God uses a deliberate and timely process to sequence the orderly implementation of activities, so that there will be no destructive conflicts as everything will perfectly align in time and place.

For example, I am naturally very restless, always wanting to be "on the go." God blessed me with an insatiable level of curiosity and interests in a wide spectrum of things. He also blessed me with various talents. Several times during the healing process, as soon as I felt even slightly rejuvenated, I would revisit some of these interests. As is my nature, I would always overindulge, overexert myself, and expose my weakened system to situations that often proved to be my undoing. When that happened, I would helplessly retreat to my safe place and nurse my regrets. For example, I would do physical activities that would cause hurt to my fractured skeletal structure.

The outdoors never failed to seduce me with its enchanting call, and I found it difficult to resist attending to my garden. But my garden is the most generous bearer of fungus, virus, bacteria, and every danger that I should avoid. With my compromised immune system, I could count the hours until I would suffer from weeks of bronchial infections after my reckless indulgence.

I could easily understand the epiphany about God's purposefulness in His process. In an instant, God could destroy every indication of the cancer markers and have the test results prove it. And what would I do? Aside from declaring it as my ultimate miracle, I would no doubt proceed to relaunch every project I had been involved in before my illness at full speed. But that could have eventually been even more destructive to me. Although the cancer indicators would have disappeared, my skeletal fractures may have required more time to mend and my immune system more time recover. Imagine the extensive damage I could have done to myself having indeed been cured from cancer but not yet receiving my total and comprehensive healing.

God purposefully orchestrates His process in my situation from the spiritual realm to manifest in the physical realm for my best interest. It will be executed in an orderly fashion and on His timeline for my ultimate best. My anxieties and need for expediencies are contrived from my emotions and ego and are recipes for my demise. Such revelations from God became another credo for how I needed to live the next chapter in my life of faith. Rather than be anxious about God's timing for my complete cure, I am at peace with life and I have given myself carte blanche to enjoy every minute of it while I pursue the greater good that God has assigned me.

At a recent Memorial Day service, our bishop spoke about relentless warriors, fighters who had the courage to go beyond the norm. In feats of bravery, some gave the ultimate sacrifice. It occurred to me that many individual heroic acts on the battlefield were never recorded and a number of those who died did not receive the laudation and rewards for their heroism. What if we could have heard or read about their real-life experiences during the heat of battle? It would be nerve-racking to hear the intensity of artillery fire destined for our destruction while in our safe place. We could be caught up in the moment and become enamored with the feeling of brotherhood, the sense of team-spiritedness in battle, as we rally to the impassioned orders of the commanding officer urging bold warriors to advance on the enemy; then be agonized with empathy as we hear the final lament of a brave fellow warrior who took a bullet for his squad, his family, and his country.

All the pain and agony I experienced on the battlefield of my affliction pale in comparison to the devastation of real-life war as I attempted to describe above. But I became convinced that my experience was tantamount to war on me and it would be robbery to not have my war story documented from the battlefield of cancer while it was in progress. God has restored me to the point where I can do so, and I dare not be negligent. He has given me the privilege to relate the ongoing drama of my fight with cancer and a platform to do so in near real time. I believe there is someone out there who would like to read about it. Like a surviving soldier with battlefield experience, the next chapter of my story will be one of awe and wonder. Rather than tell stories about the scars of my war, it will be about how faith sustained my hope to produce visible results.

The substance of my faith has already produced visible evidence. Many areas where the doctors provided me no hope for recovery, like my collapsed spine, have been significantly healed. I am mobile again and have much improved cognitive capabilities, to the extent that I could write this book. It would be selfish and ungrateful of me to suppress the works of God in me.

Generous support and encouragement ignited the idea for this book. The prophetic words from God breathed life into it. God's inspiration, guidance, and spiritual leadership sustained me to diligently compile the material. And He provided friends to believe, encourage, and support me to complete it. In my weakened state, surrounded by gloom and doubts, voices chosen by God inspired me to rise up, as I had much to live for. They convinced me that it was not the time for my death, because I had gained enough wisdom through the process to tell a story that could inspire others through

Christ. Such tremendous faith in me, I thought, was unmerited. My gratitude to those who chose to journey with me is unspeakable.

I wrote this book because I dare to believe I am a witness for God, being the beneficiary of His mercies through grace. It was compiled during various stages of the illness and recovery process and published under the conviction of the power of faith in God. This book is my testimony of what I saw only in faith, now becoming tangible, through Jesus Christ. I had to accept and come to terms with the enormity of my late-stage cancer diagnosis; that was fact. But then I had to believe that the prognosis was not of God and that it was not His will that I be destroyed by it. Believing that God provides for all our needs through the gift of grace, I wholeheartedly embraced the truth that my desire for healing was aligned with His will. I took as a warranty the promise of Jesus that I could ask anything in His name, and He would grant it. So, I sought my healing through faith, which unlocked the repository of grace and released the progressive healing I desired.

My testimony in this book seeks to assure the reader that there is transcendental hope beyond what can be seen or reasoned through our natural senses, just as I have experienced from God. I confidently documented my story for the inspiration of others. This book is for those people out there, somewhere, who want to believe, but who are challenged by current realities and encumbered by the evidence of their circumstances. Indeed, everything about your situation may be factual; what it says is logical and can be substantiated. But it does not have to be your destiny if it is not in God's plan.

I pray that by reading this testimony you will be convinced that, regardless of how daunting the evidence of your situation presents, the power of your faith can unleash and materialize your hope from grace. God desires that we believe; our relentless faith demonstrates the level of our conviction. He can and will make it right if you trust and rely on Him with relentless faith. As Hebrews 11:6 (NIV) says, "And without faith it is impossible to please God, because anyone who comes to him must believe that he exists and that he rewards those who earnestly seek him."

God is purposeful and merciful, and He is love. Here I am, a living testimony of what faith in God can produce. My improved health speaks to God's compassion; my eventual complete healing will provide evidence of how He rewards faith. I am restoration work in progress. I will depart this reality one day. But for now, my life is by God, I am of God, and I live for God. I give all worship and honor to our Divine Father, the Lord God Almighty, through Jesus the Christ. Amen.

APPENDIX I

About Cancer

According to Cancer.org, almost 17 million people alive in the United States have had some type of cancer.

Cancer is the uncontrolled growth of abnormal cells in the body. In the body, there are trillions of cells with various functions. These cells grow and divide to help the body function properly. Cells die when they become old or damaged, and new cells replace them. Cancer develops when the body's standard control mechanism stops working. Old cells do not die and cells grow out of control, forming new, abnormal cells. These extra cells may build a mass of tissue, called a tumor. Some cancers, such as leukemia, do not form tumors.

There are five main categories of cancer:

- Carcinomas begin in the skin or tissues that line the internal organs.
- Sarcomas develop in the bone, cartilage, fat, muscle, or other connective tissues.
- Leukemia starts in the blood and bone marrow.
- Lymphomas start in the immune system.
- Central nervous system cancers develop in the brain and spinal cord.

Cancer can occur anywhere in the body. In women, breast cancer is most common. In men, it's prostate cancer. Lung cancer and colorectal cancer affect both men and women in high numbers.

How is cancer treated?

The same cancer type—whether it's liver cancer, stomach cancer, or kidney cancer—in one individual is very different from that cancer in another individual. Cancer is not one disease but hundreds of different types of diseases. Within a single type of cancer, such as breast cancer, researchers are discovering subtypes that each requires a different treatment approach.

Treatment options depend on the type of cancer, its stage, if the cancer has spread, and your general health.

The goal of treatment is to kill as many cancerous cells while minimizing damage to healthy cells nearby. Advances in technology make this possible. For example, intraoperative radiation therapy (IORT) delivers a concentrated dose of radiation to a tumor site immediately after surgery. Healthy tissues and organs are shielded during treatment, which allows for a higher dose of radiation.

As previously mentioned, chemotherapy is often given several times over weeks or months in what is known as a course of treatment. This is made up of a series of treatment periods, called *cycles*. During a *cycle*, you may get chemo every day for one or more days. Since chemo also kills healthy cells, these chemo days are followed by periods of rest when you receive no treatment. This rest lets your body recover and produce new, healthy cells.

About Multiple Myeloma

Before I write about multiple myeloma, it may be a good idea to have a brief review of the types of blood cells.

- White blood cells help protect the body from infection. A low white blood cell count is known as neutropenia.

If your white blood cell count gets too low, you could get an infection.

- Red blood cells carry oxygen throughout your body. A low red blood cell count is known as anemia. Anemia can lead to fatigue, chest pain, and more serious complications.
- Platelets are structures in the blood that help stop bleeding. A low platelet cell count is known as thrombocytopenia. A low platelet count can cause bruising and bleeding.

Celgene states, "Multiple Myeloma (MM) is the second most commonly diagnosed blood cancer, after non-Hodgkin lymphoma, yet few people know much about this deadly disease. Approximately 22,000 Americans were diagnosed with MM in 2013. In the United States, nearly 74,000 have MM, and an estimated 10,700 will die from the disease this year [2014]. Globally, it's estimated that 103,000 people were diagnosed with MM in 2008, which equates to 12 percent of all blood cancers diagnosed, according to Cancer Research UK."

It quotes Brian G. M. Durie, MD, chairman and cofounder of the International Myeloma Foundation, as saying at the American Society of Hematology (ASH) Annual Meeting in New Orleans in December 2013, "Myeloma is important because it's increasing in incidence. There are more patients around the world being diagnosed with myeloma, and for some reason, it's being diagnosed in patients who are younger."

Celgene continues, "The reason behind this increase is unclear. What we do know is that MM is a type of cancer in which plasma cells—an important part of the immune system—become immortal and eventually replicate uncontrollably and accumulate in the bone marrow, the soft tissue at the center of the bones. The cancer cells grow out of control, crowding out normal cells."

Normal plasma cells produce immunoglobulins, which are antibodies that fight infections. M proteins are defective immunoglobulins that are produced by the plasma cells and are useless to the body. They also prevent the growth of useful antibodies or immunoglobulins.

Verywell Health provides the following information about the disease:

> The M protein is an immunoglobulin—or part of an immunoglobulin—that is described as monoclonal, meaning it is produced by a single clone of bad cells. It is not normal for the body to have so many copies of the exact same protein as generally occurs in myeloma.
>
> In multiple myeloma, the M protein comes from a great excess of plasma cells. Ordinarily, plasma cells will produce a wide range of antibodies. In the normal or healthy state, the population of plasma cells is capable of producing a wide array of different antibodies—so-called polyclonal antibodies, or polyclonal immunoglobulins. When plasma cells become cancerous, often there is a single, very bad cell that has given rise to many identical minions. All of the minions are clones of the same cell, and they make only the same monoclonal proteins. Since there are a lot of plasma cells, multiplying abnormally, they make a lot of this monoclonal protein. The abundance, or spike, in the volume of just one protein, can be detected in lab tests.

Symptoms of Multiple Myeloma

Many people with multiple myeloma have debilitating bone pain and fractures that require radiation or surgery. Bone fractures can be particularly dangerous when they occur in the spinal column, causing the vertebrae to collapse or compress, damaging the spinal cord. In some cases, paralysis can occur. Patients may also experience weight loss, numbness or weakness in the legs, and repeated infections such as pneumonia, shingles, or sinusitis, according to Celgene.

It is generally accepted that there is currently no known cure. As such, treatment is provided to prolong and improve the quality of life of the multiple myeloma sufferer. Only after the disease is in an advanced stage is it typically diagnosed, as it may not present any symptoms. At that stage, damage to vital organs, such as the kidneys, may have already been done. Damage to the skeletal structure, such as the spine and ribcage, could also be an indication of the disease's presence. Measuring M protein levels is useful in determining the extent of the disease and in monitoring the effectiveness of treatment.

Among the signs and symptoms are: bone pain, bone damage and fractures; swollen ankles; repeated infections such as pneumonia; weight loss; breathlessness; headaches; dizziness; weakness; drowsiness; fatigue; oozing cuts; blurred vision; bruising; anemia; hypercalcemia (too much calcium in the blood); nervous system problems such as numbness, sudden and or severe pain, tingling, muscle weakness, confusion, dizziness, and carpal tunnel; increased thickening and or stickiness of the blood; high blood protein levels; and low white blood cell counts.

For more detailed and precise detection and treatment, clinicians use various indicators from serum and urine. Paraproteins (free light and free heavy chains) help detect and characterize the type of myeloma that exists. The light and heavy chains are subsets of normal immunoglobulins (Igs). They are both produced separately in the plasma cells. There are five types of heavy chains (IgG, IgA, IgM, IgD, and IgE) and two types of light chains (kappa and lambda). When a light and a heavy chain bond, they produce a whole (intact) immunoglobulin. Plasma cells, for whatever reasons, tend to make more light than heavy chains so that there will always be excessive light chains that are released into the bloodstream. These unbonded light chains are referred to as "free light chains." The presence of a certain amount of free light chain does not necessarily mean the individual has active myeloma. When light chains are produced, myeloma cells will be kappa or lambda, depending on which is the excess, hence the type of myeloma can be classified by either free kappa or lambda free light chains. If either one of free kappa or lambda is very high or the other is low, the resulting ratio will be abnormally high and is an indication of myeloma.

If the ratio of free kappa/lambda falls within a range in response to treatment, remission is said to occur. This is referred to as a stringent complete response. Hence the goal of treatment is to reduce or possibly eliminate the levels of the myeloma paraprotein.

Cancer.Net advises that "staging" is a way of describing where a cancer is located, if or where it has spread, and whether it is affecting other parts of the body.

Stage 3—many cancer cells are present in the body at stage 3. Factors characteristic of this stage include:

- Anemia, with a hemoglobin <8.5 g/dL
- Hypercalcemia
- Advanced bone damage (three or more bone lesions)
- High levels of M protein in the blood or urine
  - M protein >7 g/dL for IgG; >5 g/dL for IgA; >12 g/24 h for urinary light chain

I was eventually diagnosed with stage 3 multiple myeloma—the most advanced stage of this type of rare cancer.

By the time I was able to review my initial lab results, it had revealed that my free light chain kappa value was 133518.0 mg/L, the reference range was 3.3 mg/L-19.4 mg/L (high), while the lambda value was 8.8 mg/L, reference range 5.7 mg/L-26.3 mg/L. The oncologists use a ratio of kappa/lambda, but I was consumed by the alarmingly high free kappa numbers and focused on that every time I received the test results. Even so, the ratio was way out of range, it was 15172.50 mg/L, exceedingly higher than the reference range of 0.26-1.65 mg/L. Bone biopsy, various CT scans, and other imaging were key metrics associated with my eventual diagnosis.

Light chain myeloma is not the only type. I went into a bit of detail because of the relevance to my specific condition. Other forms of myeloma include smoldering, active, solitary plasmacytoma of the bone, multiple solitary plasmacytomas, extramedullary plasmacytoma, non-secretory myeloma, immunoglobulin D (IgD), and immuno-globulin E (IgE). IgD and IgE are considered rare forms of the disease.

The science of today is unclear about what causes the disease. Some of the risk factors include being male, older than sixty-five, of African-American descent, a history of plasma cell disease, exposure to certain things such as radiation, hazardous conditions in the work environment, farming, obesity, and family history. (*Cancer Tutor*). I matched a few of those categories.

Treating Multiple Myeloma

The conventional treatment for multiple myeloma ranges from well-known traditional methods such as surgery, radiation, chemotherapy, stem cell transplant and palliative therapy, to targeted therapy and more revolutionary evolving treatment such as chimeric antigen receptor T-cell (CAR-T). Targeted therapy aims to distinguish between certain features of the cancer cells and normal cells. They target either the internals of the cell or receptors on the outside of the cell. This allows scientists to target cancer cells with more precision and kill them with less casualty to normal cells, resulting in reduced adverse side effects. A combination of traditional treatments and targeted therapies is commonly used these days.

With evolving research, the concept of targeted treatment of multiple myeloma is now moving towards precision or personalized medicine tailored to individualize care. The reason: everyone has different types and subgroups. The mutation characteristics of the disease means that it is composed of many subgroups and require a combination of different therapies based on its unique manifestation in different individuals. As the disease evolves, it becomes resistant to the changing therapies. DNA and RNA are now recognized for the critical roles they play and are particularly useful to administer the precise individual therapy for the patient. The DNA stores the blueprint or genetic information. RNA is more like the messenger and doer, so it can express what section of the DNA is active with the myeloma disease.

The side effects of current cancer treatment are numerous and may include nausea, diarrhea, bleeding, bruising, black stools, blood in the stools, blood in the urine, pain, burning with urination, extreme fatigue, and mouth sores. As can be expected, not everyone will experience similar side effects. Through the illness, I have experienced several of the side effects and have had to discontinue some of the medications. I would not advocate doing this, unless your doctor approves.

Diabetes—Blood Sugar

I wrote this brief section about diabetes because I was plagued with the condition throughout the disease process. It became very severe at various stages, which meant I had to be prescribed several types of insulin concurrently. Only when I paused the chemotherapy medications was I able to see reduced glucose levels from tests.

The Cleveland Clinic states that diabetes mellitus is a disease that prevents your body from correctly using the energy from the food you eat. Diabetes occurs in one of the following situations:

- The pancreas produces little insulin or no insulin at all, OR
- The pancreas makes insulin, but the insulin made does not work as it should. This condition is called insulin resistance.

In type 2 diabetes, the pancreas makes insulin, but it either doesn't produce enough, or the insulin does not work properly.

Diabetes.co.uk explains how food consumption eventually results in the presence of high levels of sugar in the blood and the role of insulin in the process as follows:

> Food is consumed. Carbohydrates are broken down into glucose—by saliva and the gut. Glucose enters the bloodstream. The pancreas responds to the presence of food by releasing stored insulin (phase 1 insulin response). Insulin

allows glucose from the blood to enter into the body's cells—where the glucose can be used for fuel. Insulin also allows glucose to be stored by muscles and the liver as glycogen. If needed, the stored glycogen can later be returned to the blood as glucose. If there is glucose remaining in the blood, insulin turns this glucose into saturated body fat. Proteins in the meal also get broken down into glucose to some degree. However, this is a much slower process than it is with carbohydrates. After the body's initial release of insulin, the beta cells in the pancreas start to develop new insulin which can be released as well; this is known as the phase 2 insulin response. If glucose is taken from the blood to the point where blood sugar levels begin to approach a low level, the body releases glucagon. Glucagon works to change the stored glycogen into glucose which is released into the bloodstream.

Some indications of high blood sugar levels are frequent urination, feeling weak and tired, weight loss, thirstiness, blurred vision, and neuropathy, which gives the experience of tingling, maybe pain in the extremities such as the hands, legs, and feet. The disease may also cause wounds to heal more slowly.

My Prescriptions

To present a broader understanding of why I may have had specific reactions or experiences during the period of my illness, I believe it is beneficial to give a brief description of some of the drugs I was prescribed. I have also documented some of the published side effects. Nothing about what I have written here or in this book is scholarly work and should not be used as a guide for a medical decision or treatment. Everyone should do the necessary due diligence, including extensive research and following both the doctors' and manufacturers' instructions and advice. The information that follows was taken from either publicly accessible sources, such as the medication inserts and manufacturer websites, or credible organizations' publications.

Each line of chemotherapy treatment was administered as cocktails, meaning a combination of drugs; in my case, at least three separate drugs for each line of therapy. They were generally administered in cycles. For example, a twenty-eight-day cycle may consist of twice weekly infusion of one or two drugs and daily oral administration of another, then there would be rest periods of seven days before the start of another cycle. The infused drugs were administered intravenously or by subcutaneous injections. In the subcutaneous method, the drug is injected into the tissue layer between the skin and the muscle. The intravenous method was administered via a needle inserted directly into the vein or through what is called an access port that was surgically implanted in my chest to access a vein there. I also had to take daily chemo drugs orally.

Aside from radiation, I have so far been exposed to three lines of chemotherapy treatment. Why three? Because, as I have been told, the cancer is very aggressive. One line of therapy may work for a while, then later, either the disease becomes resistant to that line of treatment or it finds a way to evade the chemotherapy. I am highlighting some of the medications I took with some of their side effects to show how these could have had an impact on me as I pursued a cure. My body was subjected to a range of different harmful drugs, which themselves led to the emergence of other consequential reactions. I am amazed that as fragile as the human body appears, it can withstand such trauma.

My first course of therapy, which lasted about four months, was based on a twenty-eight-day cycle. That means I would typically be administered drugs for twenty-one days and rest (be off these drugs) for seven days, then resume another twenty-one days of the drugs. I was administered a cocktail of three drugs. They comprised of Velcade (bortezomib), administered subcutaneously, and Revlimid and dexamethasone, taken orally (RVD).

Upon close examination, it will be seen that, at times, the combination I took in any one line of treatment had overlapping side effects. In my opinion, that should only serve to make the likelihood of that particular side effect more probable. For example, RVD, my first line of treatment, consisted of drugs that had almost similar side effect profiles, including the possibility of causing damage to vital organs such as the lung and heart. They also sapped my energy, leaving me exhausted. Some, such as the dexamethasone and the opioid, had mood and mind-altering effects. In many cases, I had to take medications to counter the side effects of some of these mainline drugs. Case in point, while killing the cancer cells, the chemotherapy also killed useful protective antibodies, leaving me susceptible to a host of ailments, including shingles and hives. To prevent these occurrences, I was prescribed acyclovir. I was also prescribed Bactrim (sulfamethoxazole and trimethoprim), which is used to treat infections that could result from bacteria that my weakened immune system could not combat.

There were so many other side effects that had to be treated, including numbness, tingling, and pain in my feet—all potential indicators of peripheral neuropathy. Nausea was a consistent plague resulting from medications, and I had to be prescribed antinausea medications just so I could have a meal. One of the most critical side effects that I developed was diabetes. Dexamethasone has been determined as a drug that could produce that side effect, and I believe it may have contributed to the high blood sugar levels that have remained with me. Because of high blood glucose levels, I had to be prescribed two different types of insulin medications to take simultaneously, one fast-acting and the other long-acting. Before my illness, I did not have diabetes. Fortunately, God has directed me to practice a healthier lifestyle, such that I could eventually wean myself off the insulin medications. A concern that has also plagued me is the likelihood of developing other forms of cancers from the extended therapies to which I have been subjected.

Although the list that follows does not include all the medications I was prescribed during the worst periods of my illness, it comprises the major ones. My attempt is to highlight some of the side effects of the medications, which may account for how I felt or acted, and which caused me to experience various levels of physical and mental dysfunctionality at one point or another. It would be interesting to review any studies on the residual effects on patients who were subjected to the many medications individuals like me have had to endure. From my experience and the testimonies of others, so far, the mental damage is long-term. The anticancer benefits derived in extending life seem to outweigh the side effects, for now. How will my quality of life be impacted long term? God took me through this almost-death phase and therefore will provide for my long-term quality of life so I can be a useful steward to humanity at His good will and pleasure.

Velcade

Velcade (bortezomib) is in a class of medicines called proteasome inhibitors. It is a targeted therapy that works by blocking or slowing down the action of proteasomes inside cells. Proteasomes break down proteins in both healthy and cancerous cells, inhibiting their multiplication and growth and causing them to die.

Side effects include:

The Velcade patients' portal enumerates some of the common side effects cited by them as follows: fatigue; peripheral neuropathy; low blood pressure (hypotension); heart problems; lung disorders or problems; liver disease or problems; posterior reversible encephalopathy syndrome (PRES); gastrointestinal problems (nausea, diarrhea, constipation and vomiting); low levels of neutrophils and leukocytes, which are types of white blood cells (neutropenia and leukopenia), and low levels of platelets (thrombocytopenia); tumor lysis syndrome (TLS); a low level of red blood cells (anemia); a painful, itchy rash usually located in an area on one side of the body (herpes zoster); fever (pyrexia); and decreased appetite (anorexia).

Revlimid (lenalidomide)

Researchers are still finding out exactly how lenalidomide works. It affects all sorts of cell processes, including how cells divide and grow. We know that it interferes with chemicals that cells use to signal to each other to grow. It affects how the immune system works and is called an immunomodulatory agent, according to Cancer Research UK.

Revlimid.com categorizes the side effects as follows:

Serious side effects include:

Birth defects; increased risk of death in people who have chronic lymphocytic leukemia (CLL); risk of new cancers (malignancies); severe liver problems, including liver failure and death; severe skin reactions, including severe allergic reactions; tumor lysis syndrome (TLS); worsening of your tumor (tumor flare reaction); thyroid problems; risk of early death in MCL (mantle cell lymphoma).

Common side effects include:

Diarrhea, rash, nausea, constipation, tiredness, fever, itching, swelling of the limbs and skin, and cough, sore throat, and other symptoms of a cold.

Further, the American Cancer Society says: "The most common side effects of lenalidomide are low platelets (thrombocytopenia) and low white blood cell count. It can also cause painful nerve damage. The risk of blood clots is not as high as that seen with thalidomide, but it is still increased."

Dexamethasone

Dexamethasone is an anti-inflammatory medication. It relieves inflammation in various parts of the body. It is used specifically to decrease swelling (edema), associated with tumors of the spine and brain, and to treat eye inflammation. It is also used as a treatment for a variety of cancers, such as leukemia, lymphoma, and multiple myeloma.

Side effects include:

According to Chemocare, the following side effects are common (occurring in greater than 30%) for patients taking dexamethasone: increased appetite, irritability, difficulty sleeping (insomnia), swelling in the ankles and feet (fluid retention), heartburn, muscle weakness, impaired wound healing, and increased blood sugar levels (persons with diabetes may need to have blood sugar levels monitored more closely and possible adjustments to diabetes medications).

The following are less common side effects (occurring in greater than 10%) for patients receiving dexamethasone: headaches, dizziness, mood swings, and cataracts and bone thinning (with long-term use).

Kyprolis (carfilzomib)

Kyprolis (carfilzomib) is a newer proteasome inhibitor that can be used to treat multiple myeloma in patients who have already been treated with other drugs that didn't work, according to the American Cancer Society. It is given as an injection into a vein (IV), often in a four-week cycle. To prevent problems like allergic reactions during the infusion, the steroid drug dexamethasone is often given before each dose in the first cycle. Like Velcade, it works by stopping enzyme complexes (proteasomes) in cells from breaking down proteins important for controlling cell division. They appear to affect tumor cells more than normal cells, but they are not without side effects.

Side effects include:

Kyprolis can cause heart problems or worsen preexisting heart conditions—death due to cardiac arrest has occurred within one day of Kyprolis administration; kidney problems (there have been reports of sudden kidney failure in patients receiving Kyprolis); tumor lysis syndrome (TLS); lung damage; pulmonary hypertension (high blood pressure in the lungs); lung complications (shortness of breath was reported in patients receiving Kyprolis); high blood pressure (cases of high blood pressure, including fatal cases, have been reported in patients receiving Kyprolis); blood clots; infusion reactions (symptoms of infusion reactions included fever, chills, joint pain, muscle pain, facial flushing and/or swelling, vomiting, weakness, shortness of breath, low blood pressure, fainting, chest tightness, and chest pain); severe bleeding problems (fatal or serious cases of bleeding problems have been reported in patients receiving Kyprolis); very low platelet count (low platelet levels can cause unusual bruising and bleeding); liver problems (cases of liver failure, including fatal cases, have been reported in patients receiving Kyprolis); blood problems (cases of a blood disease called thrombotic microangiopathy, including thrombotic thrombocytopenic purpura/hemolytic uremic syndrome (TTP/HUS), including fatal cases, have been reported in patients who received Kyprolis); brain problems (a nerve disease called posterior reversible encephalopathy syndrome (PRES), formerly called reversible posterior leukoencephalopathy syndrome (RPLS), has been reported in patients receiving Kyprolis). It can cause a seizure, headache, lack of energy, confusion, blindness, altered consciousness, and other visual and nerve disturbances, along with high blood pressure.

The most common side effects occurring in at least 20% of patients receiving Kyprolis in the combination therapy trials are low red blood cell count, low white blood cell count, diarrhea, difficulty breathing, tiredness (fatigue), low platelets, fever, sleeplessness (insomnia), muscle spasm, cough, upper airway (respiratory tract) infection, and decreased potassium levels.

The most common side effects occurring in at least 20% of patients receiving Kyprolis when used alone (monotherapy) in trials are low red blood cell count, tiredness (fatigue), low platelets, nausea, fever, difficulty breathing, diarrhea, headache, cough, and swelling of the lower legs or hands.

These are not all the possible side effects of Kyprolis.
(Based on information retrieved from the Amgen/Kyprolis website.)

Pomalyst (pomalidomide)

Pomalyst is also an immunomodulating agent like Revlimid and is used to treat multiple myeloma.

Side effects include:

Celgene asserts that low white blood cells (neutropenia), low platelets (thrombocytopenia), and low red blood cells (anemia) are common with Pomalyst, but can also be serious. Severe liver problems, including liver failure or death, can occur. Your health-care provider (HCP) should do blood tests to check your liver function during your treatment with Pomalyst.

It is advisable that your HCP be immediately notified if any of the following occur: yellowing of your skin or the white parts of your eyes (jaundice), dark or brown (tea-colored) urine, pain on the upper right side of your stomach area (abdomen), bleeding or bruising more easily than normal or feeling very tired.

Severe allergic and skin reactions: Your HCP needs to be notified if you have any symptoms of an allergic reaction, including swelling of your lips, mouth, tongue, or throat; trouble breathing; or skin reaction.

Dizziness and confusion: Avoid taking other medicines that may cause dizziness and confusion during treatment with Pomalyst. Avoid situations that require you to be alert until you know how Pomalyst affects you.

Nerve damage: Stop taking Pomalyst and call your HCP if you develop numbness, tingling, pain, or a burning sensation in your hands, legs, or feet.

New cancers (malignancies): New cancers, including certain blood cancers (acute myelogenous leukemia or AML), have been seen in people who received Pomalyst. Talk with your HCP about your risk.

Tumor lysis syndrome: TLS is caused by the fast breakdown of cancer cells. TLS can cause kidney failure and the need for dialysis treatment, abnormal heart rhythm, seizure, and sometimes death. Your HCP may do blood tests to check you for TLS.

The most common side effects of Pomalyst include tiredness, weakness, constipation, nausea, diarrhea, shortness of breath, upper respiratory tract infection, back pain, and fever.

Bisphosphonates for Bone Disease

The American Cancer Society notes that myeloma cells can weaken and even break bones. Drugs called bisphosphonates can help bones stay strong by slowing down this process. They can also help reduce pain in the weakened bone(s). Sometimes, pain medicines such as NSAIDs or narcotics will be given along with bisphosphonates to help control or lessen the pain. Bone pain can be a difficult symptom to treat during and after treatment for myeloma.

The standard for treating bone problems in people with myeloma are pamidronate (Aredia), zoledronic acid (Zometa), and denosumab (Xgeva, Prolia). These drugs are given intravenously (IV, or into a vein). Most patients are treated once a month at first, but they may be able to be treated less often later on if they are doing well. Treatment with a bisphosphonate helps prevent further bone damage in multiple myeloma patients.

Side effects include:

These treatments can have a rare but serious side effect called osteonecrosis of the jaw (ONJ). Patients complain of pain, and doctors find that part of the jawbone has died. This can lead to an open sore that doesn't heal. It can also lead to tooth loss in that area. The jawbone can also become infected. Doctors aren't sure why this happens or how best to prevent it, but having jaw surgery or having a tooth removed can trigger this problem. Avoid these procedures while you are taking a bisphosphonate. Many doctors recommend that patients have a dental checkup before starting treatment. That way, any dental problems can be taken care of before starting the drug. If ONJ does occur, the doctor will stop the bisphosphonate treatment.

Acyclovir (Zovirax)

According to Everyday Health, acyclovir is an antiviral drug, used to treat conditions that include varicella zoster (shingles).

Side effects include:

Nausea, diarrhea, vomiting, headache, dizziness, tiredness, muscle or joint aches, visual changes.

Bactrim (sulfamethoxazole and trimethoprim)

Bactrim is used in various forms of bacterial infections.

Side effects include:

Sore throat and cough; severe, prolonged diarrhea that may occur with fever and stomach cramps, which possibly indicates a *difficile* infection; fever or chills; trouble breathing; unusual bruising or bleeding; yellowing of the skin and eyes (jaundice); joint or muscle pain.

APPENDIX II

My Journey to Date

Chemo day: My pre-chemo selfie

Chemo blues: Feeling dreadful post-treatment

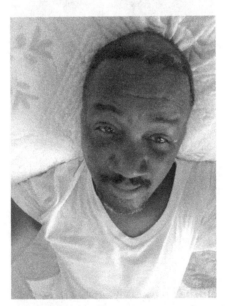

Lonely existence: In the solitary confines of my bedroom

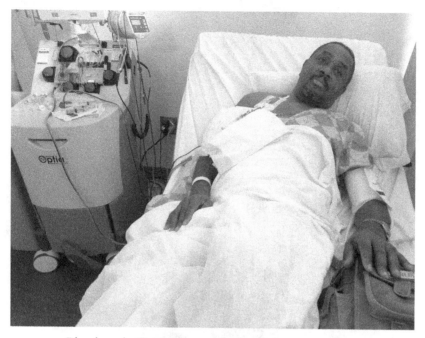

Blood work: Hooked up to the hemapheresis machine

The bald truth: Three months post stem cell transplant

Faith in the future: On the road to recovery in 2019

REFERENCES

American Cancer Society. January 3, 2019. "Drug Therapy for Multiple Myeloma: Chemotherapy." Accessed January 12, 2019. Retrieved from https://www.cancer.org/cancer/multiple-myeloma/treating/chemotherapy.html.

American Cancer Society. "Questions People Ask About Cancer." Accessed August 22, 2019. Retrieved from https://www.cancer.org/cancer/cancer-basics/questions-people-ask-about-cancer.html.

Amgen n.d. "Keeping Track of Your Numbers." Accessed December 12, 2018. Retrieved from https://www.kyprolis.com/getting-support/resources/~/media/amgen/full/kyprolisdtpredesign/Kyprolis_Lab_Tracker.pdf.

Cancer.Net. July 2018. "Multiple Myeloma: Stages." Accessed November 6, 2018. Retrieved from https://www.cancer.net/cancer-types/multiple-myeloma/stages.

Cancer Research UK. n.d. "Together We Will Beat Cancer." Accessed November 10, 2019. Retrieved from https://www.cancerresearchuk.org/about-cancer/cancer-in-general/treatment/cancer-drugs/drugs/lenalidomide.

Cancer Treatment Centers of America. n.d. "What Is Cancer?" Accessed October 10, 2018. Retrieved from https://www.cancercenter.com/what-is-cancer.

Cancer Tutor. February 2, 2019. "Multiple Myeloma." Accessed January 12, 2019. Retrieved from https://www.cancertutor.com/multiple-myeloma/.

Celgene. n.d. "Side Effects of Pomalyst with Dexamethasone." Accessed March 09, 2019. Retrieved from https://www.pomalyst.com/patient/side-effects/.

Celgene. January 2014. "Myeloma: From Deadly to Chronic." Accessed February 04, 2019. Retrieved from https://www.celgene.com/myeloma-deadly-to-chronic/.

Chemocare. n.d. "Dexamethasone." Accessed December 18, 2018. Retrieved from http://chemocare.com/chemotherapy/drug-info/dexamethasone.aspx.

Chemotherapy.com. n.d. "How Chemo Is Given." Accessed February 16, 2019. Retrieved from http://www.chemotherapy.com/new_to_chemo/what_is_chemo/how_chemo_is_given/.

Chemotherapy.com. n.d. "What Is Chemotherapy?" Accessed February 10, 2019. Retrieved from https://www.chemotherapy.com/new_to_chemo/what_is_chemo/.

Dana-Farber Cancer Institute. March 6, 2017. "Autologous vs. Allogenic Stem Cell Transplants: What's the Difference?" Accessed February 5, 2019. Retrieved from http://blog.dana-farber.org/insight/2017/03/autologous-vs-allogenic-stem-cell-transplants-whats-the-difference/.

Diabetes.co.uk. n.d. "Diabetes and Metabolism." Accessed August 10, 2018. Retrieved from https://www.diabetes.co.uk/diabetes-and-metabolism.html.

Everyday Health. n.d. "What Is Acyclovir (Zovirax)?" Accessed March 10, 2019. Retrieved from https://www.everydayhealth.com/drugs/acyclovir.

Goodreads. n.d. "The Clock of Life." Accessed September 10, 2019. Retrieved from https://www.goodreads.com/quotes/385568-the-clock-of-life-is-wound-but-once-and-no.

Mayo Clinic. n.d. "Chemo Brain." Accessed September 17, 2018. Retrieved from https://www.mayoclinic.org/diseases-conditions/chemo-brain/symptoms-causes/syc-20351060.

Multiple Myeloma Research Foundation. n.d. "About Multiple Myeloma: Prognosis." Accessed April 10, 2019. Retrieved from https://themmrf.org/multiple-myeloma/prognosis/.

Revlimid.com. "Side Effects of Revlimid (lenalidomide)." Accessed January 31, 2020. Retrieved from https://patient.revlimid.com/mm-patient/about-revlimid/what-are-the-possible-side-effects/?mm-self-id=yes.

Velcade. n.d. "Let's Talk About Side Effects." Accessed January 12, 2019. Retrieved from http://www.velcade.com/treatment-with-velcade/possible-side-effects.

Verywell Health. Raymaakers, K. March 2018. "M-Protein Antibodies and Significance in Blood." Accessed February 10, 2019. Retrieved from https://www.verywellhealth.com/m-protein-2252091.

UCSF Helen Diller Family Comprehensive Cancer Center. n.d. Accessed January 14, 2019. "About Multiple Myeloma." Retrieved from http://cancer.ucsf.edu/research/multiple-myeloma/.

Biblical References

Several Bible translations were referenced for clarity. The following were the most frequently used:

ESV (English Standard Version)
KJV (King James Version)
MEV (Modern English Version)
MSG (The Message)
NASB (New American Standard Bible)
NIV (New International Version)
NKJV (New King James Version)
NLT (New Living Translation)
NRSV (New Revised Standard Version)

ABOUT THE AUTHOR

Courtney Mullings is a former telecommunications consultant and devout Christian who is traveling on an intense hope-filled, faith-based journey as he copes with the effects of multiple myeloma—a cancer of the plasma cells. His relationship with God, who provides grace through Jesus Christ, sustains him with the significant comfort he needs to manage the consequences of his illness. Grace and all it offers through faith has since become central to his healing. That grace is what has sustained his faith through these years of affliction with cancer, and it forms the basis for this book.

Born and raised in Jamaica, where going to church was an integral part of his early upbringing, because it was mandatory, he once saw the church as a religious, high-minded, and judgmental group. His turning point and submission to Jesus would eventually be manifested, but it was rather uneventful. It was not the threat of fire and brimstone or a condemnation to hell that drew him to Christ. Rather, it was the quiet voice of the Holy Spirit, with love, that impacted his soul. The incredible concept of the unconditional love of Jesus Christ, who had never forsaken him, despite his years of waywardness, ingratitude and rejection was, for him, the great appeal of Christianity.

Courtney enjoys gardening and is an avid artist and had one of his pieces recently featured in CURE (Cancer Updates, Research and Education) magazine. He is married to his beloved Dorothy and they have two adult children.

CPSIA information can be obtained
at www.ICGtesting.com
Printed in the USA
LVHW091458011020
667476LV00010B/69